AMERICAN PANTHEON

BOOKS BY NEWTON ARVIN

Hawthorne (1929)

Whitman (1938)

Herman Melville (1950)

Longfellow: His life and Work (1963)

American Pantheon (1966)

NEWTON ARVIN
AMERICAN PANTHEON

Edited by Daniel Aaron and Sylvan Schendler

A Memoir by Louis Kronenberger

A Seymour Lawrence Book

Delacorte Press, New York

The editors wish to thank the following for permission to reprint copyrighted and other material:

The New Republic for "Hartford's Sweetest Singer," "Brooks's Life of Emerson," "Thoreau," "Thoreau v. Thoreau," "Whitman's Individualism," "The Tedious Archangel," "A Quaker Somewhat Militant," "The Usableness of Howells," "Mark Twain Simplified," "The Friend of Caesar," "Thalia Americana."

The New England Quarterly for "Melville and the Gothic Novel."

Hudson Review for "The House of Pain" from the Hudson Review, Vol. XII, No. 1, spring 1959, © 1959 by The Hudson Review, Inc. Reprinted by permission.

Grecourt Review for "The Unfinished Window."

Partisan Review for "Counterfeit Presentments" and "Notes for a Review."

Hill and Wang, Inc. for the Introduction from the American Century Series Edition of The Grandissimes by George W. Cable. Reprinted by permission.

Houghton Mifflin Co. for the Introduction to The Heart of Hawthorne's Journals, © 1929 by Houghton Mifflin Co.

Alfred A. Knopf, Inc. for the Introduction to Hawthorne's Short Stories, © 1946 by Alfred A. Knopf, Inc.

Farrar, Straus & Giroux, Inc. for "Introduction," reprinted from the Selected Letters of Henry Adams, edited by Newton Arvin. By permission of Farrar, Straus & Giroux, Inc. Copyright 1951 by Newton Arvin.

CONTENTS

ix

INTRODUCTION

During his long stay at Smith College, Newton Arvin was never considered a popular or "dynamic" lecturer. He disliked the platform manner and the premeditated "style" of the academic performer. But abler students found him rewarding, even though he was severe in his demands, and those who broke through his shyness and reserve discovered that he could be witty and amusing as well as formidably learned.

What he exhibited in his lectures and even more in his literary criticism, however, was a love of good writing that distinguished him from the average run of Dryasdusts. With all of his painstaking accuracy and his respect for careful research and intellectual tidiness, he believed that the scholar must love not only the facts but the words that he found for them. Nor could "style" be applied to the facts like a coat of calcimine, "a laying on of paint at the last moment," as he once observed. Writing was for him always an ardous and grim discipline, although his readers, very likely, never realized the effort required to set down his flowing yet firmly composed sentences. Bad writing, he once said to me, is a kind of immorality. He could be exceedingly testy in his private comments about the turgidity and pretentiousness of some of his fellow-critics just as he could be impressed to the point of despair by the clarity and force of critics he admired.

His own aesthetic criteria emerges in the terms of praise he applies to them: range of comprehension, richness in reference and analogy, quiet responsibility, justice. After reading such men, he wrote once in a letter, "what is there left for us minnows to do?" Then he went on to say, "Of course I know the serious and adult answer to this."

Arvin's answer, as this volume partially illustrates, was his own critical writing that began to be published over forty years ago and which continued to be published until his death. Judged by his own exacting standards, a good deal of it was ephemeral stuff, but its range almost from the beginning was impressive and its style, as Edmund Wilson has noted, untainted "by the jargons of the various 'critical' schools." Some of his reviews and essays touched on the issues of his times (during the Thirties his literary opinions were infused and not always improved by a Marxist coloration); others analyzed his American contemporaries or dealt with English and Continental writers or interpreted American literature and culture. Taking this large output of writing as a whole, it must be conceded that his criticism of poetry is rarely memorable, that he attempted no full-dress essays on major writers like Eliot, Pound, Stevens, Hemingway, Fitzgerald, or Faulkner, and that many of his reviews are thin and dated. But it presents nonetheless the response of an alert and restless intelligence to almost a half century of American experience and as such is of considerable interest to any intellectual historian.

In the opinion of the editors and of William Abrahams, whose wise counsel has helped to make this collection a reality, the enduring work of Newton Arvin are his books and essays on nineteenth-century American writers.

Whether he took up minor figures like James Whitcomb
Riley or the giants of the Golden Age, Arvin discussed
them with discrimination and authority, neither over-
estimating their significance nor failing to do justice to
their special gifts. Melville, for example, was a favorite
writer and the subject of his finest critical study, and yet
he refused to align himself with the "Eucharistic Melvil-
lean Congress," as he called it, and all its "cardinals" and
"archbishops." Writing to me while the Melville book was
still incubating, he remarked:

> The chief thing I'm sure of at this stage is that Melville is
> right in saying that "genius is full of trash"—and that this
> was an autobiographical remark. The way my mind works
> I'll not be able to refrain from commentary on the very con-
> siderable element of trash in H M's genius. I'm afraid I'm
> not one of the church-goers here.

The selected essays and reviews reprinted in the volume
bear him out. He never became a cultist or an uncritical
apologist for things American. At the same time, he knew
and relished American letters, diaries, and personal narratives as well as the work of neglected or forgotten writers
that crowded the literary landscape of his good friend and
mentor, Van Wyck Brooks. Brooks, after World War II,
had fallen under the ban of stern academic professionals
and certain urban critics who resented what they considered his parochialism and his celebration of books and
writers and literary tendencies he had once condemned.
But to Newton Arvin, Brooks remained (as William Ellery
Channing did to Emerson) "our bishop." If Brooks was
sometimes perverse "when he speaks of writers who have
offended something deep and personal in him, he's the
only man we have who can tell off the pedants as they need
to be told off. Their day is sunny just now, but it will be

brief, you may be sure. They are simply not in touch with the nature of things." By "they," he wrote shortly after, he meant "These arid little writers of syllogisms" who

> have no more notion of what literature is about than a mole has of astronomy. They make me quite willing and even eager to be "impressionistic," "intuitional," "appreciative," "unsystematic," and all the other sins in this tight little Elio-tine decalogue. That way lies Death!—I'm sure of it—and not the death of a lion, either, but the death of an inch-worm. . . . Remember that I am not speaking quite soberly or literally.

In his last years, Newton Arvin became increasingly engrossed in comparative literature. He wrote and lectured on Vergil and Dante. He read German and Spanish poets, translated from Robert Musil's journals and from the diary of Elio Vittorini. As for American writing, he confessed as early as 1946 to a preference for the "new movement in writing" which was revealing itself, he wrote to me, "as (in some as yet undefined new sense) a romantic and even Gothic one, and . . . I am infinitely more at home in the midst of it than ever I was in the midst of the hard-boiled or the 'objective' or the tough-minded school of my own generation." He continued to read contemporary writers haphazardly, always responding with pleasure to new talent but turning his own serious literary attention to the past.

In 1962, Arvin began work on a new critical study of Hawthorne after completing his biography of Longfellow. He reported to me:

> I am re-reading Hawthorne (a process I began in 1913) and finding some things I hadn't read for years even better than I had remembered them—the English and Italian Notebooks,

e.g., and *Our Old Home,* and the two radiant books of retold myths, which abound in characteristic notes, emblems, obiter dicta, etc., none of which have been pawed over and staled (so far as I know) by graduate students or contributors to PMLA, but about which some pleasant things could be casually said.

He had completed two rough chapters before the onset of his last illness.

Newton Arvin's career had more than its share of painful interruptions. There were moments when he believed he would never write again, when life itself seemed insupportable, and yet soon after—preserved by a toughness and resiliency—he would be back at his uncluttered desk. These shattering intervals confirmed for him the force of Emerson's reflection: "He has seen but half the universe who has never been shown the house of Pain. Pleasure and Peace are but indifferent teachers of what it is life to know." He was expressing his own variation on that theme when he wrote:

> The staple of life is certainly suffering, though surely not its real meaning, and we differ mainly in our capacity to endure it—or be diverted from it. I myself never found it consoling to have this denied or minimized: it seems to me to give one *some* strength just to know that pain is normal, and disappointment the rule, and disquiet the standard— and that the things that have the other quality (work, friendship, the arts) are the wonderful incredible exception & mitigation. And I can tell you, from a fund of experience, that one can be taken down from the rack, closer to death than to life—and then still have the most exquisite joys ahead of one.

He spent many hours on the rack, but his writing hardly shows a trace of that suffering. It is never jaundiced or misanthropic; it never succumbs to what he called "the cant of pessimism." Not that he shunned the dark side of literature. He was fascinated by Gothic revelations and reports from the pit (*frisson* was one of his favorite words), but he reserved his most positive praise for the exemplars or celebrators of the human spirit who, in the midst of tragedy, are still affirmers of life.

DANIEL AARON

A MEMOIR

by Louis Kronenberger

My first meeting with Newton Arvin decidedly lacked
dignity. One summer evening in 1928 I arrived, shortly
after dinner, at Yaddo, then a very young artists' colony.
Myself a very young colonist, I was awed by the prospect
of working among well-known writers and painters and
composers; and awed in a quite different way by the sort
of late-Victorian baronial great hall where I found myself
on arriving, and where I saw a number of other guests
standing about in knots drinking after-dinner coffee.
Fortunately Elizabeth Ames, then as now the Director,
came at once to greet me, to say that they had kept dinner
for me, and that I should go up the lordly staircase we
were standing near to drop my bags in my bedroom and
come down as soon as possible to eat. Having done this,
I re-emerged, noticing now a group of people near the
foot of the stairs waiting, I could only conclude, to greet
me. One second later, thanks to something too outgoing
in my footwork, I was descending the noble staircase by
rolling over and over on it, and finally scrambling off the
great-hall carpet in a fury of embarrassment and a mute
denunciation of the universe.

Newton was one of the people who had been standing

xix

near the foot of the stairs; and he characteristically, as soon
as he was able, came up to introduce himself and ease my
embarrassment with his friendly inquiries. This led, in
the next day or two, to our stopping to chat at odd moments, or choosing the same table at dinner; which led in
turn to what became rather habitual with us—a late-after-
noon walk. I was 23, and he not quite 28, a difference
in age at that point rather marked, and all the more by
Newton's great maturity of mind. He already seemed
"formed," and over the years was not to change much even
in appearance. He was beginning to grow bald, his round
schoolboy face making him look young, his gold-rimmed
glasses making him look studious, something in his careful
use of words proclaiming the born man-of-letters, something in his pronunciation of them tagging him a fellow
Middle Westerner. Many of the touches that go into describing him will suggest a type. But he at most looked
or spoke like one—like, I suppose, a professor; not only
at bottom, but even just below the surface, he was most
decidedly an individual. He was in manner naturally dig-
nified and preternaturally, however shyly, friendly; always
courteous, but never flabby and, with anything that mattered to him, quite decisive and firm.

Our walks that summer were thoroughly conversational
ones. As walkers, we were never—or Newton at any rate
was never with me—silent, meditative, concerned with
nature. The talk was chiefly about books and writers, and
of that exhilarating exploratory kind, that matching of
interests, that nodding at allusions, which marks a budding
literary friendship among the young. The only people we
then knew in common were our fellow-guests at Yaddo;
but these, whether for their talents or achievements, or
once or twice for their somewhat wild personalities, gave
us a good deal to discuss. In respect of our fellow-guests,

Newton could be very perceptive without being malicious. By 1928 he had already taught for several years at Smith; his biography of Hawthorne was well under way, and *The Heart of Hawthorne's Journals*, which he had edited, was soon to appear. Decidedly scholarly, he yet struck you at once as not scholar but critic, and a critic whose immersion in literature argued no dissociation from life. He had an acute sense of all the issues, the controversies, the crises in New England's and America's history that bore upon New England and American literature. Politics, morals, intellectual movements, social atmospheres, cultural patterns, economic pressures all went into his thinking about literature itself.

Yaddo, with its accessibility of meeting and its encouragement of talk, made us, by the end of a few weeks, friends. Ours was to remain a friendship of the happiest kind, one between two people who lived at a certain distance from each other, met after a certain interval, greeted each other with expectancy, took leave with a sense of having conversationally dined well, and with regret. There can have been few years in which we did not meet at least once, and in some years we met several times. Our conversations, though aired with fresh topics and brightened with new tidbits, were in some sense *resumed*, even to a degree repeated—which, coming at longish intervals, was as natural as, at longish intervals, is rereading poetry one likes, or rehearing music. It came to be part of the agenda to inquire about one person or another as the cue for discussing him; to mention this or that writer as a signal for once again canvassing his work. Thus, though I can remember very little of our actual talk at any time, I can remember a great many of the things we talked about.

If distance lent something attractive to our friendship,

difference of personality and temperament did also. We were harmoniously unalike. Even the "bond" of our having both grown up in the Middle West was weakened by Newton's having grown up in a small town, Valparaiso, Indiana, where he lived across the street from David Lilienthal, and I in a city. There may have been a much greater kinship in our both having wanted to get away from the Middle West; but here, again, Newton's whole bent was toward New England, as was mine toward New York. How much his predilection was a matter of inborn temperament, how much it was induced by his Harvard student days, I can't be sure. But it is hard to think of Newton not living in New England, though one would much sooner put him in Boston or Cambridge or Concord than at Northampton. All the same, one can still feel that he was not inextricably bound to New England and that, though he must almost surely have kept coming back to it with a sense of coming home, he might far oftener have gone away from it, to London or Edinburgh, Oxford or Cambridge, Florence or Rome. If no one had a deeper or finer literary sense, few people had, more than Newton, a historical sense, either. He was so *imaginatively* culti- vated that in a way he did not need to travel; but, in just the same way, no one could have brought more to his travels, or taken more away with him. Newton went to Europe only once, in the summer of 1929 or 1930. One reason why he may not have gone again was a certain dis- inclination, during many years, to leave Northampton for very long, except for a kind of second home like Yaddo or Harvard. But another reason, which he once mentioned, was financial: he taught for many years when, even for a full professor, academic salaries—particularly at women's colleges—were pinchingly low.

His not knowing Europe was a great pity; he should

somehow have gone often, especially after he had become an admired literary figure and could have had the experience of London's writers and clubs, of Oxford's scholars and High Tables, and glimpsed the society as well as the sights of Paris and Rome. It would have made for a wonderfully fair exchange. Newton was not in the least a worldling, but neither was he a naif or a provincial. Moreover, he had a particular igniting sensibility for just such traditional occasions, social ceremonies, varieties of cultivated living as he would have been made part of in Europe, and—though there less resonantly—*was* made part of, on occasion, in Boston and New York.

On the other hand, although Newton ought not to have lived a pedagogue's life—for he had none of a pedagogue's limitations—the reflective, somewhat donnish life was right for him. He needed art, literature, philosophy at first hand and in solitude, more than in talk with other people. He was a contemplative man, dedicated to the life of the mind. Books were inseparable from him: this is as good a place as any to speak of how extraordinarily well read he was, and in how many related fields. Yet such was the natural, needful, eager, thirsty manner of his reading that, though the word was surely applicable, one never thought to call Newton "learned." There was in his writing and speech no sign of knowledge grown at all prideful or obstrusive; he showed no deference to that frequent infirmity of academic mind, its need to make known its knowledge; and no allegiance to those credentials of academic fitness, the barren footnote or the bulging bibliography. He just *knew,* as other people knew that he did. I remember telling him that I had once followed a newspaper feature in which well-known writers were asked to list famous books they had never read; and how some writers had been entirely human and honest in their answers, setting down things like *Jonathan Wild* or *Barchester Towers;* while other writers pleaded guilty to not knowing the obscurest drama of Sir Henry Taylor's or the dullest novel of John Galt's. This was a game that Newton particularly enjoyed, whether in terms of others or himself. And no one was more human and honest than he—except, alas, that there just *was* nothing really well known that he hadn't read. He was as embarrassed by his knowledge as are other people by their ignorance, and finally managed to recall—after all these years, I can only invent my examples—that he had bogged down in *Celestina,* and read only Book I of Manilius. Most delightfully, a week later from Northampton—the result I am sure of lying awake for hours racking his brain—he submitted, with great satisfaction, three or four additional titles, of a kind that a pretty cultivated man might feel pleased to have heard of.

Newton's mind, moreover, was as orderly as it was absorbent. His method of doing research for his books may be a common one, but to me it seemed astonishing. It was to work up all the needed material, fill out all the file cards, assemble all the references, cross-references, authorities, incidental notes—in other words, do every bit of his homework—before writing a single line of the book. And as there was no one more talented at research, there was no one more thorough—he, like Boswell, would have pursued a date half-over London (or all over Camden and Cambridge). In much the same way, he would reread all the books he was lecturing on in class, no matter how well he knew them. I remember him, when a visiting professor at Harvard, doing this with Henry James while confessing there was no need to do it. It is, incidentally, a genuine loss to criticism that, despite the all too many books on

James, Newton never wrote one; it would have ranked with those that matter. But a *James* is only one of several books we may have lost by Newton's death—Emerson, too, certainly awaited him, along with the work he was thinking about very late in his career, a *History of Literary Ideas in America*. This was something he was splendidly qualified to write; furthermore, in the last year or so before his final illness, he was at the floodtide of his energy and power; never more enthusiastic about what he planned to do, or more eager to set about doing it.

The virtues of Newton's short critical writings lie open to the reader in the body of this book. The appealing quality of his conversation, on the other hand—and of his conversational manner—is not easy to recapture or even to paraphrase. To say that Newton never spoke a slipshod sentence sounds priggish in him and fatiguing to his listener; actually it was inherent with him, and fascinating to his listener. It might on occasion, and quite engagingly, be prim in language while playful in thought, a sort of cousin to English understatement. Where Newton's speech did amuse one, now and then, was in proclaiming the born highbrow, the never really naturalized man in the street, as in his pronouncing *cantaloupe* to rhyme with *soup,* or always pronouncing my last name—which was severed of its German ties in the 1840's—*Kronenbairger*. Conversely, though he never misused slang he spoke it with just a suggestion of putting it in quotation marks. His language was ordered and highbred because his thought and feeling were, and all the more because a lifetime's discriminating reading had made faultless English effortless. What might have marred his writing—the vast amount of current criticism he kept up with—did it no harm because he detested the jargon, the chic ponder-

osities that infest the criticism of our time. Newton's own
style, it seems to me, is one of the strongest assurances for
his survival.

During thirty-five years I saw Newton—whose actual
first name, which he loathed, was Frederick—in a variety
of settings. We met a good many times at Yaddo, particularly in later years when we went to board meetings there.
He was relaxed at Yaddo, from being at once a kind of
member of the family and a distinguished guest, and from
the affection he felt for it and for Elizabeth Ames. And
the meetings meant seeing old friends and acquaintances:
his very old friend Granville Hicks; Malcolm Cowley,
Morton Zabel, Quincy Porter, Richard Donovan and
others. And it is at Yaddo, and not just because we first
met there, that Newton seems to me most appropriately
"placed." This may be partly true from my not placing or
visualizing him at Northampton, where I saw him only
a very few times. I find it a rather charming limitation that
Newton is the one close friend I have had whom I knew,
as it were, almost entirely away from his home. Of him in
his own house, of his particular domestic habits, his arm-
chair or dressing-gown crotchets, or his classroom methods
and manner, I have virtually no sense at all.

Of him in New York I have no such settled memories
as I have of him at Yaddo, but there survive many glimpses
and snapshots. For a number of years, Newton's visits to
New York tended to be brief. He would write to announce
his coming; but after he came, the city itself—with its
clatter, its pace, its unfamiliarity—often proved disturb-
ing. All this sometimes kept us from meeting—Newton
would suddenly bolt, and wire his regrets from Northampton. But even then he usually managed to see the
plays and art exhibits he had looked forward to; music in

those days in some way did not sit happily on him. But in later years he grew to enjoy music and Manhattan alike: he often seemed to grow younger in spirit, he did not go away early from parties, or ahead of time back to Smith. When he came with two or three others for dinner, he could be in fine form, and the evening a very successful one.

I associate Newton most vividly, however, and think of our seeing each other most rewardingly, at the "farm" in southeast Connecticut where I went with my family for some twenty summers and where, during many of them, Newton paid my wife and me a visit. The "farm" was no such thing; it was just a lot of untilled or untillable acres which had been christened Millpond Farm, and did boast a millpond and an abandoned mill and millwheel, and made up in privacy and extent for what it lacked in appearance and utility. Here Newton would come for four or five days, sharing a rural existence whose major event was going for the mail, and whose total social life, during his visit, might mean going once to Stonington for dinner, or having Stonington friends come once to us. Equally for the pleasure he always gave and the trouble he never caused, Newton was a perfect guest. He had a wonderful way of never being *in* the way—for one good reason, he was always happy to go off walking somewhere, or to sit with a book in a corner of the living room, or climb with it to his bedroom, or shift with it to the porch, or *seem* to be reading it on the lawn.

It was during these summer visits that Newton and I could really talk, indoors or outdoors, sedentary or ambulatory, drink in hand or still clutching a book. There were, as I have said, standard items: personal friends and literary figures, underrated authors or overrated books. We did not always agree, even among the classics: Newton, I

recall, did not like Stendhal and Goya, and I certainly—
somehow one doesn't so well remember disagreeing as
being disagreed with—was untouched by admirations of
his. And there were always new quarterlies, cults, feuds
to discuss, new happenings in the wide world or bits of
gossip in our own. The talk might range from Harvard
to Columbia, from Henry Adams to Hermann Hesse, from
whom Leavis had most recently denounced to whom Eliot
had surprisingly approved of. All this drew upon Newton's
comic sense, which was quite equal to his other qualities,
and evoked in him witty comments that were properly—
or, on occasion, improperly—donnish and dry. On some of
his visits, he would do a little work and occasionally let
me see what he was working on. And I remember once,
before he arrived, being aware of what he was working on
and writing to ask whether I could be shown some of it.
Smilingly, on the first day of his visit, he handed me a
typed manuscript, which I went off at once to read. Within
an hour I rushed excitedly back to proclaim, as have so
many other people since, its magnificence: it was the
Moby Dick chapter of the *Melville.*

Our meetings revealed much more of what was admirable about Newton than his mind: they revealed a gentle
manner which enabled him to disagree without seeming
censorious; which let him, indeed, enlighten or correct
you without making you out a monkey or him a schoolmaster. All in all, he had a very real sense of his own
powers and, as he grew older, of his earned place in the
literary world; but this was absorbed into his total self,
it did not obtrude, it did not insist. Somehow his personal
amenity consorted rather than collided with critical sever-
ity. Among those who knew him, he became something
of a grey eminence, an influence, a court of appeal; but
in precisely the sense that he was not authoritarian, a

power, a promulgator of dogmas. He was a man who liked
to be consulted, and often was. He was never disputatious,
or inclined toward that favorite haunt of criticism today,
the contentious correspondence column.

All this may help explain why Newton was not better
known in his lifetime while being, wherever he was known,
respected and admired. Though he wrote so lucidly as to
be accessible to any serious cultivated reader, and though
he could write well of what was timely and even urgent,
Newton had little of the journalist in his writing; and in
his thinking, almost nothing at all. For better or worse, he
lacked what is fairly enough called showmanship; he had
small gift for inducing or enforcing a certain kind of attention, for attracting—if only by irritating—a certain
kind of audience. There were no rhetorical blandishments
or fashionable tricks; there was no calculated sudden
change of key, no practiced vibrato; no Arvin-and-syrup
or even Arvin-and-soda; and no need for them. He had
the mellowness to be taken neat.

He had, indeed, qualities enough, and in the field of
American literature distinction and stature enough, to have
been among the most undervalued critics of his time. A
more accurate phrase is among the most underdiscovered
by a large appreciative public, for he had always the high
regard of many of his most eminent fellow-critics. Still, he
was never taken up in the good sense of being focused on,
quoted from, written about. One reason for this, beyond
a lack of showmanship, may be that what he wrote had
no sharp controversial edge or iconoclastic point of view;
nor did he whoopingly resurrect writers, or send acclaimed
reputations reeling. But as Newton was no showman or
innovator, neither was he part of the closet criticism or the
tiresome methodology of the academic world. As there was
perhaps too little glitter in his work to win him a wide

audience in his lifetime, so now the complete absence of tinsel in it will lose him no earlier-won regard, and may achieve for him a recognition that will steadily increase and long endure.

AMERICAN PANTHEON

THOMAS HOLLEY CHIVERS

A GEORGIAN MINSTREL

HERE AT LAST is a full-length book * on the man from
whom Poe confessedly borrowed hints for "The Raven"
and other poems, and of whom Swinburne said to Stedman: "Oh, Chivers, Chivers, if you know Chivers, give me
your hand." Rossetti, too, meeting H. E. Scudder in the
sixties, made inquiries about the poet whose "Lost Pleiad"
he had read with at least amusement twenty years before;
and Bayard Taylor, though he ridiculed and parodied
Chivers in "The Echo Club," gave him credit for having
struck off, in a poem named "Apollo," "one of the finest
images in modern poetry." Both Swinburne and Rossetti,
as Mr. Damon shows, did Chivers the honor of using him
as a "source"; "The Blessed Damosel" has a real hint of
Chivers in it, and the cadences of "Dolores" are extraordinarily like those of "Lily Adair." Yet even the association
with Poe did not suffice to save Chivers from virtual ob-
livion in the years following the Civil War, and for a long
time his name could have been known only to the most
special of special students. A year or two ago Mr. Conrad
Aiken, in his Modern Library anthology of American
verse, included the elegy entitled "Avalon," and, in his

* *Thomas Holly Chivers: Friend of Poe*, by S. Foster Damon.

1

preface, mentioned Chivers, along with Anne Bradstreet and Trumbull Stickney, as an unduly neglected writer. Now Mr. Damon has brought together all the available information about the man's life and personality: it ought finally to be possible to do him full justice.

It is a curious story that Mr. Damon has pieced together. Chivers's life, like his work, seems to have combined, in what are perhaps peculiarly American proportions, singularity and dulness, the surface of an eccentric with the "content" of a vestryman. It is almost a definition of tediousness, this filling in of whimsical or crazy outlines with the brownish hues of essential commonplaceness; and I for one must confess to feeling that the friend of Poe, like other obscurities one has heard of, has most of the earmarks of a prodigious bore. This is by no means the fault of Mr. Damon's narrative, which is, if possible, more interesting than its subject. Born in Georgia, early in the century, when that state was still as truly in the backwoods as Maine was at the same period, Chivers was brought up by well-to-do parents in the code of a Southern gentleman and according to the precepts of the Baptist faith—a doubly bad beginning for a poet. After an early, mysterious, and unhappy marriage, Chivers spent two years at Transylvania University in Lexington, and became a doctor of medicine, but he seems never to have practised his profession. The economic security of his family made it possible for him to travel freely—first in the more or less unsettled regions of the Mid-West and South, where he entered into some sort of relations with Indian tribes, and later in the North, where he married a second time and temporarily became a householder. The story of his relations with Poe is too long to be even summarized here, but one is struck by its being the only sustained literary friendship in Chivers's career,

since he was on bad terms even with his Southern contemporaries such as Simms. He hovered, indeed, on the
fringes of the literary life: his natural associations, apparently, were not with men of letters but with mesmerists
and mediums, and he succumbed to more than one of the
current superstitions of his day. After Poe's death he lost
what little contact he had had with the intellectual life
of the Golden Day; and his last years were spent on his
Georgia estate, attacking abolitionism, painting portraits
of his family, writing medical articles, and inventing a ma-
chine for spinning silk. He died at the age of fifty-two, a
Southern gentleman, and apparently a Baptist, to the end.

II

If he had really been a man of genius, his frontier background and the intellectual tone of the period would
certainly have been pretty much against him, and one can
imagine a Georgian Blake dying young of sheer inanition,
perhaps after producing a sheaf of odd and powerful
poems. But Chivers was not a man of genius, and, with all
deference to judgments so weighty as Mr. Aiken's and Mr.
Damon's, it must be said that he was not a very good poet,
at least on the strength of the evidence they adduce. I
have been able to lay my hands on only one of his faded
little volumes (none, of course, has ever been reprinted);
and though this—the *Nacooche; or, The Beautiful Star* of
1837—is apparently not so important as *Eonchs of Ruby*
or *Virginalia,* Mr. Damon regards it as characteristic and
remarkable. The "Avalon" which Mr. Aiken prints is from
a later volume, and Mr. Damon calls it "the most original,
the most poignant, and the most melodious" of the *Eonchs
of Ruby.* But after several readings I must admit that this
throaty elegy seems to be almost an illustration of what

poetry ought not to be, and this not mainly because one turns pale at such lines as "Thou Philomelian Eclecticist of Song!" or "Whose Mendelssohnian Songs now fill the skies!" but because one cannot find a single genuinely expressive line or phrase in the whole poem, and because its total effect is of a slightly crazy flatulence. And so of the poems in *Nacooche;* the title poem I have had no success in getting to the end of, but I am prepared to say that I have never read worse Spenserian stanzas; and the blank verse of the poems that follow—which Mr. Damon calls "effective"—seems to me at once dishevelled and monotonous. The lyric poems in the book—"To Little Liza in Heaven," "Ode to the Mississippi," "Song of the Dying Soldier," "The Voice of the Exile," and so on—are about what their titles suggest: declamatory, lachrymose, and tasteless. "Oh" and "lo" and "whither" and "awake" and "farewell" and such words predominate far too consistently to allow true feeling to come through. And when Chivers himself steals from other poets it is always to vulgarize them:

> She died in beauty, like the morn that rose
>   In golden glory on the brow of night,
> And passed off gently like the evening's close,
>   When day's last steps upon the heavens are bright.

It is true that Chivers was an extraordinary experimentalist, and that there can be no doubt about Poe's indebtedness to him for metrical effects, for proper names, and even for themes; but if ever there was a case of a poet experimenting for want of better things to do, Chivers was the man. There is something entertaining, to be sure, about his incremental refrains, his 'Cydonian Suckets," his drumming paeons, his "fair-browed Rosalie Lees," and the like; but the upshot of it all is only a wild sort of old-fashioned nonsense. There is a good deal of nonsense in Poe, too, of course, but there is something else, and it makes him a true, though only a minor, poet. The "something else" in Chivers is too insubstantial to give his poetry serious interest. He had, says Mr. Damon, "a really metaphysical imagination," and, on such a subject, the expositor of Blake has a peculiar right to a judgment; but other readers can only speak for themselves, and I suppose many will feel that Chivers's imagination was metaphysical only in the sense in which a Ouija board is a philosophic instrument. Nothing that Mr. Damon quotes gives evidence of brooding or daring thought any more than of deep and disciplined feeling; the flare is the flare of a gas-jet, not of the lightning; and there is more insight in one of Emily Dickinson's slightest poems than in all Chivers's work that I have read. Mr. Damon says at another point something that seems to me far truer and more definitive: "Whoever [after reading 'Rosalie Lee'] cannot enjoy the psychical month July, ovaline arms that are rhymes, and an azure silence, cannot enjoy the real Chivers." In one sense, of course, anyone should be able to "enjoy" these oddities; but when it comes to poetry—thank you, no! The "real Chivers" is just where Mr. Damon puts him.

He did nevertheless supply suggestions to men of genius: it is not the first time that fake poetry has served such a purpose—witness "Ossian" and Blake—and this gives Chivers a genuine antiquarian interest in the story of American letters. Mr. Damon has done a real service to students and readers in digging out the facts, elucidating the man's relations with Poe, and citing his most interesting pieces. His book is extremely readable, and it is only between the lines—or from the evidence of the frontispiece portrait—that one gathers how skilful Mr. Damon has been in treating an unpromising subject. Compare with the 1848 daguerreotype of Poe—which is here reproduced—the ferrotype of the Georgia physician: the darkness and delicacy of the one face with the broad flat brow, the pale eyes, the petulant mouth and softly-contoured chin of the other. It is the face of a crank and a bore.

MRS. LYDIA HUNT SIGOURNEY

HARTFORD'S SWEETEST SINGER *

WHY DID Mr. Wyndham Lewis and Mr. Charles Lee omit
from their excellent anthology of bad verse, *The Stuffed
Owl,* the honorable name of Lydia Hunt Sigourney, who
probably produced more poems about death, both lingering and sudden, especially the death of infants, than any
other single bard, male or female, of the nineteenth century? It is true that Mrs. Sigourney's muse is not to be
compared with the grossly ludicrous drab who presided
over the cackling of Mrs. Julia Moore, the Sweet Singer
of Michigan, whom they do include at some length; but
that is only to say that she is more seriously and perma-
nently entertaining. Surely they could have found space,
if not for the lines "On the Death of a Sister while Absent
at School" (which indeed, like so much verse, are not so
fine as their title), at least for a few lines from the "Marriage of the Deaf and Dumb" or from "Female Education
for Greece." I should think they might have found a page
or two for such lines as these, from "To a Shred of Linen,"
expressing Mrs. Sigourney's regret for the passing of the
old household arts of New England:

* *Mrs. Sigourney, the Sweet Singer of Hartford,* by Gordon S. Haight.

7

> Fain would I ask,
> Mine own New England, for thy once loved wheel,
> By sofa and piano quite displaced.
> Why dost thou banish from thy parlor-hearth
> That old Hygeian harp, whose magic rul'd
> Dyspepsia, as the minstrel-shepherd's skill
> Exorcis'd Saul's ennui?

And, in a different vein, there are passages from one of many poems on "Autumn" that need not be wholly forgotten:

> Hydrangea, on her telegraph
> A hurried signal trac'd
> Of dire and dark conspiracy
> That Summer's realm menac'd.

In her own day, Mrs. Sigourney was a personage of distinct importance; for many decades she was Hartford's most eminent literary citizen, an exhibit to be brought ceremoniously to the attention of General Lafayette, Charles Dickens and every other visiting celebrity; she was easily the foremost standby of the gift-books and annuals, of *Godey's Lady's Book* and *Graham's;* she was a correspondent—on curious terms, to be sure—of Maria Edgeworth and Mary Russell Mitford, of Samuel Rogers and Mrs. Jameson; she was "the American Hemans"; on one occasion, when she visited a session of the Supreme Court, she was espied and recognized by Daniel Webster and formally escorted by him to a seat of honor; Whittier regarded her as a benefactress and Poe solicited contributions from her pen to *Graham's* during his editorship; and, finally, she was the first American versifier to make poetry pay. A true Yankee, she naturally had something of Jonathan Edwards in her makeup—a faint and slightly stale

hangover of his deep piety—but she had still more of
Benjamin Franklin; and she managed to make the Road to
Xanadu coincide with the Way to Wealth—or at least to
remarkable prosperity. It should be added that, like many
another creative spirit in big business, she gave away
much of what she raked in.

Her personality and her career have a real if very minor
interest for the student of American culture, and they
could hardly have been more happily treated than by Mr.
Haight in this unpretentious volume. One gathers that
graduate study lies behind its composition, and certainly
the book is most richly documented; but it has the least
possible taint of the mere thesis. Mr. Haight writes with
just the proper degree of unemphasized irony, with just
the proper informality in narrative and analysis, with just
the proper economy of historical allusion. If such "subjects" were always treated with so nice a reference to their
true scale, we should have more adequate literary biographies than we do have. The Sweet Singer of Hartford,
at least, will not need to be "done" another time.

RALPH WALDO EMERSON

"A WRITER who obtains his full purpose," said Dr. Johnson, "loses himself in his own lustre": of no American writer does this appear to be so true as of Emerson: he succeeded so well, at least superficially, in what he aimed at, that it is now almost impossible, in turning one's eyes back in his direction, to see Emerson himself: what one sees is so largely just the great "glad" glow of Emersonianism. What one sees is really President Eliot and the elective system at Harvard; or William James and the will to believe; or Elbert Hubbard and the "Message to Garcia"; or Theodore Roosevelt and the strenuous life; or Mrs. Eddy and the illusions of mortal mind; or even Herbert Hoover and rugged individualism. "Can we not learn," Emerson asked, "the lesson of self-help?" and seventy years of our history respond to the query with—"Only too well!" "Strong men," he said, "believe in cause and effect"; and we now know, to our cost, what "effects" may sometimes be the products of this praiseworthy faith. If the American middle class were to deify one man as its Orpheus, its Balder, its David, it could hardly do better by itself than to fix upon Ralph Waldo Emerson. He can hardly be said

---

* *The Life of Emerson,* by Van Wyck Brooks.

to have made America what it is; but, without the essays
and addresses, without the Emersonian clichés, how much
less spiritual authority the ruling culture would have had!
Now that this culture is on the wane, it would look as if
Emerson had had his day, and were about to be eclipsed
once for all. If Emerson and Emersonianism were identical, this would be the fact; fortunately for him, there is
a genuine difference between them.

Yet nothing could be more natural than that Emerson
should have become, on his most apparent side, the
spokesman of our dominant classes. Individualist critics
and biographers have never made enough—*will* never
make enough—of his close personal connection, along the
whole line, with the men who have ruled the United
States. He was no child of obscure pencil-makers, of half-
literate Quaker farmers, of unpropertied carpenters or of
strolling actors: his childhood, it is true, was spent in
poverty, but by no means in penniless obscurity. He was
the offspring of Bulkeleys and Emersons on one side, of
men who were the upper crust of the Calvinist theocracy;
on his mother's side, the Haskins side, he had for a grandfather one of the prosperous merchants of Boston. His
father, William Emerson, was a clergyman and a gentleman in somewhat unequal proportions: chaplain of the
Massachusetts Senate, a friend of President Kirkland of
Harvard, a clubman and Federalist *littérateur*. One of
Emerson's brothers studied law in the office of Daniel
Webster. His first wife was the daughter of another Boston merchant; his second wife was a Jackson of Plymouth.
He was a considerable property holder in Concord; and
lived mainly, though not wholly, on the income from his
first wife's estate ($22,000 at 6 percent, he told Carlyle).
Finally, in his old age, as if to describe the perfect curve
from the Puritan theocrats to the captains of industry, he

became a close friend and lively admirer of the builder of the Michigan Central, the president of the Chicago, Burlington and Quincy, the squire of Naushon, John Murray Forbes. To Forbes's son, later president of the Bell Telephone Company, his daughter Edith was married; and Emerson thus became the grandfather of a governor-general of the Philippines under Taft, an ambassador to Japan under Hoover. From Peter Bulkeley to Cameron Forbes, the line of class privilege is virtually unbroken. What wonder if Emerson's is on one side a philosophy of power, a metaphysics of success, a religion of enterprise and self-help? What wonder if he believed that "Everything good lies on the highway"; or that "Life is a search after power"; or that "In a free and just commonwealth, property rushes from the idle and imbecile to the industrious, brave and persevering"? What wonder, in short, if Emersonianism should often seem to be the whole of Emerson?

Certainly the class to which he belonged has exploited him for all he was worth to it: from one point of view, it is not fantastic to father upon Emerson—who said, "The only progress ever made was of the individual"—such tangible realities of our political life as resistance to the "demoralizing" dole. But there is another point of view, and from this there *is* something fantastic in such an arraignment. For probably no one who knows Emerson himself will feel that Emersonianism exhausts him. Probably no one of the sort will fail to feel that the Emersonian tradition is mainly a vulgarization of Emerson; that Mrs. Eddy and Theodore Roosevelt and Elbert Hubbard are but Emerson made Bishop of Rome. To read the essays and the journals now, amid the stench sent up by a rotten individualism, is to feel, if only confusedly, that the mountebanks of self-help and self-expression are not entitled to the whole of Emerson. It is to feel that something quite strong and essential in him escapes from the limitations of class, and allies itself potentially with more creative forces.

Is it a paradox that the writer who most perfectly expressed the aspirations of the American middle class should also, more than almost any other, have anticipated its passing? A paradox, perhaps, but a vital one. It is exactly because Emerson was so authentic a spokesman of his class in its prime that his writing is potentially so destructive. From the beginning there has been a deep disequilibrium in middle-class culture, as there have been deep contradictions in its economy: just as the French Revolution was partly made by the Parisian artisans, and the American Revolution by the workers and farmers—to the advantage, in both cases, of rich traders—so Rousseau may be said to have paved the way for Marx as well as for Mill. The middle classes began by committing themselves to a philosophy of change, to a dynamic and essentially revolutionary program: their theoreticians went farther than the concrete objectives required, but the cat was out of the bag, and the impulse to dialectical thinking, once given, was not to be easily revoked. Hegel and Darwin, the philosophy of history and the evolutionary science of biology, were on the cards; and Emerson, in a flexible sense, was both Hegelian and Darwinian: in short, he was a philosopher of intelligible change.

Emersonianism, to a large exent, is a vulgar optimistic superstition, a cant of self-seeking concealed beneath a butter of altruism, a gospel for the aggressive, the unscrupulous, the interested. It is a philosophy for those who stand to profit by things as they are and seek to frustrate a fundamental change. But go back to Emerson himself, and what does one find? Moving richly through his whole

utterance like an insuppressible bass, a sense of the exhilarating fluidity of human affairs, of the world itself; an
irreverence toward the *status quo* and toward any possible
status quo; a conviction that development is the secret of
life, and movement the hallmark of reality. It is no accident that, incited by Goethe and Lamarck and Lyell and
the Jardin des Plantes, he was ready for evolution long
before the *Origin of Species:* the matrix of his whole
thought is, in that sense, biological. It is no accident that
he was a Hegelian with but little firsthand knowledge of
Hegel: like Hegel, he was a true child of philosophic romanticism. "The fact of two poles, of two forces, cen-
tripetal and centrifugal," he says in "Politics," "is universal,
and each force, by its own activity, develops the other."
This is an informal dialectic, if you will; but it is a dialectic nevertheless; and "the principle of polarity," as Emerson himself called it, is not a principle of conservatism. If
it is true that he took but a cool interest in the radicalisms
of his day (save on the crucial question of slavery), it was
almost because he was too radical for the radicals: his
radicalism was, at any rate, too profound to be adequately
expressed in vegetarianism or the Bloomer costume. It was
too profound to be expressed in mere "rebellion" of any
kind; and there it still is, accessible as always to those who
wish not merely to "interpret the world variously" (in
Marx's phrase) but to change it. "Everything," he said,
"looks permanent until its secret is known"—*everything,*
that is; literally everything, including the elective system
at Harvard, the strenuous life of the Roosevelts, rugged
individualism, and the middle-class culture which made
this generalization possible.

It was thus a characteristic inspiration that led Van
Wyck Brooks, after interpreting Mark Twain and Henry
James, to the life of Emerson. After the man who stultified

himself by accepting his class culture uncritically, and the
man who crippled himself by trying to escape from it, the
man who spoke for it so authentically as at once to crystal-
lize and to transcend it. Having dealt with two kinds of
relative failure, Mr. Brooks closes the dialectical circle
by dealing with a case of relative success. ("To see the
country of success [England] I, who delighted in success,
departed.") It is true that Mr. Brooks's descriptions of
both the failures and the success are somewhat too purely
psychological; that the historical and sociological differences are more important than he makes them appear;
that middle-class culture in the prime of Mark Twain and
Henry James had become a very different thing from what
it had been in Emerson's prime. Still, the fact remains
that Emerson rode on the crest of a wave which was descending to its trough in Mark Twain's generation; and
this makes not only possible but desirable a very different
manner of treatment in this new biography.

Gone is the argumentation of *The Ordeal of Mark
Twain* and *The Pilgrimage of Henry James:* here is only
narrative, only painstaking and infinitely delicate portraiture. Here is Emerson seen from within his own experience, seen with an understanding which will probably
never be surpassed, seen as only an American writer with
his roots in Emerson's soil could hope to see him. Not
Emerson the philosopher mainly, but Emerson the man
and the poet; the living figure, not the chapter in intellectual history. Something is missing, as a result; but something by no means so easy for other writers to do justice
to, is here. This book is not an analysis of what our social
and spiritual life was like in its best days, but a rendering
of it; and the learning that lies behind the tale is lost in
the imaginative skill with which the tale is told. "Ask the
fact for the form," said Emerson; and that is what Van

Wyck Brooks has done with Emersonian insight and art.
Perhaps, in consequence, it is the only book on the subject
which will survive the final collapse of Emersonianism.

THE HOUSE OF PAIN:

EMERSON AND THE TRAGIC SENSE

NO ONE KNEW BETTER THAN EMERSON that every generation goes through a necessary and proper ritual-slaying
of its parents; that Zeus, as he would say, is forever destroying his father Cronos; and that, if the writers of one age
reject, with a kind of sacrificial solemnity, the writers who
have just preceded them, this is quite as it ought to be—is
the Method of Nature herself. "Our life," he said, "is an
apprenticeship to the truth that around every circle another can be drawn; that there is no end in nature, but
every end is a beginning; that there is always another
dawn risen on mid-noon, and under every deep a lower
deep opens." He could not have been surprised, therefore,
and probably he would not even have been much disturbed, if his sons, or his son's sons, turned upon him,
metaphorically speaking, and put him to the knife on the
reeking altar of literary and intellectual change. Certainly
this is what happened. Emerson had been the Socrates
and even the Zoroaster of the generation of young men and
women for whom he first spoke, and to tell the truth, it
was not until a third age had arrived that the Imitation of
Emerson was followed by his Immolation.

This rite was performed by the literary leaders of the
period of the First World War. Almost forty years ago

Mr. T. S. Eliot, whose voice was rightly to carry so far, remarked that "the essays of Emerson are already an encumbrance." Three or four years later D. H. Lawrence expressed a somewhat less drastic but in its implications almost equally repudiative view: "I like Emerson's real courage," he said. "I like his wild and genuine belief in the Oversoul and the inrushes he got from it. But it is a museum-interest. Or else it is a taste of the old drug to the old spiritual dope-fiend in me." Emerson, not as a tonic, but as a narcotic—this is the Emerson who came more and more to serve as an image of the man for the new era. The greatest poet of that generation put the case against him with almost filial finality. Speaking, in his autobiography, of his friend, the Irish poet AE, William Butler Yeats observed that he sometimes wondered what AE "would have been had he not met in early life the poetry of Emerson and Walt Whitman, writers who have begun to seem superficial," said Yeats, "because they lack the Vision of Evil."

There was much in Emerson's writings, Heaven knows, to account for these rejections; but the ground on which Yeats put *his* was the most serious and the most fundamental—the deficiency in Emerson of what a Spanish writer of that period called famously the Tragic Sense of Life. And indeed it did not have to be left to the age of Eliot and Yeats to express a dissatisfaction with this blindness of Emerson's. There were writers, as there were doubtless readers, of his own time who found him terribly wanting in any true awareness of what one of them called the Power of Blackness. Hawthorne, who was his neighbor in Concord, had a due respect for Emerson as a man; but Emerson the transcendental optimist addressed no word of authority to the ear of Hawthorne—who described him as "Mr. Emerson—the mystic, stretching his hand out of cloudland, in vain search for something real." And Hawthorne's younger contemporary Melville could be even more severe; in the margin of his copy of Emerson's essays, adjoining a particularly cheerful passage in the essay on "Prudence," Melville wrote: "To one who has weathered Cape Horn as a common sailor, what stuff all this is." A much younger man than either Hawthorne or Melville, Henry James, would not have spoken of Mr. Emerson, his father's friend, in just this vein of disrespectful impatience, but he too could not refrain from remarking that there was a side of life as to which Emerson's eyes were thickly bandaged. "He had no great sense of wrong," said James—"a strangely limited one, indeed, for a moralist—no sense of the dark, the foul, the base."

They all mount up—judgments like these, and there are a hundred of them—to what sometimes seems like not only a damaging but a fatal indictment of Emerson as a writer whom we can ever again listen to with the old reverential attention. A writer who lacks the Vision of Evil, who has no great sense of wrong—how can he be read with respect, or perhaps read at all, in a time when we all seem agreed that anguish, inquietude, the experience of guilt, and the knowledge of the Abyss are the essential substance of which admissible literature is made? It is a painful question to any reader who cannot suppress his sense of a deep debt to Emerson. But it is a question that must be asked, and one has to confess that, as one turns the pages of his essays, the reasons stare one in the face why Hawthorne and Melville, Eliot and Yeats, should have answered it so negatively.

Certainly it is hard to understand how a writer of even the least seriousness could dispose so jauntily as Emerson sometimes does of the problem of moral evil—genially denying, in fact, or seeming to, that it is a problem at all. Are we really listening to a moralist who expects to be heard respectfully when we find Emerson saying, à propos of young people who are troubled by the problems of original sin, the origin of evil, and the like: "These never presented a practical difficulty to any man,—never darkened across any man's road who did not go out of his way to seek them. These are the soul's mumps and measles and whooping-coughs. . . . A simple mind will not know these enemies"? We rub our eyes as we read, and then open another volume and find the same sage and seer reassuring us even more blandly that "The less we have to do with our sins the better. No man can afford to waste his moments in compunctions."

Did any writer on morals, we are tempted to ask at such moments, ever go farther than this toward inculcating a hard complacency, a shallow self-righteousness, in his readers? The feeling of unreality that rises in us at these times is almost dreamlike, and so it is on at least some of the occasions when Emerson turns his gaze reluctantly to what used to be called natural evil—to the facts of human misery and suffering—to the Tragic. Is it possible to recognize, in the sun-warmed landscape of the Emersonian center, the terribly familiar world of primordial human experience—that world in which sunshine and warmth have alternated, for most men, with bitter cold and darkness? It is easy to get the mistaken impression that, for Emerson, there were indeed no Cape Horns in experience, no jungles, no Arctic nights, no shark-infested seas; only the amiable rustic landscape of the Concord fields and woodlots. "I could never give much reality to evil and pain," he wrote in his late fifties, and though he had also said quite different things from this, it is true that at the *center* of his mind the space was wholly free from either pain or evil. His thought may be in some sense on the hither side of the tragic; it may be in another sense beyond the tragic;

non-tragic it undeniably is. He himself was quite clear about this. "And yet," he writes in a characteristic poem,

> And yet it seemeth not to me
> That the high gods love tragedy.

Nor did he love it himself. I am speaking now not of the literary form but of tragedy as an aspect of experience—a subject to which only once in his mature career did Emerson give sustained attention. This was in a short essay he contributed to the *Dial*, an essay called "The Tragic" that was based in part on a lecture he had given a little earlier. It is true that Emerson published this essay in a magazine, but characteristically he never reprinted it, and it was left for his literary executors to include it in a posthumous volume. The theme of this piece is that, after everything has been said that may be said on the topic of human misery, in the end one returns to the knowledge that suffering is a kind of illusion, that it has no absolute or ultimate reality. All sorrow, says Emerson, "is superficial; for the most part fantastic, or in the appearance and not in things. . . . For all melancholy, as all passion, belongs to the exterior life. . . . Most suffering is only apparent." And he goes on to speak of the self-operating compensations for suffering in a passage about the horrors of the slave-trade that tempts one, for a moment, to throw his book into the fire, as Whittier is said to have thrown *Leaves of Grass*.

To fix one's attention on passages such as this is to wonder how it is humanly possible for a man to have so weak a memory of his own sorrows or so little compassion for those of other men. Along with this there is that other strain in Emerson that has driven so many readers away from him—the strain in which he seems to be saying that progress, amelioration, an upward movement of things is a law of nature, like gravitation or natural selection, and that the painful human will is very little engaged in it. "Gentlemen," he said to one audience, "there is a sublime and friendly Destiny by which the human race is guided . . . to results affecting masses and ages. Men are narrow and selfish, but the Genius or Destiny is not narrow, but beneficent. . . . Only what is inevitable interests us, and it turns out that love and good are inevitable, and in the course of things." This is the very lotus-dream of progress, you will say, and so is that Emersonian conviction that good ends are always served whether by good men or bad; that rogues and savages are as effectual in the process as prophets and saints. "The barbarians who broke up the Roman Empire," he says, "did not arrive a day too soon." This apparently effortless emergence of good from evil, we are told, is a law not only of nature but of history. "Through the years and the centuries," says Emerson, "through evil agents, through toys and atoms, a great and beneficent tendency irresistibly streams."

"Irresistibly," did you say? Did you say that "love and good are *inevitable*"? Are we to understand that the Destiny that guides human history is simply "friendly" and "beneficent"? To the ears of contemporary men there is a mockery of unreality in such language that makes the language of the *Arabian Nights* seem to ring with the strong accents of realism. In the fearful light of what has happened in history since Emerson said these things—not to speak of what happened before—can one be merely indignant if some thoughtful men have long since settled it that Emerson is not for them? Can one even be wholly surprised if he has sometimes been relegated to the shabby company of faddists and faith-healers, or the equally questionable company of those who have preached the gospel of success, the strenuous life, or the power of positive thinking? The truth is, these charlatans have often drawn, either directly or indirectly, on Emerson himself, and, alas, one can only too easily see why. Let us face it. If Emerson has been coarsened and vulgarized by these people, it is because there are aspects of his thought that have lent themselves to this process. And it is as certain as any human forecast can be that no writer of comparable scope and authority will ever again tell us *in just those tones* that moral evil is negligible and that suffering is a mere illusion.

Yet no one in his senses supposes for a moment that Emerson really belongs in the company of Bruce Barton or Dale Carnegie any more than Plato belongs in the company of Norman Vincent Peale. A powerful instinct tells us that, as he himself remarked of Channing, Emerson is still in some sense our bishop, and that we have not done with him yet. There is no danger of our ever having too many guides or fortifiers, and we know perfectly well that, though we are determined to hold on to Hawthorne and Melville, we cannot afford to dispense with Emerson either. We can afford to dispense with him so little that I suppose most of us are willing now to look at the whole of his work dispassionately and raise for ourselves the question whether his essays are really, after all, a mere encumbrance—or drug. If there proves to be more than this to say, we can hardly be losers. And the more critically one looks at his work, the more it becomes clear that there is a good deal more to be said. No great writer is ever rectilinear—is ever unequivocal or free from contradictions—and Emerson, who consciously disbelieved in straight lines and single poles, is at least as resistant to simple formulas as most. Not only so, but, after all, the problem of evil—the tragic question—is hardly a simple one itself, and the truth is that men have given more than one answer to it. It is a matter of elementary critical justice, surely, to try to arrive at a view of Emerson not only in the flat but in depth.

To tell the truth, there is a greater willingness nowadays to work toward such a view than there was thirty or forty years ago.[1] It has become more usual than it once was to recognize that that celebrated optimism of Emerson's was somewhat less the product of good fortune or of a natively happy temper than it was an achievement both of intellectual and emotional discipline. It was a conviction he had arrived at after youthful years during which he had as good reasons as most men—poverty, ill health, bereavement, anxiety—for questioning the absolute rightness of things. No one who has read his early letters and journals can fail to be conscious of the minor strain that runs through them—the strain of sadness, apprehension, and doubtfulness of the goods of existence. The young Emerson can sound strangely like the mature Melville. He was only twenty, and a year or two out of college, when he wrote in his journal: "There *is* a huge and disproportionate abundance of *evil* on earth. Indeed the good that is here is but a little island of light amidst the unbounded ocean." Three or four years after this, forced by his alarming physical weakness, he gave up preaching temporarily and went South in search of recovery. It was a period of dire low spirits and anxiety for him, and one can understand his writing from St. Augustine to his aunt, Mary Moody Emerson: "He has seen but half the Universe who never has been shown the house of Pain. Pleasure and Peace

---

[1] An admirable example of the more recent approach is Mr. Stephen E. Whicher's volume, *Freedom and Fate: An Inner Life of Ralph Waldo Emerson,* and one ought also to mention his essay on "Emerson's Tragic Sense" in the *American Scholar* (1953).

are but indifferent teachers of what it is life to know."
One might suppose that this outcry was only the bitter
expression of a passing state of physical and emotional
misery; but it was more than that. A dozen years had
elapsed after his stay in the South when he contributed
to the *Dial* the essay on "The Tragic" I have already
alluded to. That essay, oddly enough, begins with one of
the sentences from the old letter to his aunt; let me quote
it again: "He has seen but half the universe who never
has been shown the house of Pain." And he goes on at
once, in the essay, to say: "As the salt sea covers more
than two thirds of the surface of the globe, so sorrow en-
croaches in man on felicity."

Whatever his theory of suffering may have come to be,
Emerson cannot be accused, at least in his earlier years,
of having denied to it a kind of reality. On the contrary,
there are passages in the sermons he preached as a young
minister that remind one much more of the sombre Calvinist homilies of his forebears than of the characteristically
hopeful and cheerful Unitarians in whose ranks he was for
a time enlisted. A few weeks after he returned from St.
Augustine, in 1827, he preached a sermon on the theme of
change and mortality that strikes an even Biblical note of
sorrow and affliction. "Have we brought in our hands," he
asks, like a kind of Unitarian Job—"Have we brought in
our hands any safe conduct to show to our ghastly enemies,
Pain and Death? Shall we not, my brethren, be sufferers as
all our fathers were? Shall we not be sick? Shall we not
die?" And a little later in the same sermon he alludes, in a
phrase that suggests Hawthorne rather than the familiar
Emerson, to "the dark parable of human existence."

It is quite true that these Old Testament accents become
less and less characteristic of him as he approaches the
maturity of his powers, and that the Emerson of the great

middle period—of the famous addresses at Harvard, Dartmouth, and Waterville, and of all the best-known essays—is the Emerson whom we have to think of as the Orpheus of Optimism. But, even in this period, and certainly later, there is another tone, an undertone, in his writings which we should listen to if we wish to sensitize ourselves to the complex harmony of his total thought. That thought, to change the image, is a polarized thought, and if at one pole we find a celebration of the powers of the human will, at the other pole we find an insistence on its limitations—on the forces in nature that are not friendly but hostile and even destructive to human wishes, and on the discrepancy between what a man aspires to do and what nature and circumstance allow him to do. "The word Fate, or Destiny," he says in the essay on Montaigne, "expresses the sense of mankind, in all ages, that the laws of the world do not always befriend, but often hurt and crush us. Fate, in the shape of . . . nature, grows over us like grass. . . . What front can we make against these unavoidable, victorious, maleficent forces?"

Are there, then, along with, or running counter to, the "great and beneficent tendency," forces of immense potency in nature which are not amiable but fierce and ruinous? Yes, so Emerson tells us—not only in this essay of the forties but in a lecture he delivered several times in the fifties and at last published as the essay on "Fate" in *The Conduct of Life*. It is an essay that should be read by everyone who imagines that for Emerson there were not really any Cape Horns in experience. "No picture of life," he says, "can have any veracity that does not admit the odious facts." And he lays himself out to suggest what those facts are—the facts of nature's ferocity—with a grim thoroughness that suggests the authors of *Candide* or *Rasselas* or *Moby Dick* much more vividly than the author of

"The Over-Soul." Here is all the familiar imagery of naturalistic pessimism—the imagery of earthquakes and volcanic eruptions, of plagues and famine, of tooth and claw. "The habit of the snake and spider, the snap of the tiger and other leapers and bloody jumpers, the crackle of the bones of his prey in the coil of the anaconda"—these are all in nature, he insists, and so are "the forms of the shark . . . the jaw of the sea-wolf paved with crushing teeth, the weapons of the grampus, and other warriors hidden in the sea." Could Voltaire or Melville or Zola say more?

Yet the savagery of nature—nature's Darwinism, to call it so—furnishes less of the stuff of the essay on "Fate" than what I spoke of a moment ago, the restrictiveness of nature; the tight limits set about the human will, human aspiration, human effort, by all the forces of heredity and circumstance that Emerson dramatizes by the old word Fate. "The Circumstance is Nature," says he. "Nature is what you may do. There is much you may not. . . . The book of Nature is the book of Fate." Within these merely natural and material boundaries men are the creatures of their conditioning. "How shall a man," asks Emerson, "escape from his ancestors, or draw off from his veins the black drop which he drew from his father's or his mother's life?" A demonstration of these painful truths that fascinated Emerson for a time, a few years earlier, had been the new science of statistics—the science that seemed to settle it that human behavior can be reduced to mathematical terms and predicted as confidently as the precession of the equinoxes. Perhaps it can, says Emerson, with a quiet smile, in the essay on Swedenborg: "If one man in twenty thousand, or in thirty thousand," he says, "eats shoes or marries his grandmother, then in every twenty thousand or thirty thousand is found one man who eats shoes or marries his grandmother." At any rate, viewed

from the outside, as objects, as mere creatures of nature
and society, men live and work within lines that are for
the most part drawn not by them but for them. We must
learn what not to expect.

In short it is not true that Emerson's optimism is quite
so unmodulated as it has often been represented as being,
or that he was so incapable as Yeats thought him to be of
the Vision of Evil. I have been speaking of Evil just now
in the sense of suffering and frustration, but even if it is a
question of moral evil, of human malignancy, depravity,
and vice, it is not true that Emerson averted his gaze from
it quite so steadily as his detractors have said. Neither
suffering nor wickedness is his primary theme; they are
not even secondary; in his work as a whole they are tiny
patches of grayness or blackness in a composition that is
flooded with light and high color. But, even if we ignore
the sermons of his youth, in which the New England sense
of guilt and sinfulness sometimes throbs and shoots as
painfully as it ever does in Hawthorne—even if we ignore
these early writings, it is not true that Emerson's view of
human nature was a merely smiling and sanguine one. To
be sure, it was the feebleness of men, their incompetence,
their imbecility, that he castigated, when he was in this
vein, more often than their depravity. But, when he chose,
he could express himself as unsentimentally as any moral
realist on the brutishness of which men are capable. It was
no mere idealist who said, with some humor indeed, in
speaking of the Norman Conquest: "Twenty thousand
thieves landed at Hastings."

This bluntness is very characteristic of him, and when he
was really deeply stirred by the spectacle of systematic
cruelty and injustice, as he was during the long anguish of
the anti-slavery struggle, he could wrench off certain
specious masks and disguises as unsparingly, as realisti-

cally, as any of his Calvinist ancestors could have done.
Read the "Address" he delivered at Concord on the anniversary of the emancipation of slaves in the West Indies
if you wish to have a glimpse of Emerson the moral realist.
They tell us, he says in his speech, that the slave-holder
does not wish to own slaves for the love of owning them,
but only because of the material advantages his ownership
brings. Experience, however, he goes on to say, does not
bear out this comfortable evasion, but shows "the existence, beside the covetousness, of a bitterer element, the
love of power, the voluptuousness of holding a human
being in his absolute control." Men are capable, says
Emerson, of liking to inflict pain, and the slave-holder "has
contracted in his indolent and luxurious climate the need
of excitement by irritating and tormenting his slave."

It is hard to see how the Vision of Evil, at least for a
moment, could be much keener or more terrible than this;
and in the whole slavery connection Emerson said a good
many things almost equally piercing. But it remains true
that his animadversions on human wickedness, like his
allusions to human suffering, are closer to the circumfer-
ence than to the center of Emerson's thought; they give his
writings their moral chiaroscuro, but they are not dominant, and I have perhaps dwelt too long on them. His con-
trolling mode of thought, even in his later and more
skeptical years, is a certain form of Optimism and *not* a
form of the Tragic Sense, and what I should like to say
now is that, however we may ourselves feel about this
philosophy, it was one that rested not only on a deep
personal experience but on a considered theory of Evil,
and moreover that this was a theory by no means peculiar
to Emerson, or original with him: on the contrary, it had
a long and august tradition behind it in Western thought
and analogies with the thought not only of Europe but of

the East. To put it very briefly, it is the theory that identifies Evil with nonexistence, with negation, with the absence of positive Being. In his own writings Emerson expressed this doctrine first in the famous "Address" at the Divinity School at Harvard in 1838, the manifesto of his heterodoxy. "Good is positive," he said to the graduating class that day. "Evil is merely privative, not absolute: it is like cold, which is the privation of heat. All evil is so much death or nonentity. Benevolence is absolute and real."

Such language as this has become terribly unfamiliar to us, and Heaven knows for what good reasons, in our own guilt-ridden and anxious time; some of us may find it hard to believe that reasonable men ever entertained such a view. The truth is, however, that it is not only a philosophical but an essentially religious view, and that its sources, to speak only of the West, are in the Platonic and Neo-Platonic tradition and in Christian theology on the side on which it derives from that tradition. It was from these sources, indeed, that Emerson drew his theoretical Optimism. When Plato identified the Good with absolute reality, and Evil with the imperfectly real or the unreal, he was speaking a language beyond Tragedy; and let us not forget that he proposed to banish tragic poetry from his ideal Republic—to banish it on the ground that the wise and virtuous man will wish to control the emotions of grief and sorrow rather than to stimulate them. As for Plotinus, the greatest of the Neo-Platonists, whom Emerson read with such excitement in the few years before the "Address" at the Divinity School, he too denied that Evil can have a part in real existence, since this—real existence—is by definition good. "If then evil exists," says Plotinus, "there remains for it the sphere of not-being, and it is, as it were, a certain form of not-being." The sentence reads very much like Emerson's own.

At any rate it was this Neo-Platonic denial of any absolute or ultimate reality to Evil that seems to have found
its way into Christian orthodoxy in the writings of St.
Augustine—"a man," as Emerson says, "of as clear a sight
as almost any other." The Manicheans had attributed to
Evil a positive and independent existence, and Augustine
as a young man had fallen under their spell; but he had
broken away from them at the time of his conversion, and
steeped as he was in the thought of the Neo-Platonists, he
arrived at a theory of Evil that, on one level, seems indistinguishable from theirs. "Evil has no positive nature," he
says in *The City of God;* "but the loss of good has received
the name 'evil.'" In itself it is purely negative, a diminish-
ment or corruption of the good, for, as he says, "no nature
at all is evil, and this is a name for nothing but the want of
good." Of course, as one need not say, Augustine does not
deny that *sin* has a kind of reality, but he conceives of it
as an essentially negative reality—as a rejection or refusal
of the Good, not as an ultimate and independent essence
in itself.

No sane man, of course, whatever his metaphysics, can
refuse to recognize that wrong-doing is in some sense a
fact; and Emerson was much too clear-sighted a moralist
not to find a place in his thought, as Augustine had done,
for what his ancestors had called "sin," though his account
of it is not quite the same as Augustine's. He accounts for
it, in a more purely transcendental way, by distinguishing
between what is real to the intellect and what is real to the
conscience—real, that is, in the conduct of life itself. "Sin,
seen from the thought," he says, "is a diminution, or *less*;
seen from the conscience or will, it is pravity or *bad*. The
intellect names it shade, absence of light, and no essence.
The conscience must feel it as essence, essential evil.
This it is not; it has an objective existence, but no sub-

jective." Objectively, that is, and when the conscience
speaks, the savagery of the slave-holder is real enough;
subjectively, and when the voice of the mind is heard, that
savagery is seen for the "absence of light," the essential
unreality, it is. Despite their differences, Augustine and
Emerson are saying at least not dissimilar things.

Convictions such as this, at any rate, are at the heart and
core of his philosophic optimism. Both sin and suffering,
moral and natural evil, *appear* in experience; but they are
indeed appearances, not ultimate realities; what reality
they have is relative, external, transitory; absolutely speaking, they are shadows, phenomena, illusions. We may, in
our time, find such convictions as these mistaken, but let
us recognize them for what they are. They are convictions
of an essentially religious sort, and like Plato's, or Plotinus's,
or Augustine's, they are in themselves inconsistent with
the Tragic Sense. We are in the habit of assuming that the
most serious and profound apprehension of reality is the
Sense of Tragedy; but it may be that, in assuming this, we
ourselves are mistaken. It may be that there are points of
view from which the Tragic Sense must be seen as serious
and profound indeed, but limited and imperfectly philosophical. It may even be that there can exist a kind of
complacency of pessimism, as there is certainly a complacency of optimism; and that many of us in this age are
guilty of it. We hug our negations, our doubts, our dis-
beliefs, to our chests, as if our moral and intellectual
dignity depended on them. And indeed it does—so far as
the alternative is to remain *this side* of Tragedy, and to
shut our ears and eyes to the horrors of experience. Our
impatience with Emerson is by no means wholly baseless.
We feel, and we have a right to feel, that, if we take his
work as a whole, there is a certain distortion in the way it
reflects the real world; a certain imbalance and deforma-

tion in the way in which the lights and shadows are distributed. The shadows are too meager, and sometimes they are too easily conjured away. We have a right to feel that, too much of the time, Emerson is speaking with a lightheartedness that seems to keep him on this side of Tragedy.

What I have been trying to suggest, however, is that we cannot justly leave him there—that the time has come to remind ourselves that it is possible to reach beyond Tragedy, as well as to remain on the hither side of it; that this is what the religious sense has always done; that Tragedy, as a poetic form, has flourished only rarely, in periods of disbelief and denial; and that, for Emerson, disbelief and denial were simply impossible, ultimately, in the light of his transcendental faith. We may well dislike the tone he often takes, but if we wait patiently enough, we shall find him taking other tones; and in the end we must recognize that, whatever our own convictions are, the best of Emerson is on the other side of Tragedy. I have tried to show that he did not simply *find* himself there; if he had got beyond Tragedy, it was because he had *moved* beyond it. "It requires moral courage to grieve," says Kierkegaard; "it requires religious courage to rejoice." We would be less than just, I think, if we denied that Emerson's courage was both moral and religious.

His acquaintance with the religious literature of the world was very wide; it was by no means confined to the Christian or even the Western tradition; and perhaps we might concede that his perspective was wider and deeper than that which most of us can command. While he was still in his thirties he began to read some of the Hindu scriptures as they appeared in translation; and he quickly recognized in them philosophical and religious insights that seemed at times to be mere anticipations of his own. When he read the Upanishads, or the *Bhagavad-Gita*, or the *Vishnu Purana,* what he found in them was a conception of the ultimate and impersonal Ground of Being—of Brahma—that had much in comon with the Absolute of the Neo-Platonists and with his own God or Over-Soul. He found more than that. He had already arrived at the conviction that, as he said, "Within and Above are synonyms"; that the Over-Soul and the individual soul are one; that the kingdom of God, as the gospel says, is within you. The Upanishads only confirmed him in this conviction—confirmed him by their expression of the doctrine that the Absolute Self and the individual self are identical; that Brahma and Atman, as they say, are one; that, as they also say, *"That* art *Thou."* This too was a doctrine that left the Tragic Sense behind it. According to the Upanishads, the man who, as a result of intense discipline and concentrated meditation, attains to a knowledge of the Self—call it either Brahma or Atman, for they are the same—has transcended the illusory realm of human wretchedness and wickedness, and is beyond either. "He who knows the Self," says the *Brihadaranyaka Upanishad,* "is honored of all men and attains to blessedness. He who meditates upon Brahma as such lacks nothing and is forever happy. He who meditates upon Brahma as such becomes himself invincible and unconquerable. . . . Indeed, the Self, in his true nature, is free from craving, free from evil, free from fear."

When one reads passages like this, and there are many of them, one finds it easy to understand why the literary form of Tragedy—the tragic drama—is unknown in Sanskrit literature. In any case, I do not wish to imply that there are no important differences, even in this connection, among the thinkers I have spoken of; that the Neo-Platonist Plotinus, the orthodox Christian Augustine, and the authors of the Upanishads were perfectly at one in their view

of Good and Evil; and that Emerson is indistinguishable
from any of them. The differences are vital, some of them,
and certainly there is much in Emerson, especially in his
tone, that would have struck his great predecessors as very
dubious indeed. I have intended only to suggest that it is
superficial to rule out the whole of him, once for all, on
the ground that he lacked the Vision of Evil; to see him as
nothing but a transcendental American optimist of the
mid-nineteenth century; to fail to see that his view of
these things was in a great philosophic and religious tradition; and that he rejected Tragedy not because he was
by temperament wholly incapable of tragic insight but
because it seemed to him that, as Karl Jaspers has said,
"tragedy is not absolute but belongs in the foreground";
it belongs, as he says, "in the world of sense and time,"
but not in the realm of transcendence. It belongs, let us
say, in the world of appearance, of the relative, of illusion;
not in the realm of transcendent reality and truth in which
Emerson's faith was complete. And perhaps it is only
readers who have a comparable faith, who will now accept
him as master and guide; accept him as Dante accepted
Vergil: "tu duca, tu segnore, e tu maestro."

Yet this is not quite true either, and I suppose has never
been. There seem always to have been readers, there seem
to be readers still, who have not been able to share Emerson's idealistic religious beliefs, and who nevertheless have
found him, in spite of everything, an intellectual and moral
stimulant—a cup-bearer, not an anaesthetist. Certainly
Baudelaire did not share Emerson's optimism, yet Baudelaire pored over *The Conduct of Life,* and said that Emerson had " a certain flavor of Seneca about him, which
effectively stimulates meditation." Certainly André Gide
did not share Emerson's transcendentalism, yet Gide describes Emerson's essays as "reading for the morning," and

clearly he found in them that *matutina cognitio* or "morning knowledge" which Emerson himself, borrowing a phrase from Thomas Aquinas, had described as the knowledge of God. Certainly Nietzsche did not share Emerson's other-worldliness, yet Emerson was one of his two or three great teachers and models. He is said to have carried copies of the essays, heavily annotated, with him whenever he travelled; and it was precisely Emerson's capacity for joy that Nietzsche seems most to have cherished in him. There is a paragraph in *The Twilight of Idols* in which he compares Emerson with Carlyle, to the disadvantage of the latter: Emerson, says he, "is much more enlightened, much broader, more versatile, and more subtle than Carlyle; but above all, he is happier. . . . His mind is always finding reasons for being contented and even thankful." For the author of *Zarathustra* this could only have been a token of Emerson's greatness.

Why is it that men of this sort, so little given to easy solutions and facile reassurances, have again and again found Emerson so bracing? Not, surely, because they have been willing to accept his transcendental theory of Evil, but because that theory, in Emerson as in some other thinkers, proved to be wholly consistent with a moral strenuousness seldom encountered in modern writers one can respect. For the truth is that, in this connection as in others, Emerson is a polarized, a contradictory, writer; and if, at the one extreme, you find the peculiar moral passiveness that contents itself with a "beneficent" and "irresistible" tendency toward the Good, at the other extreme you find the equally if not more characteristic celebration of the active and energetic will. It is what Emerson often calls Power, and in the essay on "Fate" from which I have quoted, after giving the devil his due, and making every concession to the determinists that seems to him possible, he goes on to insist that, among the forces operating in the universe, the human will is one—and that, ideally speaking, it counterweighs all the others. "For though Fate is immense," he says, "so is Power, which is the other fact in the dual world, immense. If Fate follows and limits Power, Power attends and antagonizes Fate. We must respect Fate as natural history, but there is more than natural history." This "more" includes the freedom of the human will, and it has to be reckoned with just as seriously as the laws of physics and chemistry; indeed, it is itself a law just as truly as they are, and more truly. "A part of Fate," as he says, "is the freedom of man." And what this should teach us, he goes on to say, is not a fatalistic acceptance, but an exhilarated and courageous activism. " 'Tis weak and vicious people," he says, "who cast the blame on Fate. The right use of Fate is to bring up our conduct to the loftiness of nature. Rude and invincible except by themselves are the elements. So let man be. Let him empty his breast of his windy conceits, and show his lordship by manners and deeds on the scale of nature. Let him hold his purpose as with the tug of gravitation." The true lesson to be learned from the facts of determinism is that we can afford to be brave. " 'Tis the best use of Fate," as he says, "to teach a fatal courage. . . . If you believe in Fate to your harm, believe it at least for your good." The one is quite as philosophical as the other.

It would be very unjust, in short, not to recognize the strenuous strain in Emerson's optimism; not to keep reminding ourselves of such injunctions as the one with which he approached the conclusion of his essay on "New England Reformers": "That which befits us, embosomed in beauty and wonder as we are, is cheerfulness and courage, and the endeavor to realize our aspirations."

The word "endeavor," like the word "work," is a thematic word in Emerson. And yet I suppose that, even in saying this, we are not quite at the center of the Emersonian vision. I have said that his thought—or better his feeling—moves back and forth between a trusting passiveness and an energetic activism; and for the most part this is true. But there are moments in his work when the dichotomy between the passive and the active is transcended, and what he expresses is a spiritual experience that partakes of both—an experience of such intensity, yet of such calm, that neither of the words, "active" or "passive," quite does justice to it. In recording such moments he expresses most perfectly that joy which, according to Kierkegaard, demands religious courage. One of the most eloquent of these passages occurs in the great address on "The Method of Nature" which he read at Waterville College, now Colby, in 1841:

> We ought to celebrate this hour by expressions of manly joy. Not thanks, not prayer seem quite the highest or truest name for our communication with the infinite,—but glad and conspiring reception,—reception that becomes giving in its turn, as the receiver is only the All-Giver in part and in infancy. I cannot,—nor can any man,—speak precisely of things so sublime, but it seems to me the wit of man, his strength, his grace, his tendency, his art, is the grace and the presence of God. It is beyond explanation. When all is said and done, the rapt saint is found the only logician. Not exhortation, not argument becomes our lips, but paeans of joy and praise.

If I had to say where we are most likely to find the quintessential Emerson, I should point to passages like this. Certainly there are other Emersons, and they are not to be made light of; there is the trumpeter of nonconformity; there is the attorney for the American intellectual; there is the New England humorist. But none of these, it seems to me, speaks in quite so special and incomparable tones as the Emerson whom one would like to call, not after all a moralist, nor a prophet, nor even a teacher, but a hymnist or psalmist—one who, at his most characteristic, utters psalms of thanksgiving, or, as he says, "paeans of joy and praise"; whose most intimate mode of expression is always a *Te Deum*. This is the Emerson who is bound to disappoint us if we look in his work for a steady confrontation of Tragedy or a sustained and unswerving gaze at the face of Evil. They are not there, and we shall lose our labor if we look for them. But there is no writer in the world, however comprehensive, in whose work we are not conscious of missing *something* that belongs to experience; and now that critical justice has been done to what is wanting in Emerson, we can surely afford very well to avail ourselves of all that is positively there. What is there, as we have to recognize when we have cleared our minds of the cant of pessimism, is perhaps the fullest and most authentic expression in modern literature of the more-than-tragic emotion of thankfulness. A member of his family tells us that almost his last word was "praise." Unless we have deafened ourselves to any other tones than those of anguish and despair, we should still know how to be inspirited by everything in his writings that this word symbolizes.

HENRY DAVID THOREAU

THOREAU v. THOREAU

MR. CANBY remarks, in the introduction to his very full and useful volume of selections from Thoreau's writings, that the reputation of the author of *Walden* is even now continually rising. Undoubtedly this is a fact, as the appearance of these two books * itself indicates, and certainly it is a cheering fact. Thoreau may not be, as Mr. Canby feels "inclined to prophesy" extravagantly, "the most durable of American writers," but there is no extravagance in saying that "he belongs in the small group of really great Americans," and we should lose something irreplaceable if we failed to make our use of what is strongest and most galvanic in his thought. There is a good deal that is weak and whimsical in it, and this ought to be winnowed out rigorously and impartially. Thoreau needs very badly to be rescued from the Thoreauvians: he needs, in fact, to be rescued from himself. To make a cult of him, to follow him wherever he leads, is to find ourselves up to our waists in an impassable swamp almost as often as on a hilltop with a wide view.

* *The Works of Thoreau*: Selected and edited by Henry S. Canby. *Walden and Other Writings of Henry David Thoreau.* Edited, with an Introduction, by Brooks Atkinson.

It would be a poor service to criticism, for example, either to play down or to rejoice in the really dangerous strain in Thoreau of contempt for exact knowledge, for scientific inquiry, for "mere phenomena." It was a strain that he had in common with all the Transcendentalists, of course, and so far as it meant only a disdain for the routine "observer" or the dull laboratory specialist, it was a healthy enough strain. But it meant more than that, and it is not in Channing or Emerson or Parker that one will find quite the equivalent of Thoreau's superstitious distrust of the organized advancement of learning, his village incuriosity about the great physical and biological generalizations of his time, or that unhealthy fear of his own growing tendency toward precision and objectivity in research. We have no excuse, in our times, for failing to see the black gulf toward which these negations drive, and Thoreau the mystical obscurantist is not our man.

No more is Thoreau the contemptuous misanthrope. For there *was* a genuinely misanthropic side of his nature, and one that cannot be explained away as Mr. Brooks Atkinson very generously attempts to do, in his introduction to the Modern Library edition of *Walden and Other Writings*. It is always possible, of course, to say of such writers as Thoreau that they have too exalted standards of human conduct ever to be quite satisfied with the behavior of real men, and that they are ethically bracing on just this account. The apology simply does not dispose entirely of that "very aggravated case of superciliousness" which Whitman reluctantly recognized in his Concord admirer. Channing too had his exalted standards, and so had Theodore Parker; but the austerity of their ideals did not keep those men from conveying, in every line they wrote, a temperamental bias of affection and respect for human beings that was quite left out of Thoreau's narrower makeup. His was not an admiring character, as one of his best friends said; and that is one reason why he furnishes so fitful an inspiration to the radical democrat today. In his passion for nature itself there was too large an element of active inhumanity. "I love Nature," he wrote quite honestly, "partly *because* she is not man, but a retreat from him. . . . What he touches he taints."

> Man, man is the devil,
> The source of all evil.

It is true that he said other things wholly contradictory to this, but it is hard to see how, when he is in this vein, Thoreau is much sweeter to the palate than Jonathan Edwards himself.

It was a heavy limitation for him—and not all the source of strength Mr. Canby represents it—that his imagination could make nothing of social experience or of the forces that move toward community among men. He could see with perfect sharpness the follies of gregariousness and the perils of conformity: he was hopelessly color-blind to the values of fellowship and unity. His individualism, as a result, lofty as it is in some of its expressions, has too large an admixture in it of insensitiveness and complacency. "What men call social virtues, good fellowship," wrote Thoreau, "is commonly but the virtue of pigs in a litter, which lie close together to keep each other warm." He did hardly more than confess his own undeveloped and unripened faculties when he wrote this, and he betrayed mainly his own want of political insight when he disposed of the Fourierists as glibly as he did: "I said I suspected any enterprise in which two were engaged together." It is the sort of thing that keeps his transcendental anarchism from having all the meaning it ought to have for us: its content is so largely not simply pride and dignity and independence but touchiness and irresponsibility. He said, after all, "I am not responsible for the successful working of the machinery of society"— and he meant it.

It is not when he rails at men of science or contemns human nature or renounces sociality that Thoreau is worth attending to. His extraordinary claim upon us rests on quite a different ground: namely, that despite his limitations he has helped to enrich the whole modern sensibility by his genius for getting at the tough substances of things and disburdening himself of shadows, substitutes and vanities. The Thoreau who said, "Be it life or death, we crave only reality," is the Thoreau we still need. He was the freshly and finely endowed poet who could slough off even his own whims and poses and make up his mind "to live deep and suck out all the marrow of life," "to drive life in a corner, and reduce it to its lowest terms"; and the explorations this purpose led him on were morally Copernican. It was necessary that the human sensibility, blunted for so long by the drug of the infinite, should be redomesticated in the world of minerals and vegetables, of kingfishers and muskrats: for all his occultism, Thoreau's wonderful instinct for reality brought him into an intimate harmony with all those purely natural existences, and our secular culture is the richer as a result. He was not the only modern who achieved anything of the sort, but he achieved it more intensely than all but a few others, and the pages that record his adventures with the real and the finite will long be Scripture to the naturalistic imagination.

WALT WHITMAN

WHITMAN'S INDIVIDUALISM *

LIBERAL and individualist critics are naturally inclined to read undiluted liberalism and individualism into whatever writers they find praiseworthy; and American critics of this stamp have pretty effectually put together an acceptable portrait of Walt Whitman out of their own range of pastel shades. According to this portrait, Whitman was merely the jolly and complacent spokesman of American middle-class democracy, undiscriminating, uncritically affirmative, and committed to the dogmas of self-help and self-expression in their simplest and even crudest form. The late Stuart Sherman, who admired Carnegie and his peers so cordially ("wholeheartedly and aspiringly democratic in their ends" as they were), once declared that "If Whitman had lived at the right place in these years of the Proletarian Millennium, he would have been hanged as a reactionary member of the bourgeoisie." Only the other day Mr. H. S. Canby was saying: "Walt never wrote for classes; the idea of a world proletariat based on economic grounds would have been repugnant to him. He

---

* *Sit and Look Out: Editorials from the Brooklyn Daily Times, by Walt Whitman.* Selected and edited by Emory Holloway and Vernolian Schwartz.

wrote for individuals." There is, according to these critics, no dynamite in Whitman: there is indeed nothing in him that would not be acceptable to Herbert Hoover or, at least, to Governor Ritchie.

Certainly it is true that Whitman, as a preacher of self-reliance, had gone to school to Carlyle and Emerson; certainly it is true that, as a democrat, he had gone to school to Thomas Paine and Jackson and, later, Abraham Lincoln. If he was a radical, it is easy to show that his was in its origins the old American radicalism, and that he never completely abandoned his early Jeffersonian conviction that "that government is best which governs least." The man who stumped, in his youth, for Van Buren and, in his old age, cherished the memory of his glimpses of Jackson, can hardly be made out to have been, body and soul, a twentieth-century collectivist. Yet is this equivalent to saying that there were not vital contradictions in his thought? that he gave expression to but one aspect of social history in the nineteenth century, and is now to be archaized by its passing? that the increasingly sharp antitheses in American society, as his life went on, made no appeal to his imagination, and had no effect on his work? Did he accept his own individualism without correction? Was he unaware that American business and American democracy were possibly at odds? Was his attitude toward social change simply that, in the good Sherman's phrase, of "a reactionary member of the bourgeoisie"? The true answers to these questions deserve a volume: I can only suggest what form they might take.

Dr. Canby has said that Whitman wrote only for individuals, never for classes; and that the idea of a world proletariat would be repugnant to him. Has Dr. Canby never looked through Traubel's three volumes, *With Walt Whitman in Camden*? If so, was he not struck by a speech

of Whitman's to his young friend on June 8, 1888? "Literature," said the old man, "is big only in one way—when
used as an aid in the growth of the humanities—a further-
ing of the cause of the masses—a means whereby men
may be revealed to each other as brothers." And a few
months later, when Traubel had outlined to him Tolstoy's
notoriously anti-individualistic views on the arts, Whitman exclaimed: "I endorse them: O yes, with ten thousand times ten thousand amens: and if he goes on like that
talking about the arts then you may say anywhere for me:
Walt Whitman is with Tolstoy—count him in." These are
scarcely the pronouncements of a man who can justly be
said to have written only for individuals; and, as regards
a world proletariat, one wonders how "repugnant" the
idea would have been to the man who said, in "A Backward Glance" (1888), "Without yielding an inch the
working man and working woman were to be in my pages
from first to last"; and who had already envisaged the on-
rush of an internationalism which does not sound, in his
lines, like that of the League of Nations:

Never was average man, his soul, more energetic, more like a
    a God,
Lo, how he urges and urges, leaving the masses no rest! . . .
Are all nations communing? is there going to be but one heart
    to the globe?
Is humanity forming en-masse?

But, indeed, to rely on particular citations such as these
is to do the question injustice: it need not rest upon them.
Quite aside from single phrases in his prose or verse, or
the oracles of his old age, it is possible to see Whitman's
"individualistic" radicalism in its true light by focusing his
whole career in perspective. It is true that he was a tran-

scendental egoist who had sat at the feet of Emerson, and was in sympathy with the expansive individualism of the middle decades of the century; true that he believed that "The American compact is altogether with individuals"; true that he came too early to have any grasp of historical materialism, or to see social history in terms of a struggle between classes. But there is a radical paradox in his work, as there was in his age, and, for all his egoism, his real sympathies were intensely democratic; his individualism, unlike Emerson's, was profoundly modified by his gospel of comradeship and solidarity; unlike most of his contemporaries, he was violently critical, from the beginning, of the individualism of business enterprise; and, even before the Civil War, certainly in the years that followed, he saw with remarkable clarity that American democracy had much of tragic implication to fear from the greed of predatory individuals. He was born too soon to make, in his own imagination, the transition from Thomas Paine to Karl Marx; but, in his old age, in conversation, he spoke far more in the manner of a Marxian than of a Jacksonian; and Traubel, who was a Socialist, had little difficulty in persuading the old poet to concur with his opinions, at least in general terms.

Jacksonian as a young newspaper editor he may have been, but the democracy that comes out in his editorials in *The Brooklyn Eagle* (1846–47) or in these newly reprinted editorials from *The Brooklyn Daily Times* (1857–59) is by no means merely the democracy of Van Buren, Cass and Polk, or of Peirce and Buchanan. His remarks in *The Eagle* on wage cuts in the white-lead factories in Brooklyn, or on the effects of slavery in degrading white workers as well as black, or on protection ("Has any one of our laboring fellow citizens such thin perceptions—does he imagine in his most abstracted dreams—that all this hubbub made by the pale-fingered richly housed Whig manufacturers, and their organs, is for *him*, the laborer?"), or on the profit-motive ("Our American capitalists of the manufacturing order, would *poor* a great many people to be rich!")—such remarks as these may be the remarks of an individualist, but only, surely, of a critical one.

Even in the editorials of the present volume, so many of which, as Mr. Holloway suggests, are colored by the high spirits and patriotic ardor of Whitman's late thirties, even here there are discordant notes. On the horrors of unemployment during the panic of 1857, on "the gaunt physical want" of the city poor ("Down Below"), on the "greater reforms needed here [in the North] than in the Southern States," on the real meaning of the slavery evil ("the great cause of American White Work and Working people"), Whitman is quite as eloquent as on the civic advantages of Brooklyn and the laying of the Atlantic cable.

Yet it was only after the war, when the patriotic emotions stimulated by that crisis had begun to subside, that Whitman was first seriously and painfully agitated by the gloomy contradictions of American democracy, and only in "Democratic Vistas" that he first allowed himself to formulate his anxieties explicitly. "The depravity of the business classes of our country," he there protested, "is not less than has been supposed, but infinitely greater. . . . In business (this all-devouring modern word, business) the one sole object is, by any means, pecuniary gain." He admonished his countrymen not to ignore "that problem, the labor question, beginning to open like a yawning gulf, rapidly widening every year"; and reminded them that for them, too, "as for all lands," there existed "the wily person in office, scrofulous wealth, the surfeit of prosperity, the demonism of greed . . . the fossil-like lethargy, the ceaseless need of revolutions." Later, as the depression of the seventies, stretching out blackly from year to year, exposed the inevitable underside of American prosperity, Whitman came more and more to see how profoundly the basis of democracy was shifting; and in such fragments as "The Tramp and Strike Questions" ("not the abstract question of democracy, but of social and economic organization, the treatment of working people by employers"), "Who Gets the Plunder?" and "Central Park Notes" (notes printed in *Collect* and *November Boughs*) he confessed that his youthful confidence in the happy future of American democracy had had to be qualified by experience.

By the late eighties, when Traubel began his diary record, Whitman's political and social views had settled down to a consistent level of bitter and disappointed, though never hopeless, protest against the dirtiness of American politics, the corruption of both the Republican and Democratic parties ("these damned huckster parties"), the unscrupulousness of American capital, and the venality of church and press. Speaking of slavery, he once said: "I never could quite lose the sense of other evils in this evil—I saw other evils that cried to me in perhaps even a louder voice: the labor evil, now, to speak of only one, which to this day has been steadily growing worse, worse, worse." "I am not interested," he said again, "in what Carnegie is doing to establish libraries abroad but in what he is doing to keep peace with and render justice to his men here." He clung to his old views of protection: "The protection of profit—the protection of the swell proprietors—I guess I don't care a shucks for that: I guess I'd just whip it out of the temple with cords any day if I could." The old journalist of the Greeley era realized what was happening to the newspapers: "They are all getting into the hands of millionaires. God help our liberties when money has finally got our institutions in its clutch." And the old free thinker realized what was happening to religion: "You spoke," said Traubel once, "of the priests of religion and the priests of the arts. We still have the priests of commerce to contend with." "So we have," replied Whitman: "doubly so: the priests of commerce augmented by the priests of churches, who are everywhere the parasites, the apologists, of systems as they exist."

Such, in terms that he constantly recurred to, were Whitman's feelings about American capitalism in the eighties. He was a mere individualist, say the liberal critics: did he, then, go back on his old faith in the masses and betake himself to the praise of "strong men," "heroes" and "rugged individuals"? Did he, on the other hand, abandon both democracy and the hero, and relapse into senile despair? He did neither. On the contrary, he reiterated his old democratic loyalties, against the background of a transformed society, with a new emphasis and a new zeal. "America," he said, "is not for special types, for the castes, but for the great mass of people—the vast, surging, hopeful army of workers." Again, speaking of some mechanics he knew fondly: "They, their like, the crowd of the grave workingmen of our world—they are the hope, the sole hope, the sufficient hope, of our democracy." And still later:

> I liked what [Edward Carpenter] said of the mechanics at Leeds: I put my faith in them—in the crowd of every-day men—in the rise, the supremacy (not the rule) of the superb masses: the men who do things—the workers: they are our hope—they will lead us on if we are led on: not the kid-gloved nobses: . . . I don't see what they can do for us except lead wrong ways—to the devil—yes, lead us into a hole.

But what were such sentiments to lead to, in the future, in the twentieth century? To socialism? He shrank, the old Free Soiler, from committing himself quite irrevocably. "Lots of it—lots—lots," he replied, however, when Traubel asked him whether he had any sympathy with the Socialism of William Morris; and, on another day:

> Sometimes I think, I feel almost sure, Socialism is the next thing coming: I shrink from it in some ways: yet it looks like our only hope. I'm a sort of an anarchist tramp, too: and you? well, you are a lot like me . . . but things drive us on—the God damned robbers, fools, stupids, who ride their gay horses over the bodies of the crowd: they drive us on: God knows to what: sometimes I don't like to think of it: but they'll drive us into an inevitable resentment, then revolt, of some sort.

One day, when he was complaining that the many were swindled by the few, Traubel asked him: "Do you think the class that has robbed the people will hand their loot back?" "I'm afraid not," he returned: "I'm afraid the people will have to fight for what they get." "Why, Walt," cried his friend, "you're a damned good revolutionist after all!" He was amused, says Traubel. "Didn't you always know it? What could I be if I wasn't?"

Such was the man who has been called a potential bourgeois reactionary, an old-fashioned Jacksonian democrat and the poet solely of individuals. It looks as if there were more dynamite in Whitman than the liberals have found in him. It looks as if, were he living today, his loyalties might be, not with the Shermans and Canbys, but with the men and women to whom he addressed himself at the beginning:

You workwomen and workmen of these States having your
    own divine and strong life,
And all else giving place to men and women like you.

BRONSON ALCOTT

THE TEDIOUS ARCHANGEL

MR. SHEPARD's book * is the work to which Little, Brown and Company have awarded the prize offered by them in celebration of their hundredth anniversary as publishers, and it turns out to be that white blackbird among prize-winners, a book that bestows quite as much honor as it receives. If you grant the point of view from which Mr. Shepard writes—and many of us will not be able to grant it—it is hard to see how a better book about Bronson Alcott could be written. The subject itself, of course, is as engagingly human—and almost as "significant"—as such a subject could be, and the two earlier books about it, ponderous in the one case, sketchy in the other, left its real substance as if untouched for the right biographer; but not many readers, at that, could have expected it to prove so fruitful a theme for narrative, for picture-making, for the study of personality, as Mr. Shepard has shown it to be.

He very evidently approached the life and character of "Orphic" Alcott—Carlyle's "venerable Don Quixote"—with all the sympathy in the world; but he is no disciple, committed to the simple view and the single line, and he brings into focus Emerson's "tedious archangel" quite as

* *Pedlar's Progress: The Life of Bronson Alcott,* by Odell Shepard.

51

clearly as the man whom Emerson also thought the greatest visionary of his time. The eccentric, the Micawber, the
idealistic egotist that Alcott was—these Mr. Shepard re-
fuses to suppress, but he keeps them rigorously in their
place; he resists the temptation to exploit the facile humor
in them; and the Alcott who emerges from these thoughtful and imaginative pages is mainly the man who ought to
emerge—the man who braved the philistines of Cheshire
and Boston with his program for the liberation of childhood, who as much as almost any other American made a
more human education possible, and whose career was a
quiet but vital protest against the self-seeking worldliness
of his time. He emerges, however, not as a misty symbol,
but tangibly, visibly and dramatically: as the sturdy country boy of Spindle Hill, as the Yankee peddler in Virginia,
as the patient and kindly Socrates of the Temple School,
as the day laborer of Concord, the reformer of Fruitlands,
the conductor of "Conversations." No doubt this portrait
depends for its fullness on those manuscript journals
which Mr. Shepard was perhaps the first man to read
through; it depends still more on Mr. Shepard's feeling
and skill.

It suffers only, but it suffers on one level seriously, from
the fact that it is drawn from a point of view too close to
Alcott's own, and that it is a point of view from which,
after all, the whole bearing of Alcott's career simply cannot be charted. In short, Mr. Shepard himself, like his
sitter, is an idealist by persuasion; like Alcott, he believes
that "pure contemplation" is "the supreme good that life
can offer"; and though, like all idealists, he resorts to
naturalistic explanations when they serve his purpose, in
the last analysis he makes his appeal to intuition and transcendental faith. Under the circumstances, they have not
led him, I think, to falsify the large outlines, the essential

spirit, of Alcott's character and career, but they have certainly blinded him to some of its interesting implications.

They have blinded Mr. Shepard, for example, to all the aspects of Alcott's failure as a social reformer at Fruitlands in that day of Fourieristic and other communitarian experiments; they have allowed him to rely, for his knowledge of Utopian Socialism, on such shallow works as Gilbert Seldes' *The Stammering Century* rather than on the writings of Fourier, of Owen and of Brisbane themselves. If he had read these men, and not Mr. Seldes, it is hard to see how, generally fair-minded as he is, Mr. Shepard could have said that "theirs was a shopkeeping morality, and a philosophy merely prudential"! With a more critical attitude, moreover, toward Alcott's idealism, he would have seen exactly why the "greed and ambition" that "tightened their grip on the land after the Civil War" aroused in Alcott "no righteous wrath"; why "the condition of labor in the factories" was met only by silence on Alcott's side. He would have seen and said that this silence, this acquiescence, are the bournes toward which transcendentalism, by its essential tenor, inevitably moves. His book, in that case, would have had a value for us that, as it stands, one cannot grant it. On every other ground, *Pedlar's Progress* deserves every cent of the generous prize it won.

JOHN GREENLEAF WHITTIER

QUAKER SOMEWHAT MILITANT

WHATEVER else may be said of it, Albert Mordell's new life of Whittier * is certainly as odd a piece of biographical writing as is likely to appear for some time. At his best, Mr. Mordell sees things with a sharp and skeptical eye, yet his book is marred by oddities, inconsistencies and crudities of a sort that does not suggest sharpness or skepticism. A trifling detail may hint at more than it proves. In preparing the final chapter, on Whittier as a poet, Mr. Mordell appears to have written to a number of American authors with the query whether they were conscious of Whittier's having influenced them and, if so, to what effect. Among these writers were O'Neill, E. A. Robinson and Jeffers—all of whom responded negatively, and Eugene O'Neill, who was once forced to memorize "Barbara Frietchie" in school, with some violence. There is a certain interest in speculating as to what sort of response Mr. Mordell expected from these writers, and whether the next biographer of O. W. Holmes will address a similar query to Dreiser, MacLeish and Dorothy Parker.

This particular matter is of course a trifle, but what is one to say of the seven chapters in the book which deal, in

* *Quaker Militant: John Greenleaf Whittier*, by Albert Mordell.

54

the most uncompromising way, with poor Whittier's relations with women? A more singular medley of fresh information, melodrama, justifiable plain speaking and Freudian mummery it would be difficult to imagine. What, apparently, are the facts? Whittier was a lifelong celibate who was, however, both susceptible to feminine charm and attractive to women; in his early youth he had at least one serious and unhappy love affair, and in later life he wished to marry a woman who rejected him as a husband; he was devoted to both his mother and sister; during most of his life, and especially after his sister's death, his need of feminine companionship and sympathy led him to maintain affectionate relations with several women, some of whom may have been "in love" with him, but none of whom was encouraged to pass a certain line; his chronic ill health was of a sort that might well have been aggravated by celibacy. Such are the plain facts, and they are psychologically interesting and important: Mr. Mordell is to be thanked for documenting them and speaking of them, for virtually the first time, with ordinary frankness.

Do the plain facts, however, really justify Mr. Mordell in his theatrical treatment of the matter? His language suggests the action of a play by some contemporary Kotzebue. He harries the good Whittier with such phrases as "male coquet" and "philandering celibate." He speaks of Whittier as "deserting" and "abandoning" young maidens whom he had "encouraged" and with whose affections he had been a "trifler." He credits him with the "fascinating powers"—and apparently the heartlessness—of "a Don Juan." As if all this were not sorry enough, the poet must be saddled with "an unconscious over-attachment for his mother," and with this a "sister-complex" is thrown in for good measure. If his poetry fails to express or represent sexual passion, then he was "unconsciously employing a defense mechanism." And so on. The true psychological quality of Whittier's rather bleak emotional history is buried beneath this avalanche of rhetoric and jargon.

When it comes to a literary judgment of the man's poetry, Mr. Mordell is not perfectly consistent. His position seems to be that the best of Whittier, the propagandist verse of protest and invective, has been consciously neglected in favor of the harmless pieces of idyllic reminiscence and of Quaker piety. Yet the finest of the harmless ballads, he says, "are true lyrics, voicing, with almost technical perfection and moving ecstasy, imperishable and important ideas." On the one hand, "he was untrue to life in his art"; on the other, "he is a poet of high order, because he effectively dealt with important themes." In the work of his age, "the old poetic fire burned with a dull glow"; yet the eight volumes of verse that he wrote in his last twenty years give evidence "that an aged poet may wield the magic wand with greater powers of enchantment than he commanded in his youth." Surely there is a little incoherence in these various dicta.

Indeed, what chiefly keeps an interesting book from being really impressive is Mr. Mordell's failure to fuse its necessarily multiform elements—psychological analysis, political history, literary criticism—into a coherent whole, to interpret the man, the politician and the poet in the light of some genuinely unifying principle of understanding. That he is capable of avoiding mere formulas, his treatment of Whittier's politics sufficiently argues. He draws the lines round Whittier's radicalism sharply enough. The passionate Abolitionist was a good Whig on almost every other ground, lukewarm in his attitude toward the evils of New England capitalism, skeptical of the possibility of reducing the fourteen-hour day in the Lowell mills, and persuaded of the benefits to women of their employment in industry. Even as an Abolitionist, Whittier, as Mr. Mordell says, was in the conservative camp—willing, unlike Garrison and Phillips, to engage in political maneuvering, and unwilling to countenance any form of direct action, such as John Brown's. On the questions of capital punishment and the rights of women, Whittier was somewhat in advance of his time; but the range and quality of his radicalism came out in unmistakable contours with the "settlement" of the slavery question by the Civil War. "Having witnessed the triumph of the cause he fought for," says Mr. Mordell, "he settled down to a serene old age." Just how serene and how complacent that old age was—as, for example, in Whittier's refusal to lift his voice for the Chicago anarchists in the eighties— Mr. Mordell demonstrates without squeamishness. The man who began as an admirer of Henry Clay ended as a Republican too faithful even to join the Mugwumps in 1884.

Mr. Mordell, as I say, makes no effort to minimize or explain away the more inglorious side of Whittier's political career, but he fails to find the clue that would integrate these apparent inconsistencies, that would make possible a fair judgment of his poetry, and even include his emotional life within the unity of the picture. I do not mean to suggest that a simple formula will do all this, but surely a *vital* formula it is the biographer's task to discover. Here, as everywhere, it is a question of connecting the man as subtly as possible with the culture of his class, with the social and intellectual life of his age and with the complex play of historic forces. There is a continuity in Whittier's life, and the clue to it lies partly in the morale of that hard-working, individualistic, religiously nonconformist, agrarian middle class from which he sprang. Whittier was a New England Quaker farmer of the early nineteenth century, a Quaker farmer who was also an Abolitionist and a poet, a Quaker farmer who believed in liberty as it had been celebrated by Milton, George Fox and Burns, and who could be outraged by a shockingly immoral form of injustice such as Negro slavery—a form of injustice, too, in which the "rights of man" and the integrity of the individual soul were openly (and not merely *in effect*) flouted and contemned. He was also, however, a Quaker farmer who could speak of "that profound political economist, Adam Smith"; who believed that "There is very little of actual suffering which may not be traced to intemperance, idleness and utter lack of economy, wasteful and careless of the future when wages are good"; who could say that "We need the gospel of Poor Richard's almanac sadly" (in 1889); who had a Quakerish distrust of other arts than that of poetry, a Quakerish obtuseness to the intellectual turmoil of his day, a Quakerish fear of "the passions"; who could speak of *Walden* as "very wicked and heathenish," and pity Emerson for his lukewarm interest in immortality, and heave Whitman's offending volume into the fire; who invested his money shrewdly, and was worth at his death, Mr. Mordell says, about $125,000.

Surely this is the Whittier whose "love life" was so abortive and, in other aspects, so touched with mild comedy; and this is the Whittier who wrote both the hot anti-slavery lyrics and the gentle ballads and idyls, both "Clerical Oppressors" and "My Playmate." Is it not clear that the two groups of poems have a common source and, after all, a very comparable appeal to us in the role of posterity? No doubt Mr. Mordell is warranted in claiming more attention for the political poems than the schoolbooks give them: no one who has not read "The Pastoral Letter" or "The Panorama" can appreciate the Quaker farmer's capacity for harshness and indignation. By all means let the most be made of Whittier as a propagandist in verse. But how can it be denied that—like his genuinely charming sentimental pieces—these poems too, for all their vehemence, have a narrow and minor appeal, that they are never lifted to a high level by a genuinely revolutionary philosophy, that a large intellect and a rich temperament are never felt behind them, that the Quaker pietist is too often audible in them along with the agitator, and that their form and language only rarely soar above the plane of partisan verse in the old newspapers? Certainly Whittier is more than merely a poet of delicate sentiment and evangelical faith; but he is not "a poet of a high order," and he is not, alas, a great political, a great radical or prophetic poet. He is the kind of poet—and to say so is to imply no cheap derogation—who could help to found the Free Soil party in one decade and vote for Grant in another.

NATHANIEL HAWTHORNE

THE RELEVANCE OF HAWTHORNE

IN *The Golden Day,* Mr. Lewis Mumford signalizes five writers as the major literary figures of that brief and prosperous period in the story of the American imagination which his title so poetically defines. These writers are Emerson, Thoreau, Whitman, Melville, and Hawthorne. These are the men, says Mr. Mumford, in whose work we can still detect the central elements of our own experience, and to whom we can still resort as an Englishman resorts to Milton, or a Frenchman to Rousseau. Of them all, I suppose, however, the one to whom most of us nowadays would be least likely to resort, the one whose work we should expect to find most alien and most remote, is the one who conquered his contemporaries the most completely, save perhaps Emerson, of the five. I mean, of course, Hawthorne.

For certainly, at a distance, it is difficult to see that Hawthorne is anything but a fine and attenuated voice out of the past. He was, as Mr. Mumford says, "the afterglow of the Seventeenth Century": and how immitigably foreign to all our most urgent concerns seems that moribund and tormented Puritanism which, superficially at any rate, was the imaginative setting for his work! Compared with

Emerson's gospel of self-assertion, or with Whitman's hearty empiricism, how archaic appears Hawthorne's preoccupation with the morbid "case of conscience," how dry and toneless that romantic "atmosphere" which he so sedulously exploited! What possible relevance to our own needs have these tenuous tales of ministers wearing black veils and scarecrows transformed into men of fashion, these dusky romances of hereditary guilt, of concealed crime and its retribution, of spooky "influences" and clashing "spheres"? Is this an imaginative world in which we can find ourselves ever so slightly at home? Or, to put the question in perhaps its sharpest form, is the experience of which Hawthorne's work is the product and the record an experience in which we can recognize any general and persistent representative quality? Did he celebrate an adventure that all Americans, or any large number of them, have had, and that is still, in any way, a portion of our destiny?

I believe that he did: that if we read his tales and romances searchingly we shall see in them the expression of something infinitely closer to us than a belated Puritanism. If we can see beyond and over the mere picturesqueness of the *décor*, we shall perceive that Hawthorne is as truly "one of ours" as Thoreau and Melville, and for not dissimilar reasons. I believe, indeed, that Hawthorne is the true laureate of one very cardinal—and not yet wholly finished—chapter in the history of the American mind.

To make this clear, we must remind ourselves of Hawthorne's own experience as a man, for it is there, in a special sense, that his fiction has its roots, and thence that it derives its symbolic force. On the face of it, no experience could well appear less typical than Hawthorne's. Its very essence seems to be that it was exceptional, eccentric, even unique. To begin with, the circumstances of his child-

hood—the early death of his father, the self-immurement
of his mother, the fallen status of the family, their living
for a good part of his boyhood in a remote frontier region
of Maine—had fostered in him an unsociability that was
perhaps, in any case, temperamental; had bred in him
what he called "my cursed habits of solitude," habits
which he was never to break more than very imperfectly.
In college, certainly, though he was not merely unsociable,
he failed to establish habits of easy intercourse with his
fellows that would see him through the critical years
ahead; and, when college was over, he found that he was
incapable of throwing himself into the life of his contemporaries and countrymen, of participating in their works
or sharing their purposes. This was as much the "fault"
of his time and his society as of Hawthorne himself: his
own secret designs were those of the creative artist, and
in a thousand crude and subtle ways his environment led
him to think of them as irrelevant, marginal, frivolous.

The important point is that it was Hawthorne's sense
of his difference from the rest of mankind that was allowed to triumph. For a decade, he "sat down by the wayside," as he said, and the rest of the world passed by, as it
seemed, without him. All the while, to be sure, he was
cultivating that one talent which it would have been death
to hide; but he was cultivating it in solitude, moral as well
as physical; growing more and more apart from ordinary
humanity, losing gradually his capacity for warm and
open relations with men and women. During the most
important years of his young manhood he failed to orient
himself humanly and, so to say, socially; to expand on all
sides as a personality, and multiply his points of fruitful
contact with reality; to achieve roundness and relief as a
man. At length this isolation, as everyone knows, proved
intolerable; and Hawthorne, first at the Boston Custom

House, later at Brook Farm, and still later at the Salem Custom House, made an effort to regain his footing in the general and morally significant march. But the essential injury had been done; these experiments, indeed, themselves, were experiments not so much in participation on a vital level as in mere association on a mechanical one; Hawthorne's real gifts were not called into play, and his real usefulness to society was not exploited. Fundamentally he failed ever to acquire a sense of genuine partnership in the experience of his coevals, and he indemnified himself for the loss in intimate personal relationships that insured his happiness if they did not reeducate his imagination.

All this should make it obvious why Hawthorne's tales and romances can be called an elaborate study of the centrifugal. Whatever their specific themes, they are a dramatization of all those social and psychological forces that lead to disunion, fragmentation, dispersion, incoherence. "The wages of estrangement is death"—that might be printed as a legend on the threshold of all of them; the causes and the consequences of estrangement is their consistent theme. The causes and the consequences, I say: and observe, for its vast significance, what Hawthorne does with both. For numerous as are the forms which estrangement takes in this drama, it is clear that they all have their roots in an error for which there is no better single word than pride. It may be the pride of family and position that cuts men off, in their own esteem, from ordinary necessities and the vulgar fate; it may be the cold pride of speculative curiosity, preying irresponsibly upon the privacies of other hearts; it may be the noble pride that shrinks from revealing guilt when secrecy may seem to accomplish a greater good, or the intellectual arrogance of a man dedicated to a limited ideal; it may be spiritual pride in its subtlest and most metaphysical form. Whatever its causes, its results are irreconciliable with a right human solidarity; it sets men at odds with one another instead of at peace; and its unavoidable fruits are frustration and despair—the maiming, the debasing, or the impoverishing of the healthy personality. "All that seems most real about us," Hawthorne once wrote to Sophia Peabody, "is but the thinnest substance of a dream,—till the heart is touched"; and to this emptiness, this fraudulence, this spectral unreality in all conduct that springs merely from the intellect and the will, he continually recurred. Not in that direction, he seemed to say, lie union and abundant life.

It would require far more space than I have here at my command to illustrate all this as fully as it deserves to be illustrated: I can hardly do more than refer, by way of reminder, to what is already familiar to readers of Hawthorne. Everyone will recognize, when it is pointed out, how recurrently some expression of mere pride, some domination of the arrogant mind or will over the human sympathies, is made the theme of Hawthorne's tales and romances; and in what a dreadful isolation, as a result, his men and women live. Recall Lady Eleanor's mantle, in the tale with that title, and how awful a symbol it is made of inhuman pride; recall the seekers for a more than human wealth and glory in "The Great Carbuncle," and the miserable fate that overtook them all; recall such monsters of intellectual pride as Dr. Rappaccini and the scientist Aylmer (in "The Birthmark") who destroy so completely, in their grotesque presumption, the most precious possibilities in what humanly lies nearest to them. Perhaps the classic example from the short tales should be Ethan Brand, who flings himself to death in the lime-kiln because he has discovered, in his long search for the Unpardonable

Sin, that he alone has been guilty of it—"the sin of an intellect that triumphed over the sense of brotherhood with man and reverence for God, and sacrificed everything to its own mighty claims! The only sin that deserves a recompense of immortal agony." His mental powers had been developed so highly that he at last stood quite alone in his eminence: "but where was the heart? That, indeed, had withered,—had contracted,—had hardened,—had perished! It had ceased to partake of the universal throb. He had lost his hold of the magnetic chain of humanity."

Like Ethan Brand, in this tragic respect, are the protagonists of Hawthorne's long romances. They have all, in their several ways, lost their hold of the magnetic chain of humanity. Separation, division, and the starvation of their spiritual lives is the fate that overtakes them all. And a destruction like Ethan Brand's, even when it is not consummated, is implicit in their miserable destinies. This, and not merely the consequences of adulterous crime, is the theme of *The Scarlet Letter*. The root of the whole tragedy is the proud selfishness of Chillingworth, the man of intellect, who tried to bring warmth into his benumbed existence by attaching to himself the radiance and vigor of Hester Prynne's youth. "It seemed," as Hester finally felt, "a fouler offence committed by Roger Chillingworth, than any which had since been done him, that, in the time when her heart knew no better, he had persuaded her to fancy herself happy by his side." And Arthur Dimmesdale's real sin is not so much his lapse from ordinary morality as the sickly spiritual pride that keeps him from disclosing it—and that not through simple cowardice, but through what might seem to be a high sense of his ghostly mission. The consequence is that Hester is cut off irredeemably from the normal life of mankind; that Chillingworth gradually transforms himself into a monster of vengeance; and that Dimmesdale finds the whole world turning false about him, the pith and substance gone out of all the realities that should be "the spirit's joy and nutriment." The tragedy of the book is that the harmony of several related lives has been fatally jangled, that they have all been set at odds with the general purposes of the life about them, and that all their fair potentialities of personal development have miscarried grievously and come to nothing.

Pride and estrangement, *mutatis mutandis,* are the leading moral motives also of *The House of the Seven Gables* and *The Blithedale Romance,* and even of so late a work as the unfinished *Septimius Felton.* In the first of these it is the hereditary pride of family and of place that have turned old Hepzibah, through the gradual years, into a half-dehumanized grotesque, pathetically incapable in the end of dealing with the one great human need that is forced upon her; the pride that turns Judge Pyncheon, a colder and more brutally selfish person, into a wholly dehumanized monster of greed and cruelty. What saves the tale, somewhat incongruously, from being a complete tragedy, is the presence and the influence of Phoebe Pyncheon, who embodies all the normal and even commonplace forces of ordinary life. No such salvation comes to the men and women in *The Blithedale Romance:* the full retribution of their surrender to pride is allowed to be visited upon them. Hollingsworth, the fanatical reformer, errs tragically through his devotion to a fixed and narrow philanthropic purpose, to which he is willing to sacrifice every other duty and every other human demand; Zenobia, the "new woman," the splendidly endowed intellectual and beauty, ruins her own life and the lives of Hollingsworth and Priscilla through her incapacity for unselfishness and humility. And Septimius Felton, the man who tries to invent the elixir of immortal life, finds that in striving to achieve a destiny beyond the reach of ordinary mortals he succeeds only in estranging himself horribly from the rest of life—in losing *his* hold of "the magnetic chain of humanity."

Such, as I see it, is the thematic unity of Hawthorne's imaginative treatment of human life; and on such grounds should I rest my contention that he is indeed one of the major writers of our great period, the epic poet, so to say, of a long chapter in our spiritual history. Like all great writers, Hawthorne clearly shared, in a full and direct fashion, one of the central spiritual experiences of his people and his time, and preserved the record of it in what he wrote. It is a paradox, but a true one, that he participated by failing to participate; that his very estrangement from his fellows was but emblematic of an estrangement that has run like an insistent motive through the whole of our career. Hawthorne is the laureate of all those forces in American life which from the beginning have made for dispersion and disunity, all those expressions of self-seeking and inhumane pride which from the time of the Puritans to our own day have hindered Americans from achieving creative integrity as a people. For is it necessary to point out that America was discovered and developed by men who, for "good" or "bad" reasons of many kinds, were escaping from the life to which they belonged; and that, ever since, the "come-outer" has been one of our grand national human types? Is it necessary to do more than refer to the chronic secessions of the pioneer, to the role that sectionalism has always played in our history, to the sway of an individualism now grandiose, now merely anarchic in our economic life? Or to the predicament in which the creative writer among us has always found himself?

I know how easy it is to protest that this is reading far too much into the stories of Hester Prynne and Hepzibah Pyncheon and Hollingsworth—stories that are full of a hundred other elements than this. I am certainly far from arguing that Hawthorne, the Jacksonian Democrat, was consciously preaching against separatism in all its phases. But I come back to his own life-story, and suggest again that the "chamber under the eaves," in which he immured himself for twelve years, is symbolic not only of the isolation of Thoreau in his hut at Walden, of Melville on the high seas and among the Polynesians, of Emily Dickinson in her solitary room, of Henry James and Whistler aloof in England; but of the spiritual isolation in which Americans on many levels have preferred to live rather than lend themselves to a general and articulated purpose. I suggest that Hawthorne's feeling that he could become "a man among men" merely by measuring coal in Boston Harbor or digging potatoes at Brook Farm is emblematic of the illusion we have all suffered from that we could achieve integrity by practising "cooperation," and attain harmony by striving for standardization. And who can miss the moral in the tragic upshot of tale after tale in the collections, and of all the romances (with one doubtful exception)?—the moral that, because the forces of decentralization have been allowed to dominate it, American life has failed on the whole to produce rich and complete personalities, men and women who touch life at many points and fulfill more than one or two of its possibilities. Who can fail to remember the Dimmesdales and Hollingsworths and Pyncheons who have divided our civilization among them?

For me, this is the relevance of Hawthorne to our own imaginative life. Essentially he was concerned, both as a man and as a writer, with the problem of personality, the problem of full and rounded personal development, the problem of avoiding the frustration that comes from isolating oneself from the world and falling under the domination of but a single part of one's nature. Who can say that the problem is no longer a reality to us? Who can deny that our life is still so organized as to produce partial and incomplete personalities on every hand, and rarely to produce men in three dimensions? Who can doubt that *The Scarlet Letter* is, in this sense, and even if it were no more, the dramatization of many a contemporary tragedy? I see no good reason, in short, why we should not go on reading Hawthorne as attentively and as profitably as most of us feel that we can read Whitman and Melville and Thoreau. For the moment, at least, he is by no means a mere "classic."

NEW PIGMENT FOR AN OLD CANVAS

HAWTHORNE expressed late in life a strong and characteristic desire that he should never be made the subject of a biography. This wish was happily ignored within the generation after his death by his son-in-law, his son, and his second daughter; and indeed Mrs. Hawthorne herself had set the precedent by publishing voluminous extracts from his notebook journals with suppressions dictated by the taste of the period. Moncure Conway, Henry James, and Professor Woodberry cooperated with Hawthorne's own family in making widely familiar practically all the facts of his life, and in consequence the clues to his personal history have long been accessible to the student in these half dozen biographical studies.

This is by no means to say that Mr. Morris' book * fills no biographical need and makes no important contribution. It would do this if only because Mr. Morris is the first biographer of Hawthorne who has used all the available material to build up a full and coherent portrait, and who has at the same time had access to the manuscripts of Hawthorne's love letters and his complete journals. These latter, to be sure, enhance our impression of the man to a disappointingly slight extent: Mr. Julian Hawthorne had reproduced enough from both in his life of his father to indicate that Hawthorne was capable, on the one hand, of more passionate emotional expression, and, on the other, of greater acerbity in the judgment of contemporaries than we should otherwise have suspected. But that book suffered from serious omissions and defects of emphasis, and these Mr. Morris has corrected so skillfully and with so disciplined a scholarship that *The Rebellious Puritan* undoubtedly supplants at once all previous treatments as a narrative of Hawthorne's life.

Nor is it only for this reason—its complete documentation—the book deserved to be written. Before Mr. Morris all Hawthorne's biographers belonged either to his own family circle or to the same generation: all were looking at him with the eyes of the late nineteenth century, and seeing in him what the late nineteenth century chose to see. It was high time that so significant a career in the history of American literature should be reexamined with the eyes of the twentieth century and narrated for a generation that knew not Joseph. It was high time, among other things, that the greater freedom in the handling of his

---

* *The Rebellious Puritan: Portrait of Mr. Hawthorne,* by Lloyd Morris.

materials now conceded to the biographer should be put
to advantage in the use of this particular material—so rich
as it is in psychological implications and appeals to disin-
terested analysis. Of all these possibilities Mr. Morris has
clearly been sensible; and one cannot help feeling that his
book has, as a result, almost the freshness and vitality of a
book on a virginal subject.

How memorable, how urgent to the imagination, how
full of intricate tones the story is! With no great dramatic
episodes, how much there is of the picturesque, the comic,
the romantic, even, certainly of the tragic, in Hawthorne's
life, and how delicately Mr. Morris exploits these for his
narrative purposes! No one, for example, has yet painted
so full and, on the whole, so true a picture of that strange,
lonely, overshadowed boyhood in the silent house on
Herbert Street in Salem and in the backwoods solitude of
Raymond, Maine. No one has yet taken the pains to describe in so great detail and with so nice an irony that
richly humorous passage of a few months at Brook Farm:
Mr. Morris' chapter entitled "A Modern Arcadia" is a mas-
terpiece of reconstruction, through which move the almost
fictional figures of a great imaginative writer in a blue
frock wielding a dung fork, a Vermont farmer turned transcendentalist, a daughter of Boston's aristocracy washing
dishes in the kitchen of the "Hive," a consumptive seam-
stress listening to Hegelian conversations, and a dozen
other characters no less droll.

Perhaps the most substantial contribution Mr. Morris
makes—because the task has been dodged or scamped by
other biographers—is his studious and judicious account
of Hawthorne's life in England and Italy. Here there is
nothing of the comic, save, perhaps, the lachrymose scene
with Douglas Jerrold, but much that has its own ironic and
somewhat sombre overtones; and the complete story is

richly worth telling. Hawthorne as a consul in a dingy Liverpool office building, as a half-pious, half-cantankerous pilgrim at English literary shrines, as a lion at London literary breakfasts, as an elderly Yankee among the palaces and galleries and holy places of Catholic Rome—Hawthorne during this whole period at the end of his life was a kind of symbol of the maladjusted American artist searching, when it was too late, for a world in which he could make himself at home imaginatively. Mr. Morris leaves no stone unturned in his task of representing this nostalgic quest, with its episodes of exuberance, its undercurrent of ill-defined dissatisfaction, and its ultimate failure; and his interpretative comments are full of insight.

Some features of this account of Hawthorne it is, naturally enough, impossible to accept without reservation. The title itself is not a happy one: Hawthorne had nothing of the rebel in his temperament, and if he reacted powerfully against much in the Puritan tradition, it was by a deeper, obscurer, and more painful process than the word "rebellious" would suggest. Indeed it is difficult not to believe that his whole preoccupation with the problems of sin and guilt had its roots far nearer to the center of his makeup and experience than Mr. Morris ever indicates, for he represents that preoccupation as largely an intellectual matter. This leads him to make much of Emerson's influence, to read the doctrine of self-reliance into Hawthorne's treatment of the erring individual, and to ignore the earlier tales, which were written before Emerson could have exerted any influence and which nevertheless anticipate in their essentials all that Hawthorne was ever to say about the problem. Furthermore, I am not sure that Mr. Morris does not miss the most curious aspect of Haw-

thorne's love for Sophia Peabody—the emphasis he put
in his letters to her upon the peace and repose she was to
bring him rather than the enlargement of experience, in
fact, the unmistakably *fugitive* character of the whole relationship. It is a question, finally, whether a man of
letters can be written about in so purely narrative a manner, with so little exposition of his work in literature,
except at the cost of a certain distortion. In such a complete and intimate biography it is disappointing not to
find more about the author's writings, since so large a part
of his life was devoted to them.

Such points of dissent, however, it would be ungrateful
to urge with vehemence. Mr. Morris has approached the
subject with so much sympathy, has mastered all the
complexities of it so imaginatively, and has ordered his
presentation of the facts so artfully and with so little
straining for meretricious effect that one cannot read the
story with anything but the liveliest enjoyment and admiration. No other literary biography of the season will
be of more general or more permanent interest.

HAWTHORNE'S JOURNALS

IN 1868, four years after Hawthorne's death, Mrs. Hawthorne, in response to the importunities of many readers for
a biography of her husband, published a selection from
his early journals under the title, *Passages from Hawthorne's American Notebooks.* In 1870 appeared a volume
of *Passages from the English Notebooks,* and in the following year a volume of selections from the French and

Italian journals. Hawthorne had expressed a wish not to be made the subject of a biography; and, in a prefatory note to the English journals, Mrs. Hawthorne explained that, in deference at once to this desire and to the legitimate demand of Hawthorne's admirers for information about his life, she was giving to the world, as a substitute, as much of his personal record as could properly be exposed to his contemporaries. A further incentive, as Mrs. Hawthorne herself pointed out, was the desire of his family to correct the general impression that Hawthorne was "gloomy and morbid."

As an editor, Mrs. Hawthorne was far less liberal with the scissors than a twentieth-century reader might be excused for expecting. Many passages in the foreign journals, later incorporated with few changes or none in *Our Old Home* and *The Marble Faun,* she wisely omitted; and many of her suppressions of trifling diaristic detail are grounds for the gratitude of every reader. More than enough was retained to give an adequate picture, deepened by a just perspective and with the light and shade duly distributed, of Hawthorne's personality. A later generation, nonetheless, can hardly be reproached for regarding a few suppressions here and there as no longer inevitable; and indeed, in the life of his father published in 1885, Mr. Julian Hawthorne included some of these—such as the full description of Tennyson at the Manchester Arts Exhibition and the passage on Margaret Fuller in the Italian journal—which even at that time might well have been generally accessible. An examination of the manuscript journals now in the possession of the Morgan Library brings to light a few further passages that seem no less interesting than many that Mrs. Hawthorne used, and particularly a large number of phrases and sentences which, in the passages she did use, Mrs. Hawthorne omitted or even altered.[1]

How early Hawthorne began to make entries in his journal we have now no way of knowing. There is record that the habit of journalizing was first formed in him during his boyhood years in Maine, when he was given a blank notebook on his birthday by an uncle, and urged to use it daily for writing out his thoughts, "on any and all subjects," with an eye to the development of a sound prose style. Many years after Hawthorne's death a manuscript of this boyish diary, which appeared to be authentic, was discovered and published (*Hawthorne's First Diary*, S. T. Pickard), and, though its genuineness has never been admitted by Mr. Julian Hawthorne, it was accepted by Hawthorne's son-in-law, G. P. Lathrop, and by many other persons whose judgment must be respected. The circumstances of its discovery, however, were, to say the least, ambiguous, and it has been thought best not to include passages from it in this volume.

At all events, no further record of Hawthorne's activity as a diarist is preserved, until abruptly, in the summer of 1835, toward the end of his long period of self-immurement in Salem, appears an entry in which Hawthorne describes a walk—one, no doubt, of a thousand such—down to Juniper Point on Salem Neck. From then on until the second year before his death the journal thus so quietly initiated (if that entry is indeed the first) con-

[1] The manuscript journals preserved begin with the entry for July 5, 1837; for the preceding entries, we are dependent on Mrs. Hawthorne's version. Two volumes of the Italian journals—covering the periods between March 11 and April 22, and between May 30 and July 2, 1858 (both inclusive)—are also missing: to the former, in all probability, belongs the passage on Margaret Fuller. Single pages and parts of pages elsewhere throughout the journals have been deleted—not, proportionately, in any great number.

tinues with very uneven fullness and regularity. As a general rule, Hawthorne appears to have journalized most assiduously in the intervals between periods of active professional writing: it was as if the energy so liberated could find only partial outlet in un-literary pursuits—as if only his tireless pen could conduct its ultimate units. Thus the entries in his journal during such periods as the visit to Bridge in Maine in the summer of 1837 and the weeks at North Adams in 1838 are abundant and regular; and during the long years in England and Italy, when (until he began *The Marble Faun*) Hawthorne was on a protracted literary vacation, the blank notebooks were enriched practically day by day, with an industry which neither Hawthorne's arduous duties as consul nor the inconveniences of nineteenth-century travel could discourage or interrupt. On the other hand, and quite predictably, there are stretches of emptiness or brief and fitful record during such months as those in Salem when he was at work on *The Scarlet Letter,* or at Lenox when *The House of the Seven Gables* was in hand. And at one period, during practically the whole of his Custom House experience in Boston and the early months at Brook Farm, after Hawthorne had become engaged to Sophia Peabody, he appears to have diverted into his letters to her the energy that would otherwise have gone into his journal. Extracts from these letters Mrs. Hawthorne herself reproduced in her edition of the journals, and, following in her footsteps, the present selection includes some of the more notable passages. For permission to correct the reading of these passages by reference to the privately printed *Love Letters of Nathaniel Hawthorne,* the editor is under obligation to Mr. W. K. Bixby, of St. Louis, the holder of the copyright.

Scarcely a page of the sixteen manuscript volumes of Hawthorne's journals is quite without interest for the special student, if only because, being relatively dull, it is dull in a Hawthornesque fashion; yet for all but the special student there are hundreds of pages—pages on which, for example, the conscientious tourist rather than the poet is at work—that can easily be spared. What remains is, if not always pure gold, some metal with a value of its own; and no one can hope to understand Hawthorne at all fully who does not study it. We must not look in Hawthorne's journals, it is true, for qualities that they do not possess: fresh from Emerson's or Thoreau's, we must not look for epigram and aphorism; fresh from Amiel's or Marie Bashkirtseff's, we must not look for studious introspection and self-revelation. Not that there is neither epigram nor introspection in these of Hawthorne's: more than a few detached sentences have a saline smack not unworthy of Emerson, and several precious passages of "confession" throw a light far into the recesses of Hawthorne's nature. Yet these things are not the staples of his work as a diarist: it is elsewhere that its charm and its value must be sought.

The difference, after all, between Hawthorne and any of those other writers of journals is the only too manifest difference between a philosopher or an essayist and a teller of tales. Not general ideas for their own sake, or personal experience on its own level, but dramatic conceptions, the fruit of imaginative revery, or observations of the external world, men and women no less than inanimate nature—these are the central substance of Hawthorne's journals. Much, no doubt, might be made of them taken merely by themselves; their real interest yields itself only to the reader who keeps in mind the figure of the prose romancer behind them. Here one can observe, almost without obstacle, the restless play of Hawthorne's imagination over the strange data of the moral world, entertaining one possibility after another, returning again and again to characteristic conceptions, and betraying always the special temper of his mind. Here in the journals, not always easily recognizable, are the original statements of the organizing ideas in tale after tale as we are now familiar with them in *Twice-Told Tales* or the *Mosses* or the *Snow Image*; here is that extraordinary series of notes, beginning as early as 1836, in which the complicated unity of *The Scarlet Letter* gradually asserts itself; here is the leading dramatic note of *The Blithedale Romance*, stated some sixteen years before the book was undertaken; here are the first suggestions for *The Marble Faun*. Such notes as thus bore fruit have a significance not to be missed: but the journals would be less revealing than they are if it were not for the dozens of entries that came to no similar consummation, entries that proclaim the wind's direction no less dependably.

Nor was it only as a storehouse for such "ideas" that Hawthorne's journal proved of service to him. If he had been a mere allegorist he might have been content with these fanciful conceptions: he was also—perhaps (fundamentally) rather—an untiring observer of the world about him; and into his journal went, usually with the utmost clarity of statement and refinement of expression, the record of his observations. Hawthorne is not commonly spoken of, in the same breath with Thoreau or Burroughs, as a student of nature; and indeed he had little or nothing of Thoreau's passionate devotion to the details of plant and animal life for their own sake. Yet he was too good a child of the nineteenth century not to be susceptible to natural beauty, and in his own vein—that of a poet or impressionist landscape-painter rather than of a scientist—he wrote much and delicately about the Massachusetts coast, the Berkshire hills, the scenery about Concord, and the English countryside. Especially in the transition from season to season did the changing aspects of nature arrest his scrutiny. And it is always curious to observe the interest Hawthorne took in birds and animals—an interest, if one may say so, not less "dramatic" than his interest in human beings, as the swine at the Salem almshouse, the hens at Lenox, and the monkeys in the London zoo, are there to witness.

By men and women themselves, however, his attention was far more steadily engaged; in them his interest was not, except at rare intervals, to be satiated. In the earliest continuous passages of his journal—those written during his stay in Augusta in 1837—we find him studying, with unmistakable zest, the personalities of his host and of the little French tutor, M. Schaeffer, and recording his impressions of Nancy the servant-girl, and the Irish laborers on the mill-dam. Similar "hints for characters" and "remarkables" recur for many years. No individuals were sufficiently humble to merit his indifference or sufficiently commonplace to escape his analysis. If he had a predilection here, it was for men and women on the edge of things, outcasts, "wrecks," people who had somehow failed to swing into the general march of life, or had somehow fallen out of it. At North Adams, it was a traveling surgeon-dentist and a one-armed soap-maker who had seen better days; in Salem, it was the old apple-dealer in the railway-station (*Mosses from an Old Manse*); in Boston, the elderly ragamuffin in front of Parker's grogshop, who later appears as Old Moodie in *The Blithedale Romance;* in Liverpool, the bedraggled inhabitants of the slums. Even when the objects of his curiosity seem scarcely to belong in this class, it is, more often than not, some note of waywardness, some hint of exile, that really preoccupies him. It was an element of his interest in his own children, of his interest in Una at all events, as her transformation into little Pearl in *The Scarlet Letter* suggests; and observe what happened to the beautiful Jewess at the Lord Mayor's dinner in London, when she turned up as Miriam in *The Marble Faun*.

In such passages it is still Hawthorne the writer who has to be kept in mind: for many readers, the same thing would not have to be said of those passages, memorable surely on their own account as well, in which he recorded his impressions and, frequently, his judgments of eminent or notable contemporaries. It is easy and natural to think of Hawthorne as a solitary and a recluse, and in fact he of course saw far less of society than most men of his distinction. Yet he knew familiarly, if not intimately, some of the greatest American writers of his time, and wrote of them in his journals with a freedom and a cool insight that bring them almost in three dimensions before our eyes. So long as men retain their interest in Emerson and Thoreau, in Margaret Fuller, in Bryant and Melville, Hawthorne's account of these personages will have a quite peculiar value. In England, if he failed through want of effort to meet some of the very great (Thackeray, Dickens, Tennyson, George Eliot, Carlyle), he became acquainted, almost by chance, with the Brownings, with Macaulay, with Leigh Hunt, with Coventry Patmore, and with a number of lesser notables—Harriet Martineau, Douglas Jerrold, Monckton Milnes, Philip James Bailey, Tom Taylor Barry Cornwall—who have not yet been wholly forgotten. In Italy, where he saw still more of the Brownings and their circle, he was mainly attracted by a number of his own countrymen, artists for the most part, of whom Hiram Powers and W. W. Story interested him most keenly. In writing of these people, Hawthorne's kindliness may now and then have deserted him; his powers of characterization, never. On the basis of these passages, one might contend that, if he had not been one of the great romancers, Hawthorne would have been one of the great memorialists of his time.

Late in his life, and doubtless in response partly to external pressure, Hawthorne developed a certain fitful and uneasy interest in the plastic arts. First awakened at the exhibition in Manchester in 1857, this interest grew with amazing rapidity during the months of his stay in Italy in the following year, and the Italian journals are very largely occupied with comments on pictures and statues. It would be idle to argue that he ever learned to enjoy such things quite naturally or to appreciate them with real discrimination. Nevertheless, Hawthorne could not have written about art as fully as he did without making many shrewd or at all events piquant observations; and, if only on account of the emblematic figure of Praxiteles' faun, these passages in his journals will always repay reading.

The editor of *The Heart of Thoreau's Journals* has justly pointed out how richly American was the personality of Henry Thoreau, and how truly his adventures, physical and philosophical, are a portion of our general experience. If a selection from his journals did nothing else, it should demonstrate that Nathaniel Hawthorne too, solitary that he was, lived through one whole chapter of our career and was a true participator in it. His mind, with all its idiosyncrasies, was nonetheless, in Emerson's sense, a "representative" one; and the pages of his journal, in consequence, have a color and a fragance that are not only Hawthornesque but also American. This is not their only significance, but it is for this reason that they will exercise their most lasting sway.

HAWTHORNE'S TALES

IF HAWTHORNE had died in his middle forties—an advanced age for a man of genius—we should know him now not as the author of *The Scarlet Letter* or any of his other novels but solely as a writer of short stories or tales. It is true that, two or three years after he left college, Hawthorne had written and published anonymously a little novel called *Fanshawe*, which under different auspices might well have been followed shortly by other works of fiction on the same scale—and of richer substance—but some chill in the New England air at that early hour disheartened the young Hawthorne for novel-writing, and in fact he had destroyed all the copies of *Fanshawe* itself that he could lay hands on. It had been a pretty unripe little work at best, and in any case for twenty years thereafter Hawthorne stuck consistently to the briefer form. By good luck it was admirably suited, all that while, to what he had to say, as it was to what Hoffmann and Gogol and Gautier had to say at much the same time, and the best of Hawthorne's tales express his nature, his personal sense of things, so subtly and truly that there can be no question of loss or limitation.

No literary fame, however, was ever of slower or less sensational growth. Hawthorne himself, who had been born in 1804, once said that for many years he had been the obscurest man of letters in America, and this remark hardly exaggerated the facts. For a long time his audience had been limited to the readers of the modish little "gift-books" or annuals, and even in those genteel pages he was anonymous and unidentifiable. A deep-rooted shyness had kept him from signing his contributions to the *Token,* as the best of the annuals was called, and for years he had hidden behind the mask of "Ashley Allen Royce" or "The Author of 'The Gentle Boy.'" Such work as his, however, could not fail indefinitely to make its impression, and a handful of readers had already been puzzling over the secret of its authorship when, in 1836, Park Benjamin, an astute and friendly journalist, named him by his real name —and eulogized him—in a popular magazine.

A year later Hawthorne was persuaded by a friend to make a collection of his pieces in book form, and the *Twice-Told Tales* appeared over the imprint of a Boston publisher. The circle now began to widen perceptibly. Longfellow reviewed the book with excited appreciativeness; there were other signs of regard and recognition from time to time, and when, in 1842, a second, expanded edition of the *Tales* appeared, they were noticed at length in several quarters—most momentously in *Graham's,* where Poe devoted to them a famous and flattering review. So much as five years later, however, and even after Hawthorne, with the *Mosses from an Old Manse,* had made a third collection, Poe could still speak of him, in another review, as "*the* example, *par excellence,* in this country, of the privately-admired and publicly-unappreciated man of genius." Few as the appreciators may have been, they were, most of them, highly competent to speak; many of them were other writers—the most ardent of all was Herman Melville—and their judgment was at last borne out, in 1850, by the great public success of *The Scarlet Letter.* The following year, with *The Snow Image,* Hawthorne made a fourth and final collection of his tales, the last that he wished to preserve or that, as he said, had survived in his own remembrance.

Not many writers have worked so long amid such a

hush or in such a shadow: the tales themselves, as Hawthorne himself strongly felt, are colored everywhere by the circumstances under which they were written. His own feeling was that they suffered as a result, and he was partly right; but they gained something vital too—a curiously cool intensity, an air of candid shyness, a quality of being at once private and communicative. They were not, he said, "the talk of a secluded man with his own mind and heart," but his attempts—imperfectly successful ones, he thought—"to open an intercourse with the world." But the truth is that his stories partook of both characters: they were attempts at communication with other men, such as only a solitary could conceive, but they were also attempts to make plain to himself the meaning of his own inward and outward experience. They were soliloquies that were meant to be overheard.

In any other period they might well have taken quite a different literary form—fabulous, visionary, legendary, poetic (in the limited sense), and even dramatic—and if they took the form of "short stories," it was because, at the moment Hawthorne began to write, that mold was a natural and almost a handy one. This does not mean that it was long-established; on the contrary, it was in its primitive or experimental stage, especially in English, and if it was handy, it was only in the sense in which the history play was so for the young Shakespeare. The Italian *novella*, the French *conte*, the realistic-moral English tale—these were ancient types, but they were nothing to the purpose of Hawthorne or his contemporaries: they were not "inward," they were not meditative or musing, they were not a matter of tone and lighting and harmony. It was only latterly that short pieces of prose fiction had begun to take on qualities such as these, and Hawthorne was as much the creator as he was the inheritor of a form.

He had been preceded by the romantic Germans, Tieck and Hoffmann and Chamisso, with their tales of fatal *Geheimnisse*, of uncanny solicitation and ruin, of "lost shadows" and spell-working portraits, of delusion and anxiety and guilt; and in his indolent but impressionable way he undoubtedly read some of these writers as they were being translated in his youth. He knew Irving, too, and the lesson of Irving's delicate, daydreaming, water-colorist's art was not lost on him. In the ten years between "Rip Van Winkle" and Hawthorne's earliest tales, a whole little literature of short fiction had sprouted in this country, a mostly very pale but sometimes rather vivid literature of ghost stories, Indian legends, "village tales," and historical anecdotes—the thin foliage of the annuals as it was put forth by the now forgotten Pauldings and Leggetts and Sedgwicks who were the lesser Faulkners or Porters of their time. It was (to change the figure) the only spring-board from which Hawthorne could take off directly, and what he, like Poe at exactly the same moment, succeeded in making of the gift-book or magazine tale of the twenties and thirties is only one more out of a thousand illustrations of a familiar literary truth, the power of men of genius to sublimate the most unpromising forms.

He had things to express that were his own, not simply the moral and æsthetic small change of the era, and he had, what none of the others except Poe had in anything like the same degree, an innate sense of the plastic, an instinct for form, the tact and touch of a born artist—an artist whom it is tempting to think of as peculiarly New England, and to associate in one's imagination with the old Yankee craftsmen, the silversmiths and the cabinet-makers whose solid and yet fastidious work his own does really suggest. He of course learned something here from his literary predecessors, even no doubt from the little

men, but what he arrived at was his own and not Hoffmann's or Irving's or Leggett's.

It happens that we can follow part way the process of
his art; from an early period Hawthorne, like James and
Chekhov after him, had had the habit of keeping notebooks, and on these, when he came to write his tales, he
constantly drew. We often find in them, therefore, what
James would call the "germs" or "seeds" from which the
stories, in their own good season, unfolded. We find, too,
the seeds from which they did not unfold: the observations of real people, queer or humorsome or even ordinary
individuals who, unlike those in Chekhov, rarely reappear
in the tales; the overheard or communicated fragments of
"true" stories out of real lives which, unlike those in James,
almost never made the transition from hearsay to art. The
germ of a typical Hawthorne tale is not a "real" individual
or an actual and firsthand story—his imagination needed
a further withdrawal from things than that—but either
some curious passage that had quickened his fancy in his
reading or some abstractly phrased idea, moral or psychological, that he had arrived at in his endless speculative
reveries.

He had been struck, to take an example of the first of
these, by an anecdote about Gilbert Stuart which William
Dunlap tells in his history of the fine arts in America.
Stuart, according to Dunlap, had been commissioned by
Lord Mulgrave to paint the portrait of his brother, General Phipps, on the eve of the General's sailing for India.
When the portrait was finished and Mulgrave, for the first
time, examined it, he broke out with an exclamation of
horror: "What is this?—this is very strange!" I have painted
your brother as I saw him," said Stuart, and Mulgrave
rejoined: "I see insanity in that face." Some time later the
news reached England that Phipps, in India, had indeed

gone mad and taken his own life by cutting his throat. The great painter, as Dunlap adds, had seen into a deeper reality behind the man's outward semblance, and with the insight of genius had painted that. Upon this hint Hawthorne wrote, and the result was "The Prophetic Pictures."

Consider, however, what he ends by doing with the hint. An anecdote, strange enough in itself and told for the sake of its deeper meaning, but naked and meager in circumstance and shape, has been worked over into an enriched and molded narrative, in which the original suggestion is only barely recognizable. Back into a remoter past goes the time of the action; back into a past which, as James would say, was "far enough away without being too far"; not the too recent past, at any rate, of Stuart himself, who had died less than ten years before and whose memory was much too fresh in men's minds. The tone of time is to count, but it is the tone of a dimmer time; and Hawthorne, with a few touches of his delicate, poetic erudition, evokes for us, only just fully enough, the simpler Boston of the mid-colonial day. The painter himself remains nameless and a little mythical; he has no actual counterpart in history—not in Smibert, certainly, nor Blackburn—and of course he could have none. As for his sitter, that sitter has become, to deepen the interest, two people, a young man and his bride: two lives, not merely one, are to be darkened and destroyed. The premonitions of madness, as in Dunlap, are to be detected in Walter Ludlow's countenance, but so too are the premonitions of passive suffering and all-enduring love in Elinor's. The painter himself, indeed, is to be involved in a way that did not hold for Stuart, but meanwhile the gloomy sequence of incidents moves from its natural prologue (the ordering of the portraits) to its first and second "acts" (the painting and then the displaying of them) through its long interval of latency (the years of the painter's absence) to its scene of violent culmination (the painter's return and the onset of Walter's madness). Such was the form—carefully pictorial, narratively deliberate, in a derived sense dramatic—that Hawthorne worked out for himself in his most characteristic tales.

Dunlap's anecdote, however, has undergone a still more revealing metamorphosis. The "moral" of Hawthorne's actual story is not, as Dunlap's was, the great painter's power of seeing beyond the physical countenance into the mind and heart of the sitter, though Hawthorne does, with a deliberate turn of the ironic screw, put just that thought into Walter Ludlow's mouth. What interested him was not so much the sitters and their tragedy as the artist and his: for him the artist's power was always a potential and here an actual curse; his art might so easily become "an engrossing purpose" which would "insulate him from the mass of humankind," as this painter's does, and transform him indeed from the mere reader of men's souls into an agent of their destinies. Hawthorne's portraits here—like Hoffmann's in "Doge and Dogaressa," which he might have known, or like Gogol's in "The Portrait," which he certainly did not know—become the symbols not only of the artist's clairvoyance but of a malignant fatality of which he may be the guilty medium. Certainly Hawthorne shared with several of his contemporaries—Poe and Balzac are other examples—their delight in the use of paintings as poetic symbols.

The earliest seeds of his tales, in any case, were sometimes of an almost metaphysical abstractness. This is true, for example, of "The Birthmark," which seems to have germinated in his imagination for six or seven years before it was ready to be hatched. It came to him first in the fleshless form of a mere "idea": "A person to be in the possession of something as perfect as mortal man has a right to demand; he tries to make it better, and ruins it entirely." A few years later this vague "something" had become a human being, and the ruin to be wrought had made itself specific in the idea of death: "A person to be the death of his beloved in trying to raise her to more than mortal perfection; yet this should be a comfort to him for having aimed so highly and holily." Even now, however, the idea was still too intangible, too unripe, for embodiment. It was only after a year or two that Hawthorne, turning the pages of a recent work on physiology, lighted upon the palpable image he had been groping for —the image of a gifted and learned young chemist who, according to this writer, aiming at the discovery of some great new scientific principle, had shut himself up in his laboratory for several days on end and, resorting to various means of artificial excitation, had endeavored to whip up his mind to the highest pitch of activity, with the result that he had ended by driving himself insane.

No such fate, of course, overtakes Aylmer in the tale; Hawthorne already had his own tragic denouement, the death of Georgiana, and all he needed to borrow from Combe was the nature of Aylmer's pursuits, the setting of a laboratory, and a touch or two like the "penetrating odors" of the perfume that Aylmer displays to his beloved. The imperfection to be rooted out must clearly be a physical one, though as free as possible from grossness, and one that a pretty fanciful "chemistry" might conceivably eliminate; the image of Georgiana's tiny birthmark must have come very lightly and naturally to Hawthorne. When, for the sake of a moral set-off, he had added the character of Aminadab, Aylmer's brutal assistant, he had all that was essential for his tale. What remained was to compose it—to send the reader's fancy vaguely back to "the latter part of the last century," to bring his young chemist on the scene, to evoke Georgiana's all-but-perfect beauty as if he were giving "instructions to a painter," to let the sense of Aylmer's mad intention grow upon us forebodingly, to *work in* the richly expressive physical details (the "gorgeous curtains," the "perfumed lamps, emitting flames of various hues," the "soft, impurpled radiance," and the like), and to advance the allegorical little drama from scene to scene, from one abortive experiment to another, until its pitiful culmination is reached. "Every word *tells*," as Poe said of another tale of Hawthorne's, "and there is not a word which does not tell."

I have just used the word "allegorical," and however inaccurate it may be, it points to another aspect of Hawthorne's manner that no reader can ever have ignored. "Allegories of the Heart" was the title that he himself seems to have planned to use for a whole group of his stories, and he frankly recognized in his work what he called "an inveterate love of allegory." It has thrown off a good many readers, from Poe onward, and certainly it sometimes takes a form that is chillingly mechanical and bare. But it would be superficial to make very much of the mere word, or to see in Hawthorne's "allegory" only a piece of conscious literary machinery. He may have inherited from his boyhood favorites, Spenser and Bunyan, the habit of a somewhat more explicit and more tangible moral imagery than most of his contemporaries found natural. But he is no allegorist in the older sense: his "moralities," after all, at his most characteristic, are far too completely dramatized, too iridescent psychologically, for that; and the fact is he shared deeply the general impulse of his time, among writers, to discern a transcendental meaning in physical objects, or to make physical objects the means for expressing what would otherwise be inexpressible.

"You know," says one of his characters, "that I can never separate the idea from the symbol in which it manifests itself." It was a way of describing the instinctive movements of his own, and indeed any poet's, imagination. If Hawthorne had lived a generation later, in Europe, he would have counted as a symbolist, though as it was he stopped short, at some point not easy to specify, of being a *symboliste* in the strictest sense: he trusts too little, for that, the suggestiveness of his symbols themselves, when left without commentary, and he yields himself far too little to the dark drift of the irrational. The truth is he is neither quite an allegorist nor quite a symbolist, but a writer *sui generis* who occupies a beautiful terrain of his own between these two artistic modes; it is tempting to catch up another word he often used, and call him an "emblematist," with a certain reliance on the old meaning—the partly pictorial, partly edifying meaning—of the word "emblem." He had inherited, at any rate, the old Puritan love of emblems and tokens and allegories, and he gave it vent as only a poet of his own romantic generation could do.

His favorite symbols tell us much, of course, about the deepest grain of his nature, but there is no space here for a detailed account of them. Two or three remarks will have to be enough. It is bound to strike any reader, sooner or later, how often this descendant of the Puritans, this provincial Yankee, this æsthetically unsophisticated and personally rather ascetic writer—how often Hawthorne instinctively makes use of the imagery of the fine arts (pictures, as we have seen, and statues), or of the minor arts (jewelry in particular), or of dress and costume (a black veil, an embroidered mantle, the finery of a dandy): it suggests, but only among other things, how much more sensuous his temperament was than it outwardly appeared to be. We are certain to be struck, moreover, by the recurring imagery of disease or physical affliction—not, as in Poe, in its more shocking and macabre forms, but in the comparatively less frightful forms of slow dissolution, of ravaging plague, of a tainted physical system, of a birthmark or a scar or a twisted mouth: only in such symbols could Hawthorne's sense of a radical moral obliquity in human nature adequately express itself. And, finally, it is extremely revealing how constantly this shy and solitary recluse found himself dealing in the imagery of social life —the imagery of a banquet or a masquerade, of a state ball or a wedding, of a merrymaking or a fireside gathering: his fancy was haunted, in his solitude, as if by tantalizing mirages, by images of social pomp or gregarious good cheer.

It was not haunted, as Poe's was, by images of cruelty, of torture, of claustrophobia and hypsophobia and phobophobia itself; and this is eloquent of the great differences between the two men as artists, between the more deeply psychoneurotic but also more intense and hallucinatory writer and the cooler, more purely meditative one. A quite different contrast suggests itself between Hawthorne and Melville in these terms: the symbols of a trackless sea, of violent tempests, of waterspouts and tornadoes, of the monstrous animal life of the ocean, of hunting, combat, and slaughter—these symbols, utterly unnatural to Hawthorne, are wonderfully expressive of Melville's wilder, more passionate, more deeply demoniac nature. The very vocabularies of these three contemporaries are revealingly unlike one another. Who can have failed to be conscious, in reading Poe, how bitterly and compulsively there keep recurring, as in a verbalized nightmare, the words *terror, anxiety, horror, anguish,* and *fear*? Who can have missed the meaning of Melville's talismanic language, of the telltale words *wild, barbarous,* and *savage; vengeful, cun-*

ning, and *malignant; noble, innocent,* and *grand; inexora-
ble, inscrutable,* and *unfathomable?* Compare with these
the palette of Hawthorne's vocabulary: the favorite adjectives, *dusky, dim,* and *shadowy,* or *cold, sluggish,* and
torpid; the favorite verbs, *separate, estrange,* and *insulate;*
the favorite nouns, *pride* and *egotism, guilt* and *intellect,
heart* and *sympathy.* They tell us everything about his
sensibility, his imagination, and the creative idiosyncrasy
of his human insight.

They tell us, for example, that, unlike the realistic novel-
ists of his day (some of whom he particularly admired
and enjoyed), Hawthorne was not interested, as a writer,
in the great social and worldly spectacle of manners and
affairs; what concerned him was what he himself once
called "psychological romance," a phrase that suggested
to him something much more serious—indeed, more tragic
—than it may suggest to us. He cared, as James said, for
"the deeper psychology"; and his tales, like his novels, are
the expression of his burrowings, to use his own words
again, "into the depths of our common nature." What he
found there was something that, more often than not,
saddened him—when it did not, as it sometimes did, appal
him. What he found made it impossible for Hawthorne to
share the great glad conviction of his age that, as Emerson
had told it, "love and good are inevitable, and in the course
of things"; he came closer to feeling that guilt and wrong
are inevitable; that, at any rate, they are terribly deeply
meshed in the texture of human experience. His sense of
the heights to which human beings can rise was an inter-
mittent one; his sense of the depths to which they can fall,
of the maze of error in which they can wander, was steady
and fascinated. What it means to be in harmony with
things and with oneself—of this he had his own intuition,
and there are gleams of it on his pages. For him, however,

it was a far more characteristic intuition, a far more continuous experience, to understand what it means to *be in the wrong*. That is the moral nucleus of most of his tales.

His awareness of the human condition, as a result, was intrinsically an anxious one—not fiercely anxious, as Poe's was, or angrily anxious, like Melville's, but anxious nevertheless in a quiet, painful, persistent, pervasive way. Sometimes this anxiety comes to a head, in his work, in a piercing moment of bitterness and almost despair, but its typical expression is grave, pensive, or mournful. Hawthorne is the elegiac poet, so to say, of the sense of guilt. And this guilty sense attaches itself, when he is being most himself, not to sins or vices of the gross and palpable sort—"incontinence," "violence," or "fraud" (to use the Dantean triad)—but to the evil that seemed to Hawthorne, from self-knowledge and observation, to be the quintessence of them all, the evil of selfishness or pride. In just this insight he was not very far from Dante, as it happened, but in any case he was very far indeed from Emerson and the prevailing spokesmen of his time. For them the essence of all virtue was reliance on oneself. Not for Hawthorne. Upon both the theory and the practice of self-help, self-trust, self-reliance he looked with a troubled gaze: he was not a good "individualist" in that sense. He was far less disturbed than Emerson by the dangers of conformity, of dependence, of compromise; he was far *more* disturbed by the evil wrought in a man's nature by the conscious or unconscious separation of himself from his fellows and the deadly tendency to hold himself not only aloof from them but superior to them. "I wrapped myself in PRIDE as in a mantle," says the heroine of one of his tales, and the gloomy upshot of "Lady Eleanore's Mantle" is a metaphor of what follows on a gesture of that sort.

Most of Hawthorne's characters wrap themselves in

some such cloak, though the pride it symbolizes may take many forms—the pride of social rank, the pride of wealth and power, the pride of moral self-righteousness. One form it takes, however, is easily the most characteristic and the most revealing. This is the pride of intellect. There is no evading the fact that Hawthorne distrusted that faculty, distrusted it with a consistency and an undertone of self-reproach that have in them a shade of the Dostoevskian. To pride oneself on one's intellectual powers or attainments, to cultivate the intellect at the expense of the sympathies, to take a merely speculative or scientific interest in one's fellowmen—this was for Hawthorne the deadliest form that human guilt could take: it was indeed, as "Ethan Brand" exemplifies, the Unpardonable Sin, the sin which the protagonist of that tale spent his life seeking and which he ended by finding in himself. This is the guiltiness also of the "prophetic" painter, of Dr. Rappaccini, and of Aylmer in "The Birthmark." It is the guiltiness to which superior natures are peculiarly prone; a more than ordinary diabolism is the fruit of it, and in their more tenuous, more evanescent, more "emblematic" way these characters of Hawthorne's belong in the same moral world as Raskolnikov or Stavrogin or Ivan Karamazov.

The penalty of intellectual pride and of all other forms of egotism—indeed, of guilt in general—is the deepest misery Hawthorne can conceive, the misery of estrangement, of separateness, of insulation from the normal life of mankind. This is the penalty of guilt, but it is also in a sense its origin, and in still another sense it *is* guilt itself, for no more in Hawthorne than in any deeply reflective tragic poet can one distinguish, beyond a certain point, between an evil and its source or its sequel. The simplest and truest thing to say of Hawthorne's human vision is that for him the essence of wrong is aloneness; you begin and you end with that. To err is to cut oneself off from "the whole sympathetic chain of human nature"; to suffer is to be merely on one's own. Solitariness, original or consequential, is his abiding theme; it is hard to believe that any other writer, including writers greater than he, has ever had a more acute sense than Hawthorne had of the whole terrible meaning of the word "solitude."

The picture of human life that emerges from his work is naturally, as he himself would say, a "dusky" one, but it would be very shallow to label Hawthorne, in hackneyed language, a "pessimistic" or "misanthropic" writer: with all his limitations, he went too deep for sentimental pessimism or facile cynicism. He took a dark view but not a low one of human nature; he took a doubtful but not a despairing view of the human prospect. He called himself "a thoroughgoing democrat," and certainly the adoption of this creed, as he says elsewhere, requires no scanty share of faith in the ideal. In his way, which was not the "optimistic" one, he had such faith. He had no faith in or respect for the forms and the forces that separate men from one another or distinguish sharply among them; he had no respect whatever for rank or caste or class, and he had almost as little for the intellectual ranks or classes that serve only too often to keep men apart. His real faith, quite "paradoxically," was in what he called the heart. Much that he saw there was terrible enough, but humanly speaking he believed in nothing else—in nothing, that is, except in the capacities that equalize instead of dividing men, in the affections that draw them together, in imaginative sympathy and the sense of a common brotherhood in error and suffering. His conviction is quite clear that what is wrong can be righted by nothing unless by love. This may be, like Melville's, a tragic version of the democratic faith; that is hardly to say that it is an unphilosophical one.

THE UNFINISHED WINDOW

SOME DAYS after Hawthorne's burial in the Sleepy Hollow Cemetery at Concord—"in a pomp of sunshine and verdure and gentle winds," as someone described it—Longfellow, who had been a classmate of Hawthorne's at Bowdoin, composed an elegy on his friend which closes with these stanzas:

> There in seclusion and remote from men
>   The wizard hand lies cold,
> Which at its topmost speed let fall the pen,
>   And left the tale half told.
>
> Ah! who shall lift that wand of magic power,
>   And the lost clew regain?
> The unfinished window in Aladdin's tower
>   Unfinished must remain!

The half-told tale to which Longfellow here alluded was an unfinished novel, later to be called *The Dolliver Romance*, the manuscript of which had lain on Hawthorne's coffin during the funeral services. What Longfellow could not have known at the time was that there were—not one —but four unfinished windows in the tower, although the relationship among the four is much too complex to be rendered by any architectural metaphor I can devise or any feat of symbolic fenestration I can perform.

To simplify a good deal, however, Hawthorne left at his death a confusion of manuscripts some of which were ultimately published under four different titles as frankly incomplete or even fragmentary novels—*The Dolliver Ro-*

mance itself, *Septimius Felton, Dr. Grimshawe's Secret,* and *The Ancestral Footstep.* It was, by the way, his daughter Una who, with the help of Browning, put *Septimius Felton* into shape, and Hawthorne's son, Julian, who pieced together the version of another novel which he called *Dr. Grimshawe's Secret.* It was a pretty artificial flower as Julian Hawthorne published it, and about seven years ago Professor Edward Davidson did much to straighten out the confusion with a book called *Hawthorne's Last Phase;* later, in 1954, he published a careful edition of *Dr. Grimshawe* based on all the various manuscript drafts which Julian Hawthorne had put to use in his somewhat lordly way.

In spite of their tantalizing fragmentariness, these four books deserve a rather high place on that shelf of the Great Unfinished which includes *The Faerie Queen, The Mystery of Edwin Drood,* Thackeray's *Denis Duval, Bouvard et Pécuchet,* James's two uncompleted novels, and so much of Kafka. One values them, after all, a good deal more highly than one does the finished work of many less original writers, just as one values an unfinished landscape by Cézanne more highly than many a finished work by unoriginal painters. For one thing, there are passages in them which, for charm or power or profundity, will bear comparison with all but the greatest chapters in Hawthorne's completed novels; and for another, three of them are accompanied by preliminary sketches and interpolated notes addressed to Hawthorne by himself which give one an exciting sense of being unobtrusively present at the moment of conception or in the process of composition itself.

Mixed up as the whole picture is, one can say that Hawthorne was attempting, in these last six years of his life, to write two fairly distinguishable though partly overlapping books—books, at least, on two distinguishable themes. One of these was the theme of the American Claimant—the theme of the young American, of English ancestry, who returns to England to claim the heritage that his ancestors had been unjustly and even violently deprived of. This is the central subject of *The Ancestral Footstep* and of *Grimshawe*, and the central symbol in both books is a bloody stain on a stone pavement in the American Claimant's hereditary manor-house—a bloody stain, like a footstep, such as Hawthorne had actually seen at Smithell's Hall in Lancashire, which was traditionally alleged to have been stamped there in anger by a Nonconformist clergyman who, under Queen Mary, had been tried for heresy and condemned to be burnt at the stake. The other theme is that of living forever, of earthly immortality, which had been suggested to Hawthorne by a story Thoreau had told him—a story about a man who, years earlier, had lived in the Wayside, Hawthorne's own house in Concord—a strange character who "was resolved never to die." This is the central subject of *Septimius Felton* and *The Dolliver Romance*, and the central symbol in both books is an elixir of life which, in the former, is distilled by Septimius and, in the second, by the aged Dr. Dolliver's grandson, an apothecary like the Doctor himself.

There is something very characteristic of Hawthorne's imagination in both these symbols: the bloody footstep associates itself vaguely and perhaps irrationally in one's mind with the tiny crimson blemish on the cheek of Aylmer's wife in the story called "The Birthmark," and the image of an elixir of life, or of rejuvenation, he had used before in an early tale called "Dr. Heidegger's Experiment." He had always been fascinated by strange discolorations or deformities, as he had always been fascinated by mysterious concoctions or potions. And the two themes,

also, which these symbols embody, are as Hawthornesque
as can be, though they express rather different sides of
his mind.

The theme of the American Claimant he had tried, un-
successfully, to work up into a novel while he was living
in Italy in 1858, and the unfinished manuscript of this is
what was later called *The Ancestral Footstep*. After his
return to America in 1860, he tackled the subject again,
wrote a series of studies and experimental drafts, but
finally abandoned them in despair; and these are what
Julian Hawthorne used as the stuff of *Grimshawe*. It was
Hawthorne the imaginative historian and social commen-
tator, chiefly, who was struggling to make a novel out of
this material. What he was getting at was what Henry
James was later to call the International Theme—the
richly dramatic contrast between the Old World and the
New, between Europe and America, the Past and the Present—or the Future—the manor-house and the New England parsonage. He failed to realize his purpose, and to
finish a satisfactory novel: this was partly because the
serious and significant story got itself hopelessly tied up
in the knots of a Gothic and rather stagey plot. It was as
if Hawthorne were reaching out toward the *Portrait of a
Lady* with brushes some of which would have been more
suitable to *The Mysteries of Udolpho*. But, even at the
worst, he was breaking new ground, and there are passages
in *Grimshawe* which have a wonderful truth, subtlety,
and insight in the way in which they render the old American "ambivalence" toward Europe; the longing to yield to
the past, to the "old home," to history and memory—and
the emotional counter-movement of resistance, rejection,
and even revulsion. If the projected book had ever really
been done, it would have put Henry James decidedly on
his mettle twenty years later.

The theme of earthly immortality Hawthorne had turned to after ceasing to struggle with *Dr. Grimshawe*; a year later he had written a rough draft of *Septimius Felton*, but his physical strength was failing, his spirits were depressed (partly by the War), and he abandoned this too. Then, in the last months of his life, ill and miserable as he was, he came back to the nagging subject, and in a miraculous dying flare-up of his powers, wrote three chapters of *The Dolliver Romance*—the writing in which is almost as enchanting as Hawthorne at his most felicitous. A few weeks later he was dead. . . . The Hawthorne of these two final books is not the historian or social observer primarily but the Christian moralist, and what he is saying, especially in *Septimius*, is that, without death, life would have no serious meaning, no meaning that would redeem it from a dreary and sterile egotism, materiality, and even brutishness. The search for the elixir has the effect on Septimius that every solitary and selfish pursuit had always had on Hawthorne's tragic personages: it carries the young scholar apart from the normal human sympathies, and converts him, as Hawthorne puts it, "from an interested actor, into a cold and disconnected spectator of all mankind's warm and sympathetic life." The elixir itself that he distills, lustrous and richly-hued as it is, makes the whole world seem unreal when gazed at through it, and besides it is cold, terribly cold, colder than ice itself; in the end it proves to be, not an elixir of life, but a fatal poison. One can imagine that Dr. Dolliver, too, though his elixir might have given him a spurious youthfulness, would have found that it was destroying him as a moral being.

All these books, in short, have a serious and characteristic interest, and one regrets that Hawthorne did not have the creative vitality to finish at least two of them—since there were really only two in his mind. Even in their inchoate condition, however, they have an extraordinary value, not only for the reasons I have just suggested, but for the sake of the notations scattered through them in which Hawthorne gives himself directions as to how he should proceed, and in doing so, exposes the workings of his mind as a writer; these sketches and notations have much the same interest as some passages in Flaubert's letters to Louise Colet. At one point, for example, in the draft of *The Ancestral Footstep,* speaking of one of the personages, he remarks: "The character must not be allowed to get vague, but with gleams of romance, must yet be kept homely and natural by little touches of his daily life." We hardly needed to be told perhaps that a very special mingling of the strange and the familiar, the marvelous and the ordinary, was an effect Hawthorne had often consciously aimed at, but it is at least pleasant to come upon his own explicit formulation of the principle. And so with the probable and the improbable. A note in the first draft of *Grimshawe* goes thus: "The narrative must be pitched in such a tone, and enveloped in such an atmosphere, that improbable things shall be accepted; and yet there must be a certain quality of homely, common life diffused through it, so that the reader shall feel a warmth in it." Just how careful, too, Hawthorne had become not to allow his expressive symbols to degenerate into explicit allegories, appears in another note in the manuscript of *Grimshawe,* a work in which a huge spider plays a conspicuous role: "The old gentleman in his study, amid his spiders, must first be touched upon; especially the gigantic spider, to which (quietly and without telling the reader so) ascribe demoniac qualities." A quite different literary consideration comes out in a note in the manuscript of *Septimius Felton:* "Italianize Aunt Nashoba's language a little; for except as Lowell uses it, I hate the Yankee dialect for literary purposes."

In asides to himself such as these, Hawthorne has the air of knowing quite well what he is about—the air of an old master of the craft—but there are other notes, especially in *Grimshawe*, that furnish the most touching and even poignant glimpses into the state of fatigue, confusion, and groping uncertainty in which, much of the time, he was working. Many of these notes, to be sure, have a psychological or biographical interest rather than a strictly critical one: they merely reveal to us how painfully a strong creative mind can fumble when its strength, as Cleopatra says, "is all gone into heaviness." "It seems as if," Hawthorne notes on one page, "there was something almost within my grasp—not quite." Or elsewhere: "There is a latent something lying hereabouts which, could I grip it, 'twould be the making of the story." Or elsewhere, speaking of a character only dimly envisaged: "I suppose I shall have to write him into the story before I can make out what he is to be."

But sometimes even these cries of distress, exasperated and self-lacerating as they are, have a more than merely clinical interest; they tell us something about the critical care with which, even in his happier period, Hawthorne had considered and then accepted or rejected a variety of possibilities. There is, for example, an aged palmer in *Grimshawe* whose role and even whose precise character Hawthorne never succeeded in defining to himself. "This old man," he writes—"what could he possibly be? The inheritor of some peculiarity that has been known heretofore in the history of the family, and the possession of which betrays itself in some of his habits, or in his person. What? I can't make it out. Some physical peculiarity?—

'twon't do. Some mental or moral peculiarity? How? The art of making gold? A peculiar kind of poison? An acquaintance with wizard lore? Nothing of this." Then, with an impatient gesture of self-parody, Hawthorne goes on: "He is an eater of human flesh—a vampire—a ghoul. He finds it necessary to eat a young child, every year, in order to keep himself alive." Hawthorne now masters himself again for a moment: "He shall have some famous jewel, known for ages in the family annals—pah! He shall have undertaken some investigation, which many members of his family have been deluded into undertaking heretofore, and the nature of which is, to change their natures disastrously—'twon't do. He shall have been to the cave of Trophonius. He shall have been to Hell—and I wish the Devil had kept him there."

The Devil did keep him there, in the end, and even in the draft of *Grimshawe* he is one of the characters who seem to have stepped out of Mrs. Radcliffe or "Monk" Lewis. But I should not like to bring these sketchy remarks to a conclusion on such a negative note as this. In all four of these fragmentary works there are passages, as I said a moment ago, that could have been written only by the "wizard hand" to which Longfellow so finely alluded; passages of magical delicacy and truth in psychological adumbration, or of picture-making richness, or of narrative energy. In *Grimshawe* there is a paragraph in which are wonderfully evoked the emotions of the young American who finds himself a guest at what is really his own ancestral hall—the sense he has of being under a spell, of moving about in a dream, of there being someone near him whom he cannot make out, "stealing behind him," as Hawthorne says, "and starting away when he was impelled to turn round." The passage in *Dolliver* in which the old doctor's morning-gown is described—the old patchwork morning-gown that has been mended by generations of his female relatives, so that it revives for him the memory of most things that have happened to him— this passage has much of the charm, the humorous tenderness, with which, in *The House of the Seven Gables,* Clifford Pyncheon's faded damask dressing-gown was rendered. Hawthorne, moreover, had always shown a special genius for conveying the states of mind of men who have somehow alienated or estranged themselves from the rest of normal mankind, and he does so with little or no loss of genial power in the passage in *Septimius Felton* in which he represents Septimius's sense of moral isolation amid the public stir and excitement that accompany the outbreak of the Revolution. It is simply not true, in short, as it has sometimes been said, that these posthumous works do nothing but betray a total decline of Hawthorne's creative forces: they do betray fatigue, ill health, dejection, and sometimes a strange dreamlike bewilderment, but along with that they tell us that, despite these things, Hawthorne's mind was still capable of moving forward into new "fields of light," and that (at least fitfully) it was capable of something like the old mastery in surveying them. The window may be an unfinished one, but at least it is, as Longfellow said, a window in Aladdin's Tower.

HERMAN MELVILLE

MELVILLE AND THE GOTHIC NOVEL

I

THERE is a curious and rather unexpected passage in *Billy Budd* in which, alluding to Claggart's hatred of Billy, Melville remarks that the cause of this dark emotion was "in its very realism as much charged with that prime element of Radcliffean romance, *the mysterious,* as any that the ingenuity of the author of the *Mysteries of Udolpho* could devise." [1] *Billy Budd* and the *Mysteries of Udolpho!* Claggart and the melodramatic Montoni! Herman Melville and Mrs. Ann Radcliffe! Surely these are little better than laughable juxtapositions, and nothing could be idler or more pedantic than to look closely and seriously at the clue that Melville dropped behind him in the passage I have just quoted. Such, at least, is bound to be one's first response to the suggestion that there is a certain strain of the Radcliffean, of the "Gothic," in Melville's own work —until, perhaps, one recalls how fond of Mrs. Radcliffe's books both Balzac and Stendhal were, and reflects that

[1] *Works* (London, 1922–1924), XIII, 43.

Melville would not be the first writer of great power to owe a certain debt to one of his small predecessors. The fact is, of course, that his mind was a very complex one; that he was tirelessly responsive to the imaginative currents of his age; and that he was indebted, as only writers of the first order can be, to a thousand books and authors who preceded him. In all that, the "influence" of the Gothic school is a slight and minor element; but every element in the sensibility of a writer like Melville has its interest and meaning for us.

There can be no doubt of his familiarity with the writers of the Tale of Terror school. He was probably familiar with them from an early date, no doubt from boyhood, though we have to guess at this. In any case, we know that Smollett's *Ferdinand Count Fathom,* with its one or two rather trumped-up scenes of what might be called premature Gothicism, was one of the books that, according to a passage in *Omoo,* oddly turned up in the possession of his amiable host Po-po, on the island of Moorea, and that he read with such delight.[2] Some years later, on his visit to England in 1849, Melville bought and brought home with him a quantity of books, among which were three or four of the favorite classics of the Gothic school: Horace Walpole's *Castle of Otranto,* Beckford's *Vathek,* Godwin's *Caleb Williams,* and Mrs. Shelley's *Frankenstein.*[3] How well Melville may have known the German writers of what is called the *Schauerroman* it is not easy to say, but in 1850 he is known to have borrowed from his friend

2 *Works,* II, 347.
3 Willard Thorp, editor, *Herman Melville: Representative Selections* (New York, 1938), xxviii, note. Mr. Merton M. Sealts, who is preparing a list of the books in Melville's personal library, tells me that there is no evidence of his having owned any of Mrs. Radcliffe's works. Only the first installment of Mr. Sealts' article, "Melville's Reading: A Check-List of Books Owned and Borrowed," has hitherto appeared in the *Harvard Library Bulletin,* II (Spring, 1948), 141–163.

Duyckinck the two volumes of Carlyle's *German Romance,* with its translations from such romantic and sometimes "Gothic" writers as Tieck and E. T. A. Hoffmann.[4]
Still later, traveling in the Near East and finding himself
followed about the bazaar in Constantinople by a sus-
picious-looking Greek, he remembered that "much of the
fearful interest of Schiller's Ghost-Seer"—a once famous
shudder-tale—"hangs upon being followed in Venice by
an Armenian."[5]

The singular passage in *Billy Budd* was not the only
place where Melville alluded to the good Ann Radcliffe
herself. There is another entry in the journal he kept of
his trip to Palestine which is almost as noteworthy; he is
speaking of the desolate, stricken landscape of the Holy
Land, and remarks: "As the sight of haunted Haddon Hall
suggested to Mrs. Radcliffe her curdling romances, so I
have little doubt, the diabolical landscape of Judea must
have suggested to the Jewish prophets, their ghastly theology."[6] In some curious way, the imagery of Mrs. Radcliffe's books must have got itself intermingled with
Melville's somber impressions of Palestine; an allusion to
one of them occurs early in the first part of *Clarel,* the long
metaphysical-descriptive poem he wrote on the basis of his
travels in that country. He is describing the Church of the
Holy Sepulchre in Jerusalem. Those pilgrims, he says, who
loiter near the sacred tomb at nightfall, and become aware
of the lengthening shadows of the stone and the low mysterious sounds stealing from its vicinity,

[4] *Herman Melville: Representative Selections,* xxviii, note. The volumes
that Melville borrowed were probably the two volumes of Carlyle's
German Romance: Specimens of Its Chief Authors (Boston, 1841).

[5] Herman Melville, *Journal up the Straits . . .* (New York, 1935), 32.
In *Der Geisterseher* the principal character, the Prince von ————,
visiting Venice incognito, is accosted at night in St. Mark's Square by
a masked Armenian, who later appears in other guises and is in fact
the Wandering Jew.

[6] Melville, *Journal up the Straits,* 88.

Shrink, much like Ludovico erst
Within the haunted chamber . . .[7]

One wonders how many of *Clarel's* readers, in the seventies, would still have recognized in Ludovico the half-comic, half-heroic manservant at the Castle of Udolpho who assists the heroine, Emily St. Aubert, in escaping from that sinister pile, and who later, in the south of France, undertakes to spend the night in the haunted chambers of the Château-le-Blanc.

II

Of course there would have been a great deal in the Gothic writers to inspire risibility in Melville rather than serious emulation, and yet the fact is that there was also a strain of feeling and imagination in them, of romantic sensibility, of morbid fancy, even of "nerves," to which he was by no means unresponsive. There was, for example, that passion for "wild," "gloomy," and "sublime" landscapes which Mrs. Radcliffe and the others derived in part from the tradition of Baroque landscape-painting—from Salvator Rosa, especially, and from such painters as the poetic English landscapist, Richard Wilson—and which certainly contributed to form and educate Melville's manner of looking at the visible world.[8] Most readers of Mrs. Radcliffe will recall her habit of alluding to those painters; a narrow valley in the Pyrenees, for example, in *Udolpho*, characteristically strikes her as "such a scene as Salvator

[7] *Works*, xɪv, 18. There are even one or two other references to Mrs. Radcliffe elsewhere. See *Works*, xɪɪɪ, 318 ("The Apple-Tree Table") and Merrell R. Davis, "Melville's Midwestern Lecture Tour, 1859," *Philological Quarterly*, xx (Jan., 1941), 51.
[8] There is an interesting account of these artistic influences on Mrs. Radcliffe in Elizabeth Stockton Ullery, *Mrs. Ann Radcliffe as a Pioneer in the Use of Description in Fiction* (Northampton, 1933), an unpublished master's thesis in the Smith College Library.

would have chosen . . . for his canvas." [9] In exactly the same manner, Melville, evoking in *Redburn* the spectacle of the dying sailor Jackson, brooding in the "infernal gloom" of his bunk, observes that he was a picture "worthy to be painted by the dark, moody hand of Salvator." [10]

His own landscapes are sometimes decidedly in the great Baroque tradition of Salvator Rosa—and of Ann Radcliffe. Even when it is a question of conjuring up a scene so far from Mrs. Radcliffe's romantic Pyrenees and Apennines as a wild ravine on the Marquesan island of Nukuhiva, the one in which Melville and Toby spend a wretched night before descending into the Valley of Typee, it seems as if Melville, on the spot, had gazed about him with eyes that had been trained in part by Mrs. Radcliffe:

> The sight that now greeted us was one that will ever be vividly impressed upon my mind. Five foaming streams, rushing through as many gorges, and swelled and turbid by the recent rains, united together in one mad plunge of nearly eighty feet, and fell with wild uproar into a deep black pool scooped out of the gloomy-looking rocks that lay piled around, and thence in one collected body dashed down a narrow sloping channel which seemed to penetrate into the very bowels of the earth. Overhead, vast roots of trees hung down from the sides of the ravine, dripping with moisture, and trembling with the concussions produced by the fall. It was now sunset, and the feeble uncertain light that found its way into these caverns and woody depths heightened their strange appearance, and reminded us that in a short time we should find ourselves in utter darkness.[11]

[9] Ann Radcliffe, *The Mysteries of Udolpho* (London, 1931), I, 30.
[10] *Works*, v, 355.
[11] *Works*, I, 59.

In the particularly "painterly" quality of this piece of landscape-writing—in the dim uncertain lighting, the heavy shadows, the dark surface of the pool, the violence of the physical motions, and the rich accompaniment of awesome sounds—there is an inescapable reminiscence, in Polynesian terms, of some of Mrs. Radcliffe's fine, gloomy landscapes. Take, for example, that in which Emily St. Aubert finds herself when Montoni's banditti attempt to abduct her from the Castle of Udolpho:

> The sun had now been set some time; heavy clouds, whose lower skirts were tinged with sulphurous crimson, lingered in the west, and threw a reddish tint upon the pine forests, which sent forth a solemn sound as the breeze rolled over them. The hollow moan struck upon Emily's heart, and served to render more gloomy and terrific every object around her—the mountains, shaded in twilight—the gleaming torrent, hoarsely roaring—the black forests, and the deep glen, broken into rocky recesses, high overshadowed by cypress and sycamore, and winding into long obscurity.[12]

It is clear enough, from such a parallel, that Melville has insensibly transmuted the old Baroque or Gothic landscape into something genuinely his own, and the point would be equally clear if one turned to such passages as Pierre's dream of the ruinous and desolate scenery environing the Mount of Titans,[13] or the marvelous presentment, in the first sketch of "The Encantadas," of the blighted, nightmarish landscape of the Galápagos Islands.[14] It is, of course, Melville's own "painterly" powers that are really important in these passages, but it is impossible not to detect in them, nevertheless, the lingering

[12] Ann Radcliffe, *The Mysteries of Udolpho*, ii, 76.
[13] *Works*, ix, 476–482.
[14] *Works*, x, 181–187.

vestiges of an older manner in fiction—the manner embodied in such scenes as that of the wild Adriatic seacoast
in Mrs. Radcliffe's *The Italian,* or the frightful abysses into
which the fiend dashes the guilty Ambrosio in M. G.
Lewis's *The Monk,* or the dreamlike horror of the bleak
Arctic landscape in *Frankenstein.*

If we look in Melville's work for the great leading symbol of Gothic fiction, the Haunted Castle itself,[15] it is quite
true that we shall not find it, at least not literally; there is
of course, in Melville, no such grand and melancholy
Gothic structure as that of Otranto or Udolpho or the
Castle of R——sitten in Hoffmann's tale, *Das Majorat.*
There is no House of Usher in his work nor even a House
of the Seven Gables. Yet something of the poetic quality
of the Haunted Castle—its strangeness, its antiquity, its
dilapidation, its somber picturesqueness—may surely be
felt, with all the differences, in Melville's description of
the *Pequod* in *Moby Dick,* with its weather-stained hull,
its venerable bows (which looked "bearded"), its spirelike
masts, its worn and ancient decks, and its general gro-
tesqueness and strangeness; [16] and perhaps one feels this
quality still more strongly in Melville's drawing of the
doomed Spanish vessel, the *San Dominick,* in "Benito
Cereno," suggesting as it does "a whitewashed monastery
after a thunder-storm, seen perched upon some dun cliff
among the Pyrenees." [17] One of Mrs. Radcliffe's beloved
convents and monasteries comes immediately to mind, let
us say the convent of San Stefano among the wild Abruzzi
in *The Italian;* and certainly there is more than a touch
of the Gothic in the *San Dominick's* dilapidated tops, its

[15] Interestingly treated in Eino Railo, *The Haunted Castle: A Study of
the Elements of English Romanticism* (London, 1927).

[16] *Works,* VII, 85–87.

[17] *Works,* x, 68.

castellated forecastle ("battered and mouldy" like "some ancient turret"), and the "faded grandeur" of its shieldlike stern-piece, intricately carved with the arms of Castile and Leon.[18] And, of course, the emotional tone of "Benito," its absorbing anxiety and half-pleasurable foreboding, is but a deeper and more serious version of Mrs. Radcliffe's "pleasing dread." [19]

Less interesting in every way is the image of the ruined tower, standing out like "the black mossed stump of some immeasurable pine," in the feeble Hawthornesque tale, "The Bell-Tower" (one of the *Piazza Tales*); yet this, too, is a dim echo of the towers, the turrets, the belfries in which the Gothic writers abound; [20] and when, in *Pierre*, the hero and his half-sister Isabel ensconce themselves in the city high up in the building that adjoins the Church of the Apostles, in chambers from which Pierre can gaze out at "the donjon form of the old gray tower" of the Church itself,[21] one is at any rate oddly reminded of the La Mottes and their protégée, the forlorn Adeline, in *The Romance of the Forest*, taking refuge amid the ruins of the Abbey of St. Clair, from the apartments of which they can contemplate the "almost demolished" eastern tower.[22] The tower is an obsessive symbol in Gothic fiction, but still more obsessive, and deeply characteristic, is the recur-

---

[18] *Works*, x, 69–70.

[19] Ann Radcliffe, *The Romance of the Forest* (London, 1904), 23.

[20] *Works*, x, 253. Mediocre as it is, "The Bell-Tower" has a certain interest because of the "experimental automaton" which Melville introduces into it, and which recalls not only *Frankenstein* but such tales of Hoffmann as *Der Sandmann* and *Die Automate*.

[21] *Works*, ix, 377.

[22] Ann Radcliffe, *The Romance of the Forest*, 20. Towers occur several times in *Clarel;* the tower on Mount Olivet (Part i, xxxvi, "The Tower") and the "towers twain" on Mar Saba (Part iii, xxi, "In Confidence") may be instanced. Nor should one forget, in *Moby Dick* (Chap. xcix), the emblematic tower engraved on the doubloon that Ahab nails to the mainmast.

ring, dreamlike symbolism of the subterranean—of ill-lighted, perplexing, labyrinthine corridors below ground, of obscure and gloomy vaults, of yawning dungeons; one finds it everywhere in Beckford, in Mrs. Radcliffe, in "Monk" Lewis; and such tales as "The Cask of Amontillado" and "The Pit and the Pendulum" suggest that this claustrophobic imagery had a quite special value for Poe. It is less characteristic in every way of Melville, but even in him there is a hint of it in the murky, stifling, vermin-infested forecastles of *Omoo* [23] and *Redburn;* [24] and for a moment or two, in the sketch called "I and My Chimney," one finds oneself in the true underground realm of Mrs. Radcliffe and Poe. Very often, says the narrator of that sketch, he goes down into his cellar to survey the vast square base of his enormous chimney: "It has a druidical look, away down in the umbrageous cellar there, whose numerous vaulted passages, and far glens of gloom, resemble the dark, damp depths of primeval woods." [25] In Melville, as in Hoffmann and Poe, the Unconscious is powerfully symbolized in this imagery of the subterranean.

If not the Superconscious, then certainly the Inexpressible bodies itself forth for many of the romantics, and certainly for some of the Gothic writers, in the imagery of music and the musical instrument. One may well question whether Melville was so spontaneously sensitive to musical form as he certainly was to color, to line, and to the plastic in general. Yet he shared too fully the sensibility of romanticism not to be capable, at moments, of expressing himself almost in the vein of Novalis, of Hoffmann, of

[23] *Works,* II, 8, 46–49.
[24] *Works,* v, 109–110.
[25] *Works,* XIII, 283. There is an interesting discussion of the symbolism in this sketch in Merton M. Sealts, "Herman Melville's 'I and My Chimney,'" *American Literature,* XIII (June, 1941), 142–154.

Shelley: "Now, music," he says in *Redburn*, "is a holy thing, and its instruments, however humble, are to be loved and revered. . . . Musical instruments should be like the silver tongs with which the high priests tended the Jewish altars—never to be touched by a hand profane." [26] Certainly musical instruments had been favorite emblems for Mrs. Radcliffe and her followers; stringed instruments especially, but woodwinds too and horns; and no cachet of the school is more individualizing than the *"picturesque sounds,"* [27] as Mrs. Radcliffe rather finely calls them, which her heroines so love to draw forth from some romantic instrument. Emily St. Aubert, in *Udolpho*, is representative, and Emily's pleasantest hours, we are told, were passed in a pavilion to which she frequently retired "with a book to overcome, or a lute to indulge her melancholy." [28]

Isabel, in *Pierre*, is not a very remote descendant of Mrs. Radcliffe's Emilys and Adclinos and Ellenas, and not least in her passionate penchant for music, especially the music she knows how to draw forth preternaturally, even without touching its strings, from her beloved guitar. This remarkable instrument, she tells Pierre, she had bought with some of her little earnings from a peddler; later, to her astonishment, she had found the name Isabel lettered in gilt on its interior surface, and when she learned that the instrument had come from the Glendinning mansion, she was at once intuitively certain that it had belonged to her mysterious mother. It is, in short, one of the delicate links in the ambiguous chain of circumstances which convinces Pierre that Isabel is in very truth his half-sister. But the poetic use of the symbol is subtler and less tan-

[26] *Works*, v, 321.
[27] Ann Radcliffe, *The Mysteries of Udolpho*, I, 75.
[28] *The Mysteries of Udolpho*, I, 126

gible than its use in the plot; the mystical melodies which Isabel, in Pierre's fascinated presence, evokes from her guitar are suggestive of the strangeness, the preternaturalness, the ambiguity of the relations that are at the same moment springing up between Pierre and her. "All the wonders that are unimaginable and unspeakable," as she herself says, "all these wonders are translated in the mysterious melodiousness of the guitar." [29] Indeed, it is while she bends over the speaking instrument, her long dark hair falling over its strings and glowing with a mystic radiance from the "scintillations" of the melody, that Pierre is first aware of the spell which is being cast over him—that spell from which he knows it is impossible for him ever to break.[30] Gothic as Isabel's guitar undoubtedly is, it serves a darker and more painful purpose than any of Mrs. Radcliffe's genuinely charming lutes.

In any case, there appears in this same novel a remarkable example of still another favorite Gothic device, the magic portrait. Paintings in general are highly characteristic symbols in romantic fiction—Balzac's *Chef-d'oeuvre inconnu* is a familiar example—and true to his romantic heritage Melville had already introduced two striking pictures in *Moby Dick,* the smoky and almost unintelligible painting hung up in the entry of the Spouter-Inn,[31] and the stormy seascape that hangs at the back of Father Mapple's pulpit in the Whaleman's Chapel.[32] The painting in *Pierre,* however, is not a landscape but a portrait, and it belongs in the line of all the mysterious, uncanny portraits that stem from the likeness of Prince Manfred's grandfather in *The Castle of Otranto*—the somber portrait

[29] *Works,* IX, 177.
[30] *Works,* IX, 211–214.
[31] *Works,* VII, 13–14.
[32] *Works,* VII, 48.

which steps down out of its frame, at one juncture, and stalks gravely out of the room. Mrs. Radcliffe's portraits, mostly miniatures, are less preternatural than Walpole's, and Melville's imagination is more likely, here, to have been quickened by Hawthorne's various portraits—and perhaps also by the terribly strange portrait with the baleful eyes which, in Maturin's *Melmoth the Wanderer*, young John Melmoth burns to ashes at his dying uncle's injunction.[33]

The portrait in *Pierre*, as a matter of fact, is one of two pictures, two portraits of Pierre's deceased father, the elder Glendinning, one of which Pierre's mother approves of and allows to hang prominently in her drawing room; the other, however, she intensely dislikes and taboos, insisting that Pierre hang it safely out of her sight in a small closet that adjoins his bedroom. This latter picture represents Pierre's adored father as a carefree, irresponsible youth, seated negligently in an old-fashioned Malacca chair; and Pierre is much given to sitting before it and communing with it, for he at least imagines that it speaks to him and smiles at him in its suggestive, ambiguous way. He had learned, as a younger boy, of the circumstances under which it had been painted, and now, after the real action begins, his recollection of them sickeningly confirms the suspicions of his father's rectitude which Isabel's tale has implanted in his heart. From being the object of a kind of idolatry—a literal "father image," indeed—the portrait has turned to an object of loathing to Pierre, an emblem of the moral ambiguities that flicker and leer about him; and before he sets off for the city with Isabel, he destroys the chair-portrait by burning it. As he does so, and it writhes blackly in the flames, it stares at him tor-

---

[33] Charles Robert Maturin, *Melmoth the Wanderer* (London, 1892), I, 93–95.

mentedly "in beseeching horror," quite as if it were a living thing.[34] It is perhaps not meaningless, psychologically, that both Pierre and Melville should so much have disliked to have their portraits painted or their pictures taken.[35]

III

Pierre, in any case, like some of Melville's other books, owes more than its symbols to his Gothic forerunners. The novel, from this somewhat pedantic point of view, represents an intertwining of three strands in Melville's literary heritage: Elizabethan tragedy, sentimentalism, and the Radcliffean novel that has so much in common with sentimentalism and that also expressed, in its own time, a kind of displaced Elizabethanism. The incest motive in *Pierre,* for example, might certainly have come to Melville from Webster or Ford, but it is still more reminiscent of the sentimental, the Gothic, or in general the romantic school. In *White-Jacket,* Melville himself alludes to Walpole's incestuous tragedy, *The Mysterious Mother,* along with *Oedipus Tyrannus* and *The Cenci;* [36] and he may well have recalled how Mrs. Radcliffe had dallied with the theme in *The Romance of the Forest,* only to slip away from it unsullied, and how the less fastidious, or less timorous, Lewis had embraced it without coyness, restraint, or apology in *The Monk.* Needless to say, the fact that Melville turned to the theme of incest in *Pierre* has a far deeper meaning than any study of literary *Einflüsse* could possibly suggest; one speaks of these connections only for what they are, no more; and Melville—who, in-

34 *Works,* IX, 98–119, 273–277.
35 *Works,* IX, 352–357. See also a letter to Duyckinck in Meade Minnigerode, *Some Personal Letters of Herman Melville* . . . (New York, 1922), 72–73.
36 *Works,* VI, 474.

credibly enough, seems actually to have fancied that *Pierre* was "calculated for popularity" [37]—may have thought that his novel would succeed as *The Monk* had done sixty years earlier, and partly for similar reasons.

At all events, Pierre's half-sister, the dark and doubtful Isabel, is a perfectly legitimate descendant, if not of Pierre's father, then certainly, as I have said, of a long line of betrayed and persecuted heroines or even heroes in Gothic fiction, from Walpole's Isabella in *The Castle of Otranto* (whose name is so close to her own), or Mrs. Radcliffe's Ellena, or M. G. Lewis's Antonia, to Charles Brockden Brown's Constantia Dudley. It is not only Isabel's dark beauty that links her with many of these, or her mysterious origins, but much more the fact that she is both innocent and victimized. The persecution of the helpless and the blameless, with its undertones of "romantic agony," of the fearfully attractive pair, sadism-masochism, is only too notoriously a pervasive theme in romantic literature generally, and full of meaning as it clearly was for Melville himself, there is nothing surprising in its appearing so continuously in his own work. It appears there essentially because the basis for it had been present in his own life and experience, and it would be pure pedantry to allege that there is anything peculiarly Gothic in the figure of the buffeted and put-upon Redburn or in that of White-Jacket, close as this latter allegedly comes to being flogged at the mast. Caleb Williams could have furnished a literary model for these unhappy youths, but it was not at all necessary that he should. Redburn and White-Jacket suffer from the commonplace and unromantic brutality of the everyday world; elsewhere in Melville there are victims of a more specifically

[37] A phrase used by Melville in a letter to the English publisher, Bentley. See Harrison Hayford, "The Significance of Melville's 'Agatha' Letters," *English Literary History*, XII (Dec., 1946), 306.

romantic sort. Yillah, in *Mardi,* with her unearthly beauty and her mysterious provenance, is one of them; surely she is a sort of Polynesian and allegorical Ellena. Surely, too, the pathetic Benito Cereno, the so untragic Spanish sea-captain—with his morbid sensitiveness, his nervous anxieties, and his fainting spells—is a masculine and sea-going Isabella. And surely the innocent and ingenuous Billy Budd, victimized by the unreasoning hatred of Claggart, can count among his ancestors the handsome young Vivaldi in *The Italian,* who is so mercilessly hounded by his mother and his mother's confederate Schedoni, and perhaps also the upright and high-minded Caleb Williams, in his time too the object of so black and baseless a malignity.

It is not only Melville's victims who put us in mind, at least a little, of his Gothic predecessors; so too do the monsters who persecute them. Again it is true that Melville derived from experience itself his intense, appalled awareness of the evil in the heart of man, and of its baffling union, now and then, with a certain largeness and even heroism. But it is the most original, not the most imitative, writers who owe the deepest debt to their literary forerunners; and Melville cannot have been unaffected by the romantic writers, including the Gothic, in whose work he found so many embodiments of the type that is known as the Majestic Monster; the type that Schiller called the *Ungeheuer mit Majestät.*[38] Wickedness to the point of deviltry, associated nevertheless with a satanic grandeur and loftiness—the splendid ambiguity, indeed, that the romantics loved to see in Milton's Satan—had a deep and firsthand significance for Melville; he was disposed by native temper, as well perhaps as by chapters in his experience, to be impressed by such devilish but still

[38] Schiller used this phrase in the so-called *Unterdrückte Vorrede* to *Die Räuber.*

somehow noble characters as Manfred in *Otranto,* or Schedoni in *The Italian,* or Ambrosio in *The Monk*—precursors as these were of Byron's Manfred, of Shelley's Count Cenci, of Balzac's Vautrin, and other personages in the work of far greater writers than Walpole or Mrs. Radcliffe.

It was certainly somewhere in the real world, if not on his Liverpool voyage,[39] that Melville encountered the misanthropic sailor, Jackson, with his eye of a starved tiger and his ferocious nihilism; but when we are told that "he was a Cain afloat; branded on his yellow brow with some inscrutable curse," [40] we realize that an impression out of life itself has joined hands, and in a creative manner, with a literary inheritance. There is a touch of Schedoni in Jackson, as there is a touch of him in the wily, ingratiating, diabolical, yet somehow grandiose Negro slave, Babo, in "Benito," to whose masterfulness we cannot refuse a reluctant admiration; and combined in very different proportions, elements of the same sort are discernible in the splendid figure of Paul Jones, in *Israel Potter,* "intrepid, unprincipled, reckless, predatory, with boundless ambition, civilized in externals but a savage at heart." [41] Nor have we left the tradition of the Majestic Monster wholly behind us when we arrive, late in Melville's career, at the baleful figure of Claggart, master-at-arms on the *Indomitable,* who wreaks so purposelessly the destruction of

[39] According to William H. Gilman, "Melville's Liverpool Trip," *Modern Language Notes,* LXI (Dec., 1946), 543–547, there was actually a sailor named Jackson on the *St. Lawrence,* the ship on which, in 1839, Melville signed up as a "boy" and made the trip to Liverpool, but the dramatic death of Jackson must have been pure invention, since (as Mr. Gilman has shown in his unpublished doctoral dissertation, "Melville's Early Life and *Redburn,*" Yale, 1947) the whole crew of the *St. Lawrence* returned to New York alive and unscathed; and Jackson the imaginative creation may well have owed something to characters Melville had encountered elsewhere.

[40] *Works,* v, 134.

[41] *Works,* xi, 158. The adjectives quoted are used literally of the United States as a nation, but they are used in metaphorical relation to Paul Jones, whom they also characterize.

Billy Budd. Indeed, it is in the central passage which concerns Claggart that one comes upon the allusion with which this essay began, and the collocation seems not without meaning. At any rate, if there is no doubt of Claggart's monstrous wickedness, his "natural depravity," or the purity (so to say) of his malignity, neither is there any doubt of his not being a merely small and sordid villain. On the contrary, Claggart is physically tall, spare, and handsome, with a brow that hints of more than average intellect; a man of "superior capacity," who indeed is "dominated by intellectuality" and wholly free from "vices or small sins." [42] He is such a hero of pure evil as only a profoundly romantic imagination could envisage.

Profoundly romantic, in one of the largest senses of the word, Melville's imagination in fact was; and to say so is to say, especially for an English or American writer, that the Gothic or Radcliffean was almost certain to be a minor ingredient in its complex totality. Brockden Brown, our earliest novelist of any true genius, was a Gothic writer in the strictest sense, and the work of Poe and Hawthorne, of course, abounds in Gothic feeling and Gothic detail. This is far less true of Melville, for many reasons, one of which is simply that he was enough younger than any of them to have passed beyond the immediate reach of the Gothic magnetism. I need hardly add that the center of his mind, in any case, lay elsewhere, or that the effect upon him even of a minor master, such as Mrs. Radcliffe certainly was, could never have been a vital one. What is striking, indeed, is that that influence lingered so long as it did in this country, and that it preserved enough of its vitality to impart even the most delicate tincture to an imagination like Melville's. When one looks at his work with some of his own hints in mind, one observes that it did just that.

[42] *Works*, XIII, 31–35, 43–47.

HENRY WARD BEECHER

WITH THE ROCKIES FOR SOUNDING BOARD

NOW that Mr. Hibben has gone and done it,* one's first reaction is to exclaim, "Why had no one thought of doing it
long ago!" Why has it not been obvious for the last ten or
a dozen years—certainly since the date-marking "Queen
Victoria" appeared—that in the career of Henry Ward
Beecher the "new biographer" had ready to hand the
richest, the most highly seasoned, the easiest to dramatize,
of materials. Next to the good queen herself, there is
scarcely a figure in the nineteenth century, not even Napoleon III, more friendly to the brush of the portraitist
than the figure of the greater preacher. And Mr. Hibben,
like all good portrait painters, has done his work in a spirit
nearer to the caricaturist's than to the photographer's.
Was it the late John Singer Sargent who once defined a
portrait as a "likeness with something wrong about the
mouth"? Mr. Hibben, in catching his likeness, has left
"something wrong."

For the book he has written cannot and should not be
read or judged as a detached, judicious, "scientific" study

* *Henry Ward Beecher: An American Portrait,* by Paxton Hibben.

of a noncontroversial personality. A thousand questions remain unanswered when one has finished it. Hundreds of lapses from mere objectivity can be pounced upon by the dissenter. At point after point, with no real sacrifice of truth, the emphasis could be shifted from the ground where Mr. Hibben has laid it, and the whole portrait would take on, now a kindlier, now a more imposing, aspect. The central episode in the book—the story of Beecher's trial on a charge of adultery—leaves one reader not at all disposed to partisanship in behalf of a man with Beecher's religious and social views, uncertain whether the entire truth has been told. The whole affair was clearly a shady one, and not all the shadow appears to fall on the great preacher. And one may suspect that Mr. Hibben has belittled Beecher's work in England for the Union cause only somewhat less unduly than Holmes and Lyman Abbott exaggerated it.

The whole truth about such a man as Beecher would probably prove too complex to be stated with the severest objectivity. He belonged to the type which it is easy and convenient to describe by the word "charlatan," and the gap between charlatanry and simple hypocrisy is the gap between bewildered admiration and mere contempt. No black-and-white Chadband or Pecksniff emerges from Mr. Hibben's pages. The man who does emerge is something of a genius, a man of strangely continental proportions, a man who—to paraphrase what was said of John Stuart Mill—was not unintelligibly used by the American people to fill the breach where a great spiritual leader should have been.

It is, indeed, a chapter in the biography of the American character that Mr. Hibben has told, with a good deal of partiality. At one end, the son of Lyman Beecher touched the moribund Calvinism of the seventeenth century, stiffening in its fight for life; at the other end, he touched the twentieth century modernism of Lyman Abbott and Dr. Fosdick, which has made its peace with science and the dogma of progress. At one end, he touched the great old Constitutional compromises that had entrenched the "peculiar institutions" of the South; at the other end, he joined hands, far too closely, with the triumphant plutocracy of the Grant and Garfield era. He was at once one of the first champions of the movement for women's rights, and one of the first clerical apologists for the gospel of business and opponents of the labor movement. The intellectual confusions, the clumsy readjustments, the wanderings between deep sincerity and doubtful conviction that all these changes imposed upon the American mind were mirrored in the dramatic inconsistencies—incoherences, at the very least—of Henry Ward Beecher's career. If he was a charlatan, he performed his tricks against a national background; his audience was a party to his conjuring just as the public of P. T. Barnum knew it was being hoaxed—gloried in its very gullibility and loved the man who did the gulling.

He was exceptionally fitted by temperament and endowment to play that role for his countrymen. It has always been recognized—and Mr. Hibben merely amplifies and elucidates the charge—that his intellectual equipment was mediocre. In childhood and youth he was even regarded by his family and teachers as below the average in acumen, insight, and mental vigor. He never saw so deeply into the heart of social and moral problems that he was forced to state his solution of them in an unpopular and uncompromising way. His audiences did not have to follow him to some rigorous and distasteful logical conclusion. His real powers, as Mr. Hibben shows, were those of a great emotionalist. His frostbitten and disregarded childhood left him at the beginning of his career with an engrossing need for admiration, sympathy, and affection; and the rest of his life was spent in multiplying and intensifying his sympathetic relationships with human beings. In him the undisciplined and misdirected emotionality of the Puritan turned pioneer found voice and a liberating gesture.

It is on that ground, and not because it contains a commonplace tale of the priest caught *flagrante delicto,* that I should hope Mr. Hibben's book might be widely read. There is a kind of symbolism that takes it out of the merely personal sphere in the spectacle Mr. Hibben reveals of young Henry Ward Beecher moping about in the chilly inhumane atmosphere of his father's overcrowded parsonage at Litchfield, discovering his unsuspected resources of emotional expression in his elocution lessons at Amherst, evading the abolition issue, and waging war on intemperance in his early tentative years as a minister in Indiana, and finally coming into his own as a great popular pulpit orator in Plymouth Church, that extraordinary monument to American business and American evangelical piety. One visualizes a Friday evening prayer meeting in the Brooklyn tabernacle, crowded to the door with prosperous pewholders, the very galleries jammed with auditors, and the tall, bulky, histrionic figure of the preacher himself on the rostrum, his soft and ruddy countenance alight with fervor, the tears perhaps streaming down his cheeks, as he enunciates—with the Rocky Mountains for his sounding board—the great new gospel of the Love that is to take the place of the Puritan conscience. Plymouth Church becomes more than a house of worship in Brooklyn, and Beecher more than its pastor: what is taking place there is the funeral of an epoch—or the christening of another.

"Beecher stood forth a prodigious figure," says Mr. Hibben searchingly, "not by blazing a path in any wilderness, but by the fact that his inner experience was identical with that of millions of his fellow countrymen. His gift was merely that he was articulate while they were not." It is because he sees this and gives it a thematic centrality, and in spite of the overcorrected hostility with which he treats the man, that Mr. Hibben has written a book of large and perhaps lasting significance. The subtitle has more relevance than subtitles generally have.

WILLIAM DEAN HOWELLS

THE USABLENESS OF HOWELLS

IT LOOKS very much as if William Dean Howells were lucky in the timing of his centenary—luckier than some other writers whose names have cropped up for the same reason in the last half-dozen years, and certainly luckier than Howells himself was in rounding out his long career during those ten or fifteen years that preceded 1920. The whole disposition of criticism at the moment is immeasurably warmer and friendlier toward him than it was when, a year or so after the outbreak of the War in Europe, Howells himself could write to Henry James, with what painful feelings we can well imagine: "I am comparatively a dead cult with my statues cut down and the grass growing over them in the pale moonlight." There was almost no exaggertion in this melancholy remark, as anyone knows who can remember the distinguished obscurity in which he spent his last few years, or as anyone can now learn for himself by reading, for example, the essay which Mencken, with characteristic amenity and characteristic moderation, devoted to Howells and his work a year or two before his death. According to Mencken's view, the older man of letters was "an Agnes Repplier in pantaloons," "a contriver of pretty things," the author of "a long row of uninspired and hollow books, with no more ideas in them than so many volumes of *The Ladies' Home Journal* and no more deep and contagious feeling than so many reports of autopsies."

Judgments such as these, of course, have now taken their place among the curiosities of literary history, and the essay can be recommended only to those who want to be entertained by the spectacle of H. L. Mencken taxing Howells with "triviality" and "narrowness of vision." There is a Howells legend, however, a legend that was set in motion by Mencken's generation, and it has by no means even now been wholly discredited: the legend that represents him as merely a servile idolater at the shrine of Bostonian self-complacency; as a pander to the shallowest pruderies of the Brown Decades; as, at the best, a writer whose vision of human life was limited to the suburban horse-car, the summer colony and the front piazza. No one, I think, will now be tempted, in rejecting this caricature, to swing over to the opposite extreme and attribute to the author of *New Fortunes* the stature of a Stendhal or a Turgenev. But it is clear enough to the critical sense of this decade that, with all his deficiencies, Howells is one of the decisive figures in the development of our literary culture. The meaning of his career it is no longer possible to neglect or to belittle: he was the first of our important imaginative writers thoughtfully to consider and intelligently to comprehend what was happening to the form and quality of American life as it moved away from the simplicity, the social fluidity, the relative freedoms, of the mid-century toward the ugly disharmonies of monopolism and empire. He was the author of the first realistic novels of permanent interest in which the effects of that development are represented dramatically with any fullness or clarity.

Nothing could be less critical than to judge Howells

simply in comparison with the severest and most powerful of his successors: his true achievement comes into focus not only when he is seen beside Dreiser or Dos Passos but when his work is set against that of his predecessors and contemporaries. What he left for Frank Norris and Jack London to do is no more important than what he did that Hawthorne and Melville, Simms and Cooke and Cable had left undone. Dreiser, in a later generation, was the creator of Cowperwood, true; but his portrait of that titanic financier was made possible partly because the creator of old Dryfoos had already, in his zeal for the cultivation of a sound realism among us, cast out the old Jacksonian and romantic illusions and faced all the implications of the fact that "business," as he said, "is the national ideal, and the successful business man is the American type." In the growing realization of this—for it had once been hoped, of course, that the farmer or the professional man would dominate the life of the republic —Howells had made a scrupulous study of the old-fashioned business man at his best in his portrait of Silas Lapham.[1] But even in that novel, in the figures of Lapham's competitors, he had more than hinted that the pace was no longer being set by men like the old paint-manufacturer; and in later novels he proceeded to call into being a series of more typical moneymakers—the coarsely avaricious and boorish Dryfoos of *A Hazard of New Fortunes,* the tight-fisted, pettily tyrannical Gerrish of *Annie Kilburn,* the thievish and cowardly Northwick of *The Quality of Mercy,* and the unpitying sensualist Langbrith of *The Son of Royal Langbrith.* With these personae in mind, can we believe that Howells was expressing no private emotion when he allowed his old Socialist, Lindau, to rage against "this oligarchy of traders and tricksters,

[1] *The Rise of Silas Lapham,* by William D. Howells. Centenary Edition. Boston: Houghton Mifflin Company.

this aristocracy of railroad wreckers and stock gamblers and . . . mill-serf owners"?

It is too much to suppose so, though in his own person he habitually spoke more mildly. He believed as profoundly as any American writer has ever believed in the principle of equality, and he discerned as plainly as any later writer—as Upton Sinclair, let us say—that the sure effect of the business man's economy was "to establish insuperable inequalities" among us. No other native writer of his time was so constantly preoccupied with the question of class, and no other watched so responsibly or so anxiously the sharpening of class lines and the stiffening of class barriers in the world about him. In his earlier work, in such books as *A Chance Acquaintance* and *The Lady of the Aroostook,* he had made the contrasts between social groups, in an ostensibly democratic order, the object of a lightly ironic or genially comic treatment, though even in such books one can sometimes detect the rumbling of more tragic undertones. The rumbling becomes easily audible in *A Woman's Reason,* of the early eighties—with its treatment of a young woman's descent, temporary though it is, from her own leisure class to that of the wage-earners—and in *The Minister's Charge* and *Annie Kilburn,* which belong to the years of the Haymarket trials, that gloomy sound has drowned out most other noises. The "apprenticeship," in the first of these, that the country boy Lemuel Barker undergoes is a course of sprouts in the drawing of class lines with the hardness and the finality with which city people, as he discovers, know how to draw them. Howells' picture, in *Annie Kilburn,* of life in a small New England mill town that is also a summer resort of the well-to-do, may be touched with some of the gentler ironies; but the grave theme of the book—the harshness of class distinctions in such a community and the hopelessness of extending any true good will or fellow feeling above them—was broached in it for the first time by a major American realist.

In his love of genuine equality, Howells, like his friend Mark Twain, simply preserved and expressed the finest social feelings of the old Middle Western life of the forties and fifties: his father before him had been a courageous champion of equal rights and political freedom. Unlike Mark Twain, however, Howells came to see that there was a real clash between freedom as Americans had largely conceived it—freedom to pile up money and to sweat other men—and the equality he so passionately desired; and he came also to see that a merely political equality is a tricky and superficial thing. Such insights make an essential difference in all the fiction he wrote after *Silas Lapham,* but they are of course most explicitly given out in his two Utopian novels and in some of those fugitive essays on social matters which it would now seem to be high time for someone to collect and reprint in a volume. "Freedom," he wrote in one of them, "is only occasionally a political affair, a civic affair: it is constantly a social affair, a pecuniary affair, an economic affair. Liberty and poverty are incompatible and, if the poverty is extreme, liberty is impossible to it." He was no less realistic, no less free from the older delusions in his view of equality. "Economic equality," he said in a different essay, "is the mother of all other equalities."

These propositions may be commonplaces today; they were anything but commonplaces to old-fashioned Americans in Howells' time, and they were not embodied in painstaking narratives by other writers until he had shown the way. For of course it is not simply a question of Howells' having arrived intellectually at certain political convictions as a result of fusing his inherited social values with the results of his observation and reading. It is a question of imaginative understanding, of fresh ethical and social perceptions; and on that ground Howells did much to make possible a new orientation for American fiction in its sober rendering of American life. If such later writers as Dos Passos have based a series of novels on their sense that the world about them is a planless and wasteful chaos, they were worthily anticipated by the man who made Basil March, one of his most transparent fictional spokesmen, denounce "this economic chance-world in which we live"; who made another character speak of "the squalid struggle which is the plutocratic conception of life"; and who, in *The World of Chance,* gave over a whole novel to the deliberate representation of a way of life dominated not by purpose and control but by accident, hazard and whim. The "formlessness" for which Howells has often been reproached, and which this book exemplifies, is as little a defect as the formlessness, so-called, of *1919.* He had the astuteness to see that a disordered world cannot be shadowed forth in the well made fictions that may do justice to a small and harmonious scene.

He cared for order, for fraternity, for union, as deeply as he cared for equality, and he cared at least as much for a genuine individualism. But he saw that a rich personal development not only is not fostered but is actively and tragically frustrated by the egotism and the self-interest that are the ruling motives in an individualistic society. It was Howells' Altrurian, and not some later critic, who, describing in *Through the Eye of the Needle* the Americans of the turn of the century, uttered that phrase about "their warped and stunted and perverted lives," and certainly few writers have ever realized so keenly what happened to the old dogmas of self-help and self-cultivation by the time the triumph of industry had taken its toll of them. Again, it was a young New England farmer in *A Traveler from Altruria,* not one of Anderson's characters, who was perhaps the first to say plainly: "If you want to see American individuality, the real, simon-pure article, you ought to go down to one of our big factory towns, and look at the mill-hands coming home in droves after a day's work, young girls and old women, boys and men, all fluffed over with cotton, and so dead-tired that they can hardly walk. They come shambling along with all the individuality of a flock of sheep." Of course it was in the nature of the case that Howells made relatively little, in fiction, of the terrible sacrifice of personal wholeness among the industrial workers; but who can fail to discern, in so many of his middle-class characters, restless or ill occupied or discontented or self-seeking men and women that they are, his implicit criticism of an egocentric culture?

It is true that his criticism remained within certain limits that later writers have fortunately overleapt; it did so too, partly because of that excessive and essentially unwholesome fastidiousness of which so much has been made, and which in fact was almost as heavy a handicap, for a serious realist, as some critics have taken it to be. Even more fundamental, though less damaging in practice, was the fact that he never broke entirely with the Swedenborgian mysticism on which he had been brought up or with the foggy idealism of the Transcendentalist epigoni he lived among: the remark by one of his characters that our prejudice against crime and injustice comes "from somewhere outside of what we call Nature" points straight at the philosophically shaky basis of his realism. It was the basis, however, on which Howells was bound to write, given the circumstances; and if it qualifies, it does not at all undermine the extraordinary interest of his work for us, or keep it from being "usable" in a sense in which the work of one of his contemporaries quite is. Its vitality is more evident, at the moment of his centenary, than it has ever been before.

MARK TWAIN

MARK TWAIN SIMPLIFIED

TWELVE years ago Mr. Van Wyck Brooks published what is perhaps the most remarkable piece of interpretative biography in our literature, *The Ordeal of Mark Twain.* Everyone remembers what the thesis of that book was; everyone remembers Brooks's argument that Mark Twain, whose endowment was as richly creative as that of any writer in our history, was inhibited in his development as an artist partly by the suspicious Calvinism of his early training and of his wife's culture, partly by the associated worship of success, of financial prosperity, which dominated not only the frontier as he knew it, but the whole of American life in his age. "For Mark Twain was not simply living the bourgeois life now," said Brooks, speaking of Clemens in the eighties; "he had adopted all the values and ideals of the bourgeoisie. Success, prestige, position, wealth had become his gods, and the tribal customs of a nation of traders identical in his mind with the laws of the universe." But the artist in Mark Twain, though ruthlessly repressed, could not be killed; and the resulting disharmony within him accounts, Brooks contended, for the limitations of much of what he wrote, and for the savage misanthropy, the icy pessimism, that grew upon

135

him, despite his "success," with the movement of the years. "He said," Howells tells us, "that he never saw a dead man whom he did not envy for having had it over and being done with it." An abnormal view of life, according to Brooks, which only some deep violation of his integrity as a man and as an artist could account for.

To Mr. Bernard DeVoto this interpretation of Mark Twain is preposterous, ignorant and indefensible; and he has written a book * to demonstrate that Brooks has distorted the facts, misunderstood the man and lamentably failed to appreciate his greatness as a humorist. In general, Mr. DeVoto does not believe in interpretation or in "theories": "Whatever he might or should have written," he says, "has, for me, no importance whatever. I am completely uninterested in what psychology, politics, economics or evangelism may reveal about him"; and, though his book attempts to explain Mark Twain entirely in terms of the frontier and its particular type of laughter, he declares: "I have no theory about Mark Twain." In the latter part of the book he passes some severe judgments on Mark Twain as a writer ("He completely lacked the discipline of art"—which is stronger than Brooks) and on particular works (such as *A Connecticut Yankee*, which, he asserts, "is chaos"); but earlier in his book, when Brooks's judgments are in question, he says, *tout court*, that "the business of criticism is description."

Such discrepancies inspire little respect for Mr. DeVoto's logic, and more than once his fairness to an opponent seems almost as dubious. It advances his own case but little for him to speak of Mr. Brooks's "strange thesis"— "that Clemens really wanted to be Shelley" (a malicious caricature, of course, of the earlier book); and he quite distorts Brooks's use of the scene (described in Paine's

* *Mark Twain's America*, by Bernard DeVoto.

biography) at the bier of the elder Clemens, when the high-strung boy's mother forced from him a solemn promise to be "a faithful and industrious man, and upright, like his father": Mr. DeVoto speaks of Brooks as associating this scene with the boy's subsequent apprenticeship to a printer, though its bearings are of course far more general, and Brooks makes no allusion to the apprenticeship. It is certainly true that there are inconsistencies in *The Ordeal of Mark Twain,* and that the resources of psychoanalysis are sometimes fancifully exploited: Mr. DeVoto, in one chapter, has pointed out several details in which Brooks is fairly open to attack. But he has nowhere grappled with a serious interpretation on its own merits, and by disposing not only of Brooks, but of writers such as Waldo Frank and Lewis Mumford, as romantic ignoramuses, he prejudices his own theory (for he distinctly has one) in the eyes of every fair-minded bystander.

What is Mr. DeVoto's theory? Simply that Mark Twain is to be taken for what he is, a great humorist; that "he began as a humorist" and "continued as one so long as he wrote"; that, considered in this light, he was born (if I may use qualitative language) at the right time and in the right place; that life in Missouri, during his childhood, so far from being poor and starved, was full of color, charm and romance—that it was, in short, an "idyl"; that neither poverty nor riches really existed in Hannibal, nor any division into social classes; that Jane Clemens' Calvinism, a merely conventional and formal brand, cast no serious shadow over Sam's boyhood; that life in Nevada during the great days of silver-mining was an ideal discipline for a frontier humorist, and put the finishing touches on Mark Twain's education for this role; that the man expressed himself completely and abundantly in his literary career, and that his later pessimism cannot be regarded as "anything but the fruit of his experience." In short, the business of criticism and biography (in Mark Twain's case as elsewhere) is to accept the accomplished fact without comparison or qualification, and to explain it without analysis.

A shallow and romantic theory, of course, and one that results (on the whole) in a shallow and romantic book. On certain aspects of life on the frontier and on its edge, in Mark Twain's early days, Mr. DeVoto is informed and eloquent; on the purely literary derivation of Mark Twain's humor (the tall tale, frontier burlesque, etc.), he makes a valuable contribution to criticism. But, taken as a whole and as a portrait of a complex character, his book is almost worthless. In his eagerness to adorn himself with the scalps of Brooks and his followers, Mr. DeVoto has overstated or misstated everything, and he leaves us with a false and superficial impression of his subject. It is impossible, of course, to accept his view of Mark Twain as merely a humorist and, indeed, in praising the realistic truth of *Tom Sawyer* and *Huckleberry Finn,* he himself claims far more for him. *The Innocents Abroad,* Mark Twain's first important book, is sprinkled with serious descriptive writing: *Roughing It* and *Life on the Mississippi,* as everyone knows, are (by design) only intermittently funny; and how is Mr. DeVoto to account for *The Prince and the Pauper, The Mysterious Stranger* or *Joan of Arc*—the last of which its author described as "a serious book," which "means more to me than anything I have ever undertaken"?

Mark Twain "boundlessly created laughter," says Mr. DeVoto, and certainly the prodigality of his humorous invention is not to be belittled; but he was a humorist who was capable of saying (privately): "My idea of our civilization is that it is a shoddy, poor thing, and full of cruelties, vanities, arrogancies, meannesses, and hypocrisies."

Howells, who knew him long and intimately, was probably nearer to the truth than Mr. DeVoto in discerning "the depths of a nature whose tragical seriousness broke in the laughter which the unwise took for the whole of him."

As regards the "idyl" that was life in Hannibal in the forties and fifties, Mr. DeVoto himself has undermined his own claim by what he relates of frontier savagery, lawlessness, vice, inhumanity, superstition and intolerance; and as regards its democratic classlessness, we have Mark Twain's own testimony, in his *Autobiography*, that "the class lines were quite clearly drawn and the familiar social life of each class was restricted to that class." Chiefly, it would appear, because Brooks emphasized the morbid Puritanism of that society, Mr. DeVoto either denies or soft-pedals it; yet in the same book (published since *The Ordeal*) Mark Twain himself says: "Mine was a trained Presbyterian conscience and knew but the one duty— to hunt and harry its slave upon all pretexts and on all occasions, particularly when there was no sense nor reason in it"; and no one can read either this book or Paine's vast biography without realizing how insidious were the effects, on Mark Twain's unstable spirit, of the petty-bourgeois religiosity of his mother and his wife. "In my age, as in my youth," he confessed—he who was the most merciful and the most generous of men—"night brings me many a deep remorse." Perhaps Mr. DeVoto will argue that this too was merely "the fruit of his experience."

In any case, the more important questions are whether Mark Twain as a writer completely realized his potentialities, and whether his negations were merely those of a sagacious elder who had seen "many cities" in his time. Nothing that Mr. DeVoto says on these heads is of much cogency simply because he deals with Mark Twain wholly in terms of the frontier, and thus evades the more important aspect of his career—his appalling immersion, beginning in his silver-mining days, in the mad scramble for money, money, money, that made American life in his age a caricature of civilization. Probably the annals of literature do not contain another equally tragic instance of a highly endowed artist debauched and demoralized (to a point where his very integrity was lost) by the infection of crude avarice.

There is not space here to develop the point, but the man whose idolatrous biographer could say that he "took a childish delight in piling up money," and "liked the game of business, especially when it was pretentious and showily prosperous"—the man who was "frightened at the proportions of my prosperity"—is not to be wholly understood on the ground that he "boundlessly created laughter." Out of one eye (and *that* kept closed more often than not), Mark Twain saw what the industrial pirates were making of American democracy; out of the other, he saw only that everything he touched (as he said) turned to gold—and he rejected, as a commercial publisher, a book arraigning the Standard Oil Company, of which his friend and benefactor, H. H. Rogers, was an official.

Among his manuscripts, says Paine, is a burlesque manual of etiquette; I quote his directions for conduct "At the Dog-Fight": "Let your secret sympathies and your compassion be always with the under-dog in the fight—this is magnanimity; but bet on the other one—this is business." The note is painfully autobiographical: Mark Twain himself—whose "secret sympathies" were intensely democratic —spent most of his life betting on the top dog. If, as Mr. DeVoto says, he "completely lacked the discipline of art," is it fantastic to explain the want on grounds like these? And are we to accept simply as mellow sagacity the reflections of an old man who could write, as Mark Twain wrote on the margin of a page in Greville's *Memoirs:* "Byron despised the race because he despised himself. I feel as Byron did, and for the same reason."?

THE FRIEND OF CAESAR

IT IS late in the day to praise so famous a book as *The Ordeal of Mark Twain* * : its reissue, with excellent but not organic revisions, is only the occasion for reminding oneself that thirteen years ago Van Wyck Brooks, quietly shelving the shallow Mark Twain-legend that Howells and Brander Matthews and others had created, observed that Mark Twain was a split personality, "the supreme victim of an epoch in American history," and that the man who might have written a *Gulliver's Travels* in which American capitalism would have been moved to Lilliput, accepted instead the status of a kind of titanic Bill Nye. If intuition of the first order and the most sensitive literary feeling were enough to make an infallible critic in our time, *The Ordeal of Mark Twain* would be the last word on the subject. With all its brilliance, the book is not quite that. In 1933 it is easy to see that Brooks, diving into waters that his predecessors were incapable of imagining, was himself unable to touch bottom. With a few more coils of cable, he would have been there.

What are those coils? Briefly, a genuinely dialectical mastery of the development of American society. *The Ordeal of Mark Twain,* despite Brooks's superb picture of the Gilded Age, is after all imperfectly historical; and

* *The Ordeal of Mark Twain,* by Van Wyck Brooks.

the result is that, as one finishes a rereading, one wonders more than ever what concrete and active conclusions one is to draw from it, for American letters, with reference to the present and the future—for Brooks intended the book, it is clear, as not only a diagnosis but (by implication) a call to action. As such, it is up in the air. It is up in the air because Brooks never shows *how* Mark Twain could have made himself the Rabelais that he never became. To have shown this would have been to raise questions with which Brooks's criticism never comes to grips. It would have been to raise the question of the writer and his class: it would have been to challenge the idealistic individualism which is the whole background for Brooks's judgment of Mark Twain. To put it otherwise, Brooks censures Mark Twain for his failure to break with the prosperous bourgeoisie of the Gilded Age, and suggests that such a break—a break into the empty air—would have liberated his bottled-up energies as a creative artist. It would have done no such thing.

Mark Twain could have become the destructive satirist of the American middle class of his time only by adopting, no matter how intuitively, the point of view of another class. This is what all great satirists have done: Rabelais, who spoke for all the anti-feudal, socially progressive forces in the France of the sixteenth century; Swift, the great reactionary, who spoke for the old pre-Whig society; and so on. In short, American society in Mark Twain's time was not, as Brooks almost suggests, one great undifferentiated whole: it was a society increasingly disunified by the dynamics of class development, and both its vices and its follies had their roots in this disunity. It was characteristic of Mark Twain that he should have been at once sympathetic with the labor unions and a servile admirer of H. H. Rogers, the Standard Oil magnate; and indeed Brooks makes both observations. But he does not observe that Mark Twain could have seen through H. H. Rogers only by understanding the dialectics of American capitalism: no matter how "free" he had made himself from bourgeois culture, he would have had nowhere to go without some clue to the culture toward which it was moving, and which would ultimately replace it. Mark Twain had never so much as imagined, says Brooks, "the normal existence of the artist, of the writer, who writes to please himself." But surely the normal existence of the artist is far from being so private an affair as this; and surely the fundamental thing about Mark Twain, in this connection, is that he failed to comprehend even the watered socialism of his friend Howells.

At the end of the book, Brooks observes that the American writer of today has not the same excuse as Mark Twain for missing his vocation—"not if he remembers the splendid parts his confrères have played in the human drama of other times and other peoples." It is a stirring thought, and Brooks expresses it stirringly. But he has nowhere expressly shown how American writers can now avoid becoming the victims of a more pitiless epoch than Mark Twain's.

Stephen Leacock, rather surprisingly, in a volume of the Appleton Biographies, shows that he has not read *The Ordeal of Mark Twain* to no effect. "Mark Twain only half-expressed himself," he says. "Of the things nearest to his mind [the Boer War, the Philippine conquest, the Catholic Church, Russian Tsarism] he spoke but low or spoke not at all. . . . Instinct told him that had he done so, the Mark Twain legend that had filled the world would pass away." But does Mr. Leacock deplore this appalling stultification? On the contrary. "It is better that it should be so. It leaves the legendary Mark Twain and his work and his humor as one of the great things of nineteenth-century America." Mr. Leacock has a certain celebrity as a humorist on his own. Is it possible that in the sentences just quoted he is making, at his readers' expense, a particularly cynical crack?

GEORGE WASHINGTON CABLE

THE GRANDISSIMES

WHEN the editors of *Scribner's Monthly,* in 1879, accepted
the manuscript of *The Grandissimes,* and began publishing it serially in the November issue, they were well aware
of the freshness and distinction of their young author's
work, but they could hardly have foreseen how far the
novel would ultimately throw its beams. They had already
published several short stories by its author, a young New
Orleans accountant and part-time journalist, George Washington Cable, who had been "discovered" and drawn out
—living as he did, in those harsh post bellum days, at so
great a remove from the literary center—by another *Scribner's* author, Edward King, who had gone to New Orleans
in the mid-seventies to do a series of articles on the new
South. Cable's stories had been collected, earlier in 1879, in
a volume entitled *Old Creole Days,* and *The Grandissimes*
was to be published as a volume in the following year. It
may not have been perfectly evident then, but in a quiet
way the novel made a sharp break with the central tradition of Southern fiction, as it then was and was long to be;
it pointed forward to a kind of thing that was to assert itself only after several decades. This is what led Hamilton
Basso to say, some years ago, that Cable was the first writer

to question the validity of the aristocratic tradition in Southern fiction—the "spiritual godfather," as he said, of more recent writers such as Ellen Glasgow, Thomas Wolfe, and William Faulkner. There is a sense in which, as Mr. Basso said, Cable may be said to have been the first of the "Southern realists."

The phrase, to be sure, requires a good deal of qualification, with Cable as with Faulkner, and even a fairly responsive reader might understandably come away from *The Grandissimes* with a sense of having been breathing the warm, soft air of the romantic, and even the sentimental, rather than the colder and more energizing atmosphere of realism. At a quick glance the novel does certainly *look* romantic. The central ganglion of the action is a bitter feud between two old, proud, aristocratic families —a feud for which the author himself finds a romantic analogy in the strife of Shakespeare's Capulets and Montagues. As for the time of the action, it is, and was even for Cable, a by no means immediate past; it may have been what James called a "visitable past," but the opening years of the nineteenth century, at the moment when Napoleon had just ceded Louisiana to the United States, were already bathed, in the seventies and eighties, in a haze of romantic and even glamorous remoteness. And if the time of the action has this quality, what is to be said of the scene?—old New Orleans, still essentially the little eighteenth-century city, dominated by French and Spanish Creole families, and abounding in elements of the picturesque to which one can no longer even allude without falling into the clichés of colorfulness and charm. The story gets under way at a masked ball in the old Théâtre St. Philippe, and something of the effect of a masquerade —of the courtly, the costumed, the masked, the choreographic—is never wholly absent from the action.

It is true, moreover, that, to the sensibility of a later
generation, there is a distasteful streak of sentimentality
in much of Cable's work—of that peculiarly sweetish and
effeminate sentimentality that throws one off in so much
of the fiction of the period, including even Howells's and
Mark Twain's. Cable himself once said: "Great is sentiment"; and though he went on to say that *sentimentality*
is "despicable," being "at best but a feeling after feeling,"
the truth is that his own sensibility had been infected, on
one side, by the dreadfully ladylike "feeling after feeling"
of which even the great writers of the age were guilty.
Howells drooled mawkishly over the two Nancanou ladies,
Aurore and Clotilde, in *The Grandissimes*—Aurore, he
said, "is one of the most delicious creations I ever knew"—
but to our taste Cable's treatment of them is unendurably
coy, arch, and, as Mencken once said of these writers,
"kittenish." Even the great and terrible story of Bras-
Coupé—the core around which the book grew—ends on a
note of false and untrue feeling that for a moment seems
almost to unman its power.

All these things are true, and yet the fact is that Cable
had a complex and curiously contradictory nature; the
duality of his mind is accountable for both what is weak
and what is unmistakably strong in his work as a whole
and in his best novel, *The Grandissimes*, in particular. He
was capable of "feeling after feeling," as he was capable
of making the utmost of every romantic tone and hue in
local color, but he was also an extraordinarily sharp-eyed,
quick-glancing, astute observer of ordinary social reality,
with a strongly developed critical sense, a love of the
thoroughly documented fact, and a habit of tough resistance to the conventional and traditional version of things.

The result is that, both on superficial and on deeper
levels, *The Grandissimes* is a singularly searching and

veracious rendering of the life it represents. Cable's scene may be a romantic one in a certain sense, but the fidelity of his depiction of it is painstakingly and even literally, perhaps too literally, accurate. Lafcadio Hearn, who ought to have known, testified to the "sharp originality" of Cable's descriptions, and in an article in the *Century Magazine* went so far as to identify the particular houses in New Orleans that Cable had used as settings in *Old Creole Days*; he could undoubtedly have performed a similar service for the buildings in *The Grandissimes*. And so with the speech of Cable's Creole and Negro characters: his passion for faithful and realistic precision was so intense as to carry him, here, beyond the limits of what the literary art can profitably do, and led him, in the use of dialect, to cultivate a laborious and literal accuracy that comes close to destroying the imaginative sense of human reality. Randolph Bourne once spoke of Cable's "phonetic atrocities"; readers of *The Grandissimes*, picking their way through some of the speeches of Aurore Nancanou or Raoul Innerarity or Clemence the *marchande des calas*, will agree that the phrase is not an unjust one.

Mistaken as all this was, it is a small price to pay for the great qualities of *The Grandissimes* as a piece of social and historical realism—the qualities Edmund Wilson had in mind in calling Cable "essentially a sociologist." The phrase points to only one pole of the work, but certainly Cable's primary aim in the novel was to paint a full, truthful, critical picture of a social and regional scene. On the surface this scene is Creole society in New Orleans in the first decade of the century, but it is evident enough to a careful reader that the New Orleans of *The Grandissimes* is the South pretty much as a whole, not only in 1803 but in Cable's own time too. Indeed he himself furnished the clue to this in an entry in his diary: *"The Grandissimes,"* he said, "contained as plain a protest against the times in which it was written as against the earlier times in which its scenes were set." A Northerner must speak with all possible humility here, but in that perspective it is difficult not to feel that Cable's representation of the Creole social character, his free and unsparing treatment of its vices and his tenderness for its high virtues, is, in every sense but the literal one, a representation of the South in the mid-century—the South of the fifties, of the War, and of Reconstruction.

The guilt of the Civil War was a divided one, if ever guilt was, but we are not speaking, nor was Cable writing, about the sins of the North: his subject is the Southern temper, and it is evident that he is criticizing his own people in his delineation of the Creole spirit, and particularly of the Grandissimes—that Creole dynasty which embodies the best and the worst of the old Southern ethos, as the Atridae embodied, for the Greek tragic poets, the best and the worst of *their* inherited ethos. The best and the worst was their pride—that pride that at one pole took the form of arrogance, bluster, swagger, and disdain, and at the other pole took the form of a generous and magnanimous self-respect. Honoré Grandissime, the "white Honoré," expresses one half of this antithesis in his colloquy with the young Yankee pharmacist Frowenfeld: "Did you ever hear of a more perfect specimen of Creole pride? That is the way with all of them. Show me any Creole, or any number of Creoles, in any contest, and right down at the foundation of it all, I will find you this same preposterous, apathetic, fantastic, suicidal pride. It is as lethargic and ferocious as an alligator."

Honoré is speaking here, to be sure, of some of the De Grapions, not of the Grandissimes, their hereditary enemies; but Cable himself, we need have no doubt, is taking this dramatic mode of criticizing that whole aspect of the Southern temper that made real compromise or conciliation impossible in the forties and fifties, and that led in the end to the suicidal steps of secession and rebellion. Nor is this all. It is Southern writers themselves, especially since Cable's time, who have told us in effect how constant and tragic a role has always been played in Southern life by violence. And Cable, here, is their ancestor. "Charming" as much of the business of *The Grandissimes* is, the novel abounds, almost like a work of Faulkner's, in the imagery of violence. The action, as we have seen, has its center in a family feud—a feud that is itself an emblem of the enmity between the sections—and the feud had its source in a duel, a duel in which a De Grapion had been shot and killed by a Grandissime. This blood guilt was later deepened and darkened when another Grandissime, Agricole Fusilier, shoots and kills, over another insult, the husband of another De Grapion. These duels seem emblematic of a sectional war that had some of its roots in irrationality and hot temper, and there is a transparent symbolism in the passage in which the Yankee Frowenfeld persuades the aged Agricole to refrain from still another duel, this time with a cousin of his own, and to seek a reconciliation by peaceful means. It is at least a wishful gesture of a symbolically political nature.

Meanwhile the novel has been pervaded by the growling of suppressed, or the roar of open, violence. An aged gentleman is set upon in a dark street and knifed in the arm; his presumed assailant is shot and wounded in the shoulder. A mob of Creoles, enraged by a Yankee shopkeeper's liberal sentiments, attacks and wrecks his shop. An old Negro woman is cut down from the tree on which she has been nearly lynched, allowed to save herself by running away if she can, and then shot and killed as she attempts to flee. A principal character is finally given his death wound, stabbed thrice in the back, by an embittered relative. Most notably of all, most grandly and terribly, the magnificent Bras-Coupé, the African chief turned Negro slave, having struck down in a moment of anger his white master, and having been hunted down in his lair in the swamp, has been punished under the old Code Noir by being flogged and hamstrung, as well as by having his ears cut off. It was this ferocious tale, composed first as a short story, and rejected by G. P. Lathrop for the *Atlantic* as "unmitigatedly distressful," "to and around which," as Cable later said, "the whole larger work is built." Violence, in short, is at the very heart of *The Grandissimes*.

Violence—and the tension of relations between the races. The feud between Grandissimes and De Grapions, and even that other feud between the Creoles and the new American territorial government, is as nothing to the hostility, the never-absent, unevadable, obsessive hostility, between white and Negro. Hostility, yes, but one of a sort that can be felt only by human beings whose lives are as intimately, as inextricably, bound together as those of brother and brother, or cousin and cousin. Such was the hostility between North and South in the days before and after the War, and such, in all but the literal sense, was that between the Grandissimes and the De Grapions. The three forms that human antagonism takes in the novel—familial, political, racial—are all seen as involving a confusion of emotions, attraction as well as repulsion, closeness as well as division, love as well as hatred. The central token of this is the relation betwen the "two Honorés" (their names are identical)—the white Honoré, the Creole gentleman, and the quadroon Honoré, his declassed and alienated half-brother. There is a curious anticipation, in this pairing, of the intense and almost amorous relation between Henry Sutpen and his mulatto half-brother, Charles Bon, in Faulkner's *Absalom, Absalom!* as there is an anticipation in the essentially sisterly relation between Aurore Nancanou and the quadroon Palmyre of the essentially brotherly relation between Bayard Sartoris and Ringo in *The Unvanquished.* Like Faulkner, Cable had an intuition of the inescapable and profound dependence upon each other—a dependence like that of inimical brothers—of the two races.

In moral insights such as this, and in his transcendence of the literal and factual, his indirection and his sense of metaphor, Cable took a long step beyond the sociological realism with which he has been justly credited. "It is not sight the storyteller needs," he once wrote, "but second sight. . . . Not actual experience, not actual observation, but the haunted heart; that is what makes the true artist of every sort." His own heart was haunted—haunted by the spectre of sectional hatreds and bitternesses, and by the spectre of racial strife—and this was what made him so much more than one more local-color short-story writer and more, too, than one more prosaic realist. *The Grandissimes* ends, like *The Tempest*, in a marriage that betokens a permanent reconciliation between families: Cable was not far off, historically, in hinting thus at a reconciliation between the sections. As for the races, a step is taken that seems to promise a similar reconciliation. But Cable, like Faulkner, was too veracious a writer to delude himself with the image of an easy and premature solution, and the end of *that* is failure and tragedy. It would be a very long time before a truthful writer could depict any other.

HENRY JAMES

HENRY JAMES AND THE ALMIGHTY DOLLAR

IT WAS the year of the Trafalgar Square riots in London
—and of the Haymarket tragedy in Chicago—it was the
portentous year 1886 when *The Princess Casamassima* appeared. The heroine of that book makes some remarks to
her young friend, Hyacinth Robinson, the little socialist
book-binder, which bear a closer relation to such events
than the remarks of Henry James's heroines are generally
reputed to do. She is speaking of English "society." "It is
the old régime again," says the Princess, "the rottenness
and extravagance, bristling with every iniquity and every
abuse, over which the French Revolution passed like a
whirlwind; or perhaps even more a reproduction of Roman society in its decadence, gouty, apoplectic, depraved,
gorged and clogged with wealth and spoils, selfishness and
scepticism, and waiting for the onset of the barbarians.
You and I," she adds, "are the barbarians, you know"—for
the Princess is a still more vehement radical than Hyacinth.

She is far enough, moreover, from being an idealized
character to keep us—even if there were no other deter-

153

rents—from attributing to her author personally all the sentiments she expresses. Yet it happens that this particular speech was echoed, late in the year, in a letter from James to Charles Eliot Norton, à propos of some scandalous divorce case that was at that moment bringing to light some aspects of the life of the English upper class. "The condition of that body," wrote the one Anglophile to the other, "seems to me to be in many ways very much the same rotten and *collapsible* one as that of the French aristocracy before the revolution—minus cleverness and conversation; or perhaps it's more like the heavy, congested and depraved Roman world upon which the barbarians came down." Unlike the Princess, of course, James hardly identified himself with the barbarians. "In England," he however went on, "the Huns and Vandals will have to come *up*—from the black depths of the (in the people) enormous misery, though I don't think the Attila is quite yet found—in the person of Mr. Hyndman. At all events, much of English life is grossly materialistic and wants blood-letting." So far, in 1886, had the passionate pilgrim moved from the emotions with which, nearly twenty years before, he had landed on British soil.

Did he seriously contemplate, in his own time, a repetition in England of the events of a hundred years before in France? Did he consider for a moment the possible meaning of the ideas for which, with all his limitations, Mr. Hyndman was then the spokesman? Even such guarded questions can hardly be answered with a round affirmative. Yet a simple "certainly not" seems equally shallow in the presence of that sinister book, *The Princess Casamassima*, with its hints at the decadence of the privileged classes, its evocation of the dreariness and hopelessness of life in the London slums, its intentionally vague intimations of retributive movements from below—intimations of which

James defended the vagueness, more than twenty years later, in a preface, on the ground that the effect he had wished to produce was exactly that "of our not knowing, of society's not knowing, but only guessing and suspecting and trying to ignore, what 'goes on' irreconcilably, subversively, beneath the vast smug surface." For a moment, Henry James makes an attempt, to say the very least, not to ignore all this; and then his little book-binder, torn between his aspirations toward a more just society and his yearning for the traditional values made possible (as he supposes) by inequality and injustice, shoots himself—and from the particular pitiless questions his dilemma has raised James turns his head for good and all.

What the motives or the influences were that made Henry James shrink from considering the social problems of his time on their own level, it would not be easy to say in words of one syllable: enough that all kinds of personal involvements, reenforcing his distaste for public questions as such and a mediocre capacity to deal with them, blinded him to the historic changes in the society he was necessarily depicting. W. C. Brownell once observed that James's work bears almost no evidence of an interest in the course of history; and, in a sense not intended by the traditionalist Brownell, this is a useful way in which to describe James's heaviest handicaps as a serious recorder of manners. He was almost wholly wanting in historic understanding, though he had plenty of historic fancy; and the spectacle of a society torn by inner contradictions could produce in him only perplexity. He could only shrug his shoulders—and put his trust in Arthur Balfour.

More than one eminent novelist, however, has got along without a true sense of history, and James had powers which came very close to serving the same ends—I mean especially his extraordinarily penetrating ethical insight, in the narrow sense in which ethics can be distinguished from sociology. He was a true son of his father, the Swedenborgian Fourierite, and he saw, with deadly lucidity, things which strictly speaking he did not understand. He made out no historic meaning in the corrupt life of the great bourgeoisie or the philistine morals of the small bourgeoisie of his time, but he saw that corruption, that philistinism, as few of his contemporaries saw them. In his later period particularly he deals with almost nothing else. This is of course what Ford Madox Ford means by saying, in *Return to Yesterday:* "He gives you an immense —and an increasingly tragic—picture of a leisured society that is fairly unavailing, materialist, emasculated—and doomed. No one was more aware of all that than he." So true is this, indeed, that one is tempted to see in it a partial explanation for that famous "later manner" of his: what are all these pictorial devices of "foreshortening" and "point of view," these elaborately dramatized expositions, these old tragedy confidants and confidantes—what, for that matter, are these tropical flora of syntax, these hypertrophied metaphors, these arch adverbs and embarrassed interjections—if not the components of a beautifully shimmering and scarcely transparent veil half-intentionally drawn between the reader's eyes and the peculiar rottenness of the world described? No doubt they are more than just this, but they serve this function admirably.

In any case, the point itself has been noted more than once before—the point, I mean, that Henry James's world, especially the world of his later fiction, is far from being a pretty one; that, on the contrary, it is morally as ugly a world as any in the English novel, up to that point, and that a tiny handful of decent people wander through it, bravely or timidly as the case may be, like men astray in a land of condors and boas. I do not know whether it has been noted that some of our later disillusionists have been quite definitely anticipated by the older writer—that most of Aldous Huxley, for example, is already latent in *The Awkward Age* (remember Mitchy, who according to Nanda "thinks nothing matters," and who "says we've all come to a pass that's the end of everything") and *The Ivory Tower* (in which Davy Bradham observes that "we're all . . . unspeakably corrupt"); and that if, in James's earlier work, one frequently catches echoes of Hawthorne and George Eliot, in his final period one sniffs, on the breeze, rancid odors wafted prophetically from the world of Cabell and Hergesheimer, of Lawrence and Eliot, even of Hemingway and Faulkner. (Is not *The Turn of the Screw* nearer to *Sanctuary* than to *Rappaccini's Daughter?*) I do not know, I repeat, whether these particular observations have been made; but it could hardly have escaped notice that, in general, Henry James became in his old age the chronicler of a festering society.

What has been less observed, I believe, is that from the beginning of his career James had intuitively taken a critical view not only of American but of European society, and that this view exposed both societies to him, despite his restrictions of vision, at their most vulnerable spot—their gross preoccupation with money. It has been pointed out a hundred times how recurrent this chord is in Balzac's work: it seems not to have been very obvious that, in this respect, James followed closely in the footsteps of his master. From the beginning, he envisaged covetousness as the leading Vice of his "morality." Plot after plot was to depend upon avarice as a spur. He has been called an apologist of the leisure class, and represented as the painter of a charming social world aloof from crude considerations of dollars and cents; but these must have been the impressions of readers who had "skipped" with a vengeance. It is no secure and stately leisure class that James depicts; it is not a world into which only exquisite scruples and fastidious dilemmas are allowed to enter; it is no Court of Love, no Abbaye de Thélème, no *fête champêtre*, that he evokes: far from it. It is a world much more recognizably real than any of these, a world in which men have their eyes sharply fixed on the main chance and women know how to add and multiply, a world in which buying is done in the cheapest market and selling in the dearest, a world obsessed by the nervous craving for acquisition and haunted by the fear of penury. James's scene is one in which greed plays something like the same rôle as snobbishness in Thackeray's scene or sentimentality in Meredith's. It is not an "aristocratic" scene in any real sense: it is something more modern than that.

How true this is can hardly be fully demonstrated in a sketch, but what I have in mind can be allusively suggested by a speech of the Baroness Münster's in *The Europeans*. Felix Young, the Baroness's younger brother, has remarked to her that their Cambridge cousins, the Wentworths, are charming, and she has asked him, "In what style?" "In a style of their own," he has replied. "How shall I describe it? It's primitive; it's patriarchal; it's the *ton* of the golden age." "And have they," she counters, "nothing golden but their *ton*? Are there no symptoms of wealth?" The Baroness, unlike many of James's readers, is no sentimentalist: what she is concerned about is not lights and shades, but—with no beating about the bush—hard cash. In this, she is far from unique; on the contrary, she is a familiar type in her creator's *comédie*. Her (spiritual) sisters are women and her brothers are men who leave nothing of this sort to chance; what they want to know about people is not what they might learn from philosophy, but from Dun & Bradstreet's, and they go to some trouble to learn it. The Baroness herself was forecast by a character in James's early published tale, *A Landscape Painter*, the hero of which is a rich young man who has broken off his engagement with a girl owing to "overwhelming proof of the most mercenary spirit" on her part: the irony of the tale is that Locksley proceeds to fall a victim to the equally mercenary Esther Blunt, whom he supposes to be ignorant of his true identity and of his wealth, but who discovers them on the sly and successfully marks him for her own. Esther Blunt is the first of a longish line which reaches to Kate Croy in *The Wings of the Dove* and Charlotte Stant in *The Golden Bowl*. If these women are not good mathematicians—I had almost said, good bookkeepers—they are nothing.

It is true that of the moneymaking career in its central form—in business—James knew extremely little at first hand; that he shrank from the study of it, and never represented it at full length. Christopher Newman has already made a fortune before he appears in *The American* (though we are told retrospectively that, to his own conception, he had been placed in the world "simply to gouge a fortune, the bigger the better, out of its hard material"); and Jim Pocock, in *The Ambassadors*, is seen only in a festal mood. James never undertook to dramatize the career of a Cowperwood or even of a Silas Lapham, and perhaps he did well to keep off that ground. The omission did not blind him to the prevalence of rapacity in his world: it only required him to study it on a less significant ground—on the ground most of which is mapped out by the phrase, "marrying for money." It is chiefly the marriage-market that he deals with, but that market has many points of similarity with any other. It is a meeting-place for those who have something to sell and those who are eager to buy, and it is ruled over by what Adam Smith called "the propensity to truck, barter, and exchange one thing for another." How much of the action in James's narratives does not involve the marriage-market at all? Singularly little. Consider in how many ways, in his novels and tales, the formula is varied. Often the rapacity is that of a woman's parents who, like Christina Light's in *Roderick Hudson* or Mme. de Cintré's in *The American* or Angela Vivian's in *Confidence*, are determined to marry her advantageously at any expense of spirit—or die in the attempt. As respects the Bellegardes, in *The American*, who finally retreat before the prospect of a merely mercenary marriage, and are thus a kind of exception, James felt (years later) that he had been guilty of "romance"—since, as he said, an "accommodation of the theory of a noble indifference to the practice of a deep avidity is the real note of policy in forlorn aristocracies." In the book as it stands, the Bellegardes seem calculating enough: James was to live to feel that he had done them more than justice.

At all events, it is not only in this guise that James introduces the marriage-market into his work. Sometimes the character in whom the propensity to truck and barter is stronger than mere sentiment is a man who spots some innocent but financially fortunate girl for his victim and flings himself into the chase. Such is Mme. de Mauves' husband, the Baron, in an early tale, and such, notably, is Gilbert Osmond in *The Portrait of a Lady*. "I won't pretend," says Osmond to Isabel Archer in that work, "that I am sorry you are rich [she has inherited seventy thousand pounds]; I am delighted. I delight in everything that is yours—whether it be money or virtue. Money is a great advantage." So, too, thought Giovanelli in *Daisy Miller*, and so thought Morris Townsend in *Washington Square*, and so, in his less crudely avaricious way, thought Prince Amerigo in *The Golden Bowl*. There is little or nothing, in the lives of other people, that these men are not willing to sacrifice for a few thousands, or a few hundred thousands, a year.

But the avarice is not always to be laid at the door of scheming parents or venal men: sometimes it is the girl herself who, like Esther Blunt, knows quite well what she is about. Barberina Clement, in *Lady Barberina*, is a bird of this feather. "*Carte blanche* is not what Barb wishes," says Barb's mother to her father; "she wishes a settlement. She wants a definite income; she wants to be safe." Guy Firminger, in *Lord Beaupré*, after he has succeeded to that title, has terrible anecdotes to tell in illustration of "the science evolved in an enterprising age by this branch of industry, the manufacture of the trap matrimonial." Cupidity of this sort turns into something grotesque, farcical, Molièresque, in the figures of the predatory women who, in *The Album*, one of James's four published "theatricals," prowl about the scene, after the rich man's death, sniffing the air like unclean beasts and ready to root in any mire for a taste of the precious substance. Here, as I say, the thing has the crudity, and almost the gaiety, of farce: it assumes the deepest shades of moral tragedy in the figures of Kate Croy, of Charlotte Stant, and presumably (in the unfinished *Ivory Tower*) of Cissy Foy—women, all of them, willing to forego marriage with the men they love rather than face the prospect of moderate prosperity, and willing also to invent, or to connive in, the basest treacheries, if only they may make sure of a "settlement."

Cissy Foy is one of the leading characters in a novel which, if it had been finished, would certainly have challenged *The Ambassadors* for highest place in the roster of James's latest fiction. *The Ivory Tower* represents not only a remarkable return to the American scene after twenty-five years or more, but a directer grappling than James elsewhere attempted with the theme of moneymaking, of acquisition on a vast piratical scale, and of what follows, humanly and morally, in the wake of these activities. "The enormous preponderance of money"—such is a phrase used by the dying millionaire, Mr. Betterman, as he speaks of his contemporaries. "Money is their life," he adds; and Graham Fielder, his nephew and heir, was apparently to learn in a painful school some of the implications of that truth.

The words, indeed, "money is their life," might with a little exaggeration but essential justice be inscribed over the portals through which one passes as one enters the whole company of Henry James's men and women. Not that there are not fine examples, in his own words, "of the reaction, the opposition or the escape": just because there are these exceptions does the general proposition hold so true. It was a greedy society in the midst of which James found himself living; and, though all the conditions of that greediness were never made clear to him—though he failed to criticize it from a more significant angle than that of a refined individualism—he was too honest, too responsible, too scrupulous a writer to white-wash his society as he found it. This—and not the formal ingenuities of which so much too much has been made—is what gives his fiction its real solidity and weight; this is what reminds one of his own remark, in an essay on Turgenev, that "The great question as to a poet or novelist is, How does he feel about life? what, in the last analysis, is his philosophy? When vigorous writers have reached maturity we are at liberty to look in their works for some expression of a total view of the world they have been so actively observing. This is the most interesting thing their works offer us." To read even a little between the lines of his own work is to be left in no doubt what was the total view Henry James took of the world he so studiously observed.

NOTES FOR A REVIEW *

1. A scrupulous, discerning study of James's later novels— *The Ambassadors, The Wings of the Dove,* and *The Golden Bowl,* as well as the two unfinished books—and a few of the later tales, partly from the point of view of the recently available notebooks, in which the germs of these works are to be found. Sensitive account of the manner in which they foliated from their sometimes scanty origins to the full, fragrant, richly-colored blooms they ended by being. Especially revealing on the *Wings,* which F. O. M. rightly regards as the most deeply-felt and most completely realized of the group.

2. Admirable discussion in Chap. III of J.'s use of symbols—as elsewhere, too, of his imagery. J. not a *symboliste* in strict sense, certainly not in the sense of French and other contemporary poetry, if only, as F. O. M. says, for his indifference to music—and, one might add, his innocence of any systematic transcendental metaphysics; nor, either, in the sense of such writers as Mann, Kafka, Joyce and Eliot. The symbol not for him the thing-in-itself, the very substance of the fable, but something reached "with the final development of his theme," to give concretion and beauty to his thought; its consummation, not its egg.

3. Importance of the book as another and very cogent answer to Brooks' and Parrington's criticism, which naturally is not defensible in its familiar, unmodulated form. Maintains, unanswerably, that only in this later phase did J.'s art attain its truest, most idiosyncratic perfection, and his spirit express

* *Henry James: The Major Phase,* by F. O. Mathiessen.

itself on a level with his deepest intuitions, his most nearly tragic finality. (Surely what J. lost in expatriation—and he lost something; that need not and cannot be denied—found wonderful compensation; perhaps he simply saved his skin as a functioning writer.)

4. Nevertheless, not at all an uncritical, blown-up overestimate of these novels or of J.'s work as a whole, in the vein that threatens to become a fashionable orthodoxy. Recognizes the absence from even the great novels of some qualities that would (he implies) lift J. to the level of the Prometheans of modern fiction—not to plunge more deeply backward into the *coulisses* of literary history. The "attenuation" of Strether's desire for experience, "its passive rather than its active scope," "the inadequacy of his adventures"; the femininity of all J.'s emotional symbols; the sense in which Milly Theale is the sufferer rather than the actor (and hence no *protagonistes* in the developed Greek sense of that word), and the elegiac rather than tragic emotionality of the *Wings;* the failure, in the *Bowl,* to find an "objective correlative" really equal to the moral burden of the fable.

5. Necessity, surely, to push the analysis still further and more unsparingly. J.'s great achievement of understanding and revelation—even of compositional beauty—not safe with the mere idolaters. Let us avoid exploiting him in the interest of our own anxieties, our own revulsions from reality, our own inner poverty. Essential components of cardinal literature missing in him: (*a*) the toughest mastery of external, contemporary, historical and biological reality, and (*b*) the deepest and clearest, most unshrinking awareness of the inner abyss—or the "inner fountain" either—the fearful and hopeful nature of man, man the primate and the saint. J.'s work fully understandable only after a still more rigorous dual analysis, sociohistorical at one pole, depth-psychological at the other. Importance for latter of Saul Rosenzweig's tentative discussion. Deep and crippling injury to the sources of social capacity and sexual realization certainly sustained by J. in early experience —resulting, no doubt, as S. R. argues, in repression of both

sexuality and aggression. Highly ambiguous quality, then, of his relations with the outer and the inner world. Vacillation between acceptance and repudiation, between thirst for experience and shrinking from it, between the active and the passive role, between the male and the female principles. Hence the *relative* meagerness of his work as "history" (his own term): imagine his sharing Proust's passion for military science, or Mann's and Joyce's for medical learning, or Gide's for political exposure. Hence, too, the *relative* attenuation of his symbols for moral evil and moral heroism. His novels compensatory—and not in the highest sense—for vital frustrations, vital withdrawals from experience. His sense of evil (if Kate Croy and Charlotte Stant are its fullest embodiments) remains a shuddering perception rather than an unblinking gaze; his vision of the good (if Milly Theale and Maggie Verver are its highest expressions) remains a tender, fastidious, singularly pure and beautiful ideal, but a tenuous, late Transcendental, and imperfectly substantial one.

6. Even his austere preoccupation with form impossible to discuss naively on its own terms. What was compulsive, compensatory, protective of the wounded ego, in that too. Remember Flaubert's remark to Louise Colet: "The very great men often write quite badly, and so much the better for them. One must look for formal perfection not in *their* work but in that of the secondary men."

7. Suggestive but unsatisfactory discussion in last chapter of J.'s *vues d'ensemble*. Why not confess that—compared with such men as Stendhal, Dostoevsky, Hardy, Proust, Mann—J. had little capacity for general ideas and that his work is really much less illuminated, much less toughened by them than the work of those others? . . . F. O. M. rightly feels that the view of life expressed in his books now seems inadequate to "both the religious man and the political and economic man," that there is no synthesis in them (as there was in his father's now archaic work) of the two orders of experience, and adds that "the next synthesis must be more rigorously based in both political economy and theology, in the theology that recognizes

anew man's radical imperfection" and in an equalitarian politics. Quite impossible to follow F. O. M. here in the strangely wishful conviction that dogmatic theology can ever be reconciled with a revolutionary democratism, or ever prove anything but a stubborn barrier to the fuller humanization of man. J.'s freedom from such regressive delusions one of the secrets of his true strength. With a more masculine grasp, indeed, of "man's place in nature" than he had, he might have been, as he is not, one of Flaubert's "very great men."

EMILY DICKINSON

WHEN the announcement was made, a few months ago, that a whole group of yet unpublished poems * by Emily Dickinson had been discovered and were to be given to the world, one heard the news with something of that ungracious incredulity with which too good news is usually greeted. Long unpublished manuscripts have a way of disconcerting the expectant, and it scarcely appeared to be in the natural course of things that a poet like Emily Dickinson, whose name had never suggested the voluminous, would have left behind her much more of the very first quality than had already been gathered together in a good-sized "collected" volume. Then a few poems began to appear here and there in the magazines—poems so characteristic, so true to her intense idiosyncrasy, so obviously perfect, that one's first sense was of having read them before and come upon them again after a long interval. If any skepticism remained, it could not survive the appearance of the whole collection. Mr. Louis Untermeyer has called it "Emily Dickinson's most beautiful and, from every standpoint, most important work"; and there is little exaggeration, if any, in what he says. What it comes to is that we shall have to rephrase the conventional description or impression of Emily as the poet of a small sheaf of tiny but perfect poems: quantity, of course, can hardly add to

* *Further Poems of Emily Dickinson,* edited by her niece, Martha Dickinson Bianchi, and Alfred Hampson.

167

her stature, but she is to be thought of, with a real shift in emphasis, as a writer of protracted, sustained, and many-sided inspiration. Only Emerson and Whitman, among our nineteenth-century poets, impose themselves upon us with a comparable reach and density; if anyone insists on adding Poe to the little group, he must be left to defend his own judgment.

It is peculiarly easy and peculiarly wrongheaded to confuse the surface frugality and such a poet as Emily Dickinson with real parsimony or narrowness of range, and that is just what we have all, I think, with a few exceptions, been guilty of doing. In an obvious sense, she said what she had to say in but one manner: to the eye, as it were, her poetry is all of a kind, and all apparently small-scale. So far as expressive versatility is an important poetic faculty, she breaks down in any comparison with Whitman or even Whittier; and Poe himself did "more" things in a much smaller space. There are good reasons, of course, why such expressive versatility as theirs should be valued; but considerations like these need not blind us to the real quality of another kind of poet. Spareness, meagerness, frugality—these are not the really important words to use in any appreciation of Emily. On the contrary, as this volume must have reminded many readers, her true note is to be defined (if the difficulty of defining it can be overcome at all) as a very personal, a wholly unique balance between opulence and reserve, between expansion and concentration, between fire and ice. Madame Bianchi, in her indispensable *Life and Letters,* quotes from a little note, one of thousands, sent over to her sister-in-law "a hedge away," the flashing question: "Are you sure we are making the most of it?" And this is the essential Emily Dickinson: this is the poet, not the myth. Her poetry sprang, not from a Yankee niggardliness, but from a clutching eagerness for experience, a determination to miss nothing momentous, a thirst for what she would have called "Golconda." It is the richness of her poetry, not merely its intensity, that authorizes it.

She used language with a force so special, she bent it so consistently to her own idiomatic purpose, that a first acquaintance with her poetry is apt to leave one mainly with a strong impression of its personal unity, its unvarying uniqueness of style. But she is not the poet of a single absorbing mood, a single hard glare of insight. Her capacity for light and shade is almost the secret of her genius. When critics compare her with Sappho, when they call her "an epigrammatic Walt Whitman," when they allude to Donne or to Blake, they are paying their various tributes to her great powers; but they miss her own quality. For she did not need, like Sappho, the ruinous heat of great passion, nor, like Blake, the ecstasy of vision, in order to make poetry. She was capable of both— in her own vein, of course. There are not many love poems in the language more "abandoned" than one of these new poems—"One life of so much consequence." There are not many mystical poems more enlarging to the imagination than "Behind me dips eternity," nor many poems about death more genuinely solemn than "It feels a shame to be alive." A few such poems—and there are more than a few of each type—would force a reader who knew only those to call Emily Dickinson one of the greatest of erotic poets, or one of the greatest of the mystics. But her whole being was not exhausted in a few moments of transcendental vision, or in a single emotional ordeal. With a resilience that reminds one of Shakespeare, she could turn from them, with a quick humorous glance, to the dinginess of a disagreeable day or to the eloquent fatuity of the Amherst clergy.

To the formulas, indeed, that would simplify poetry in terms of "emotion" or "vision," she is especially troublesome. In an age when poetry was considerably an affair of spontaneity, or of moodiness, or of patriotism, or of declamation, she refused, so to say, to take it seriously: she lived on more than one plane, and poetry might take the consequences. Hence, what seems to many readers the excessive mentalism, and to her admirers the strong metaphysicality, of her characteristic verse. Mr. Mark Van Doren has said that "wit" is the word that sums Emily Dickinson up, and certainly it comes very close to suggesting the concentrated and purified intellectual heat that glows in so much of her poetry. Emerson is the only other American poet who can be compared with her at all in this respect, and the difference between them is an unmistakable one. "Gnomic" is the word for Emerson: the wisdom that springs from prolonged reflection is the substance of his verse, and the language-oracular, abbreviated, at once homely and stately—has often the aspect of translation from some sententious poetry of the East. But that is not the note of Emily Dickinson: no more than Donne does she deal in what is called "lore." Her intellectuality, like his, is rather the intense intuitive activity of an intelligence playing continuously over the personal experience in which it is itself involved; even more than Donne, she gives us the impression of being *on the spot*. Such a poem as this owes nothing to the Persians; it owes everything to experience:

> Expectation is contentment;
> Gain, satiety.
> But satiety, conviction
> Of necessity.

> Of an austere trait is pleasure
> Good, without alarm,
> Is a too serene possession—
> Danger deepens suns.

So true is it that "witty" rather than "oracular" defines her quality, that one gropes for a word to express more sharply still the feeling one has, in reading her verse, of being in direct communication with her mind. The cult of spontaneity has had so general a bearing on poetry since the late eighteenth century that we shall obviously gain nothing by calling Emily Dickinson spontaneous. And how shall we explain the fact that so many of these poems have an immediacy, a sharp promptitude, that one must look for in vain among the poets of "the lyric cry"? For in this respect too, she reminds one of certain seventeenth-century poets—Donne, Herbert, Habington, Vaughan—more than of any writers since their time. The author of "The Collar"—"I struck the board and cried, 'No more; I will abroad!' "—had no greater capacity than she for dramatizing a mental or emotional crisis so arrestingly that the reader is coerced into reacting it. Her very diction is dramatic rather than lyrical: the quick gleam of her metaphor is like that of the Elizabethan playwrights and of these same Caroline metaphysicals who are so close to them in spirit—not really like that of Shelley or Swinburne. Again and again she sets the stage as Herbert or Vaughan would do, bids us look on as spectators, and takes the leading role herself. One remembers a poem, not wholly characteristic in language, in an earlier collection:

> Heart, we will forget him!
> You and I, tonight!
> You may forget the warmth he gave,
> I will forget the light.

When you have done, pray tell me,
That I my thoughts may dim;
Haste! lest while you're lagging,
I may remember him!

And in this new collection one is, as they say, "embarrassed" by the prodigality of a dramatic imagination that turns to account so incomparable a range of mental and emotional experience—by the qualitative richness and quantitative inclusiveness of a single volume. It takes all one's own flexibility to accompany her—but she makes the effort imperative—as she turns from a defense of Moses against the Jehovah who kept him out of Canaan to an epigram on great pain; from a celebration of the bee or the humming-bird to a strangely stony description of death and burial; from a dialogue with autumn to a kind of hymn of renunciation. Socially and physically, her life was more limited than that of any other poet of whom one can think, except Emily Brontë; but its ideal boundaries were wider than most.

For after everything has been said about her sheer linguistic brilliance, her specific genius as a writer, one comes back to what is of course always the secret of such writing as hers—to her undefinable distinction as a person. Everything was against her that usually acts to discourage distinction: provincial surroundings, the humid atmosphere of a defunct Puritanism, a too agreeable home life, drastic denials in the realization of her whole nature as a woman, and doubtless still subtler handicaps. But she was not to be carried under by such forces as these. There was more overtness and activity than receptiveness in her makeup, and she forced life—so far as a human being can do it—to accept her conditions and live up to her demands. We hear much, in connection with her, about "renunciation"; and it is true that she did without much that makes life tolerable for lesser beings. But her spirit had no grimness, no real austerity; she made renunciation a positive, indeed an ecstatic thing. "I find ecstasy in living," she wrote to Colonel Higginson; "the mere sense of living is joy enough." And even if she brooded over death, even if she *was* "eternally preoccupied with it," as Madame Bianchi says, it was not in the saturnine manner of low-keyed natures; it was because the tide of life ran high in her, and she could not be indifferent to death. Her poetry lingers in the memory, not in sober New England hues, but in flashes of light and color; there emerges from it, not an ironic repudiation, as some writers have suggested, but a vigorous assent. In this view, it is tempting to regard as exquisitely symbolic the last message she sent across the intervening garden to her sister-in-law, Susan Gilbert Dickinson. She never spoke more deeply and more characteristically than in these final words: "My answer is an unmitigated *Yes*, Sue."

EDWARD ROWLAND SILL

THE FAILURE OF E. R. SILL

" 'I HAVE endeavored—I have utterly failed!' How the whole miserableness of human life has been compressed into such words at the last." So begins an essay on "Failure" contributed by an undergraduate to the *Yale Literary Magazine* for October, 1860. "Boyhood of wistful dreams," it continues, "Youth of eager hope, Manhood that so resolutely labored, and then,—'I have failed utterly!' That is all. Bitter acceptation of the truth, a little patience, and it is over; God be thanked that life isn't long! But, gloomiest of the shadowy thoughts that form out of the confused past, cannot but be the reflection of all which *might* have been. A little deviation at this point or that,—such a mere touch, here or there, from a stronger hand—might have saved it all, might have gathered up into completeness all that dim-crowned future,—sunken and scattered, now, into crownless wreck."

A history of our letters might easily be written with the interplay of success-as-a-motive and failure-as-a-motive for its sole plot. Not all the characters could be lined up, without ambiguity, as in a bad novel, on one side of the conflict or the other; but the first chapter, if one began with

Franklin and Jefferson and Freneau, would unmistakably announce the theme of success; and the second, with Irving and Cooper, would but introduce variations upon it. Not until a third chapter, with the appearance of Hawthorne, Poe, and Melville, would be gloomier forces come into play; and, even here, the darkness would be only partial; the sunlight of Emerson, Whitman, and Lowell would be at least a match for such shadows as these. In the last chapter or two—with their Dreisers and Andersons, their Robinsons and O'Neills—we all know how the balance would be upset, even though the conflict would continue. Our undergraduate does not belong to those later chapters, yet it is surely more than an accident that on the very eve of the Civil War—beyond which we now have to look as if across a cañon—so gifted and so susceptible a youth as Edward Rowland Sill should have taken time to consider, and have tried to render in words, the meaning of failure. If I could quote the whole of the essay, it would come out that young Sill was not at all a shoulder-shrugging pessimist; he ends, it is true, on an excellent note of strenuousness. Yet there the sad theme is, at the very least; it was really an omen on the horizon that, at such a moment—and at Cooper's alma mater—the mere chance of defeat could seem so real.

An omen, certainly, if only of a limited and personal import. For, judged in the light of all ordinary canons, Sill's own life was to end in anything but clear victory. His classmates at Yale seem to have remembered him in college not only as full of fine promise but as bent on some more than routine achievement: "Sill then and always," said one of them, "hungered for real distinction. Commonplace successes that tickle the vanity and fill the wants of most men had for him no attractions." From the beginning, he had aimed high; and, if he cast about longer than most

men for a vocation, it was not through mere indecision so
much as through a deep concern that his career should be
as fruitful as possible. To see him, then, retiring at the age
of forty-one from a not very conspicuous college chair in
an uncongenial atmosphere—retiring partly in order to
give himself to literary labors for which, by that time, he
did not consider himself more than moderately gifted—is
to feel that, certainly, something had gone amiss. Sill himself, at any rate, in those last four or five years (he was but
forty-six when he died), resigned himself to something
very like ineffectualness. You cannot escape the sense of
painful anti-climax when you find him writing, to a
younger correspondent, that "One must not expect to do
very much more than the average"; and you are still more
troubled by the remark to Miss Shinn three years before
his death: "I should have made an excellent citizen of
some other planet, maybe, and they got me on the wrong
one." In this connection, a little essay which he wrote at
about this time for the *Atlantic's* "Contributor's Club" has
a curious interest. "Books of Refuge" is its title; and its
point is that, as one advances in life, literature, like other
things, comes to be valued not merely as promising "some
increment of positive enjoyment," but as fortifying the
spirit "against positive suffering." Some books, says Sill,
"so quicken the flight of time as to obliterate the present
moment, with all its 'gain-giving,' its remorse, its too acute
memory of personal mortification, its thickening Brocken-
shadow of one's own unprofitableness, of whatever sort."
Such a phrase as "one's own unprofitableness"—is it not
a singular echo of that undergraduate essay?

Yet Sill had been a far from ineffectual teacher of English—first in Ohio, then at the Oakland High School, and
later, for eight years, at the University of California—and,
if he had retired prematurely, it was owing rather to ill

health, and to rebellion against the spirit of a new administration, than to a conviction of his own valuelessness as
a teacher. The clearest success in any practical role, you
feel certain, would have left Sill with something to desire.
It was a poet that he was meant to be, and it was as a poet
that he felt he had virtually failed. There is another of his
undergraduate essays that tells us what his intimate aspirations were: it is called "Vinum Daemonum," and it is of
course a descant on "the sacredness of [the poet's] calling."
Six years after graduation, during a short period as a divinity student at Harvard, he was writing to Holt: "I haven't
had the requisite cultivation [to be a good poet]; and besides my knocking around and feeling the cold shoulder of
things hasn't improved the imaginative powers—the delicacy is blunted, and the bloom gone—if they were there."
But "I believe," he added, "that born into a rich Englishman's son's shoes, like all those chaps, I could have added to
the world's stock of poetry." Three years later: "I suppose
that if taken young and trained right I might have made a
writer; but the training has certainly been wanting. I have
got myself, by dint of nearly killing labor, into the shape
of an almost tolerable schoolmaster, but higher than that
I never shall get, till the resurrection." After his retirement,
when all his time could at last be given to writing, he
could not bring himself to speak of his own work seriously.
"I am supposed to be entered upon a mad career of
literary work," he once wrote, in a moment of troubling
levity. "Have so far only written some very mild verses,
suitable for nursery use in some amiable but weakminded
family." Like all men whose purposes have been foiled,
Sill avenged himself by belittling the worth of what he
did accomplish. Our modern psychology would see a fine
symptom in the habit he confessed to of forgetting things
he had written; and we know what the psychiatrist would

make of the remark: "I hate every bit of verse I write, as soon as it is printed, and would gladly never see it again."

It was a clue to Sill's self-distrust as a writer that he shrank from challenging any estimate of himself on that ground, that he preferred not to be known mainly as poet, and that he called himself "a teacher who occasionally wrote verses." Read the letters to Thomas Bailey Aldrich, written during the final years in Ohio at Cuyahoga Falls, and you will be irresistibly struck by the recurrence in them of a morbid insistence on anonymity: it was as if the writing of verse were a thing no grown man could openly own to, like a lingering penchant for marbles. "More and more I wish all literary work was anonymous" is a characteristic expression; and there are queer passages in which he discusses, with the *Atlantic* editor, the tenuous advantages of this, that, or the other pseudonym. He was undoubtedly sincere when he protested, "I don't feel the least fitness for a writer"; and some of those who knew him best are most willing to accept his own judgment of himself as a teacher first and a man of letters second. "The limitations of his poetry," one of his favorite students, Miss Milicent W. Shinn, writes to me, "are due . . . to the fact of his own temperament, in which the artistic was a strong element, but wholly secondary. Much of it was written almost as he would have sat down at the organ and worked off a mood or passing thought—it flowed out with what he called a 'fatal facility,' without serious artistic purpose. In reading the biography, in spite of its conviction that he was primarily a man of letters, it is very evident how uncertain and self-distrustful he is over his literary work, compared with his clear convictions and resolute efficiency in teaching." Yet he came to teaching only after making trial of several other professions: during the five years that followed on Yale, Sill tried his hand at the study first of

law and then of medicine; becoming an actor was, according to one friend, another project that he "very seriously
considered"; and, still later, he came so close to the min-
istry as to spend some months, as I have said, studying
theology in Cambridge. It is true that teaching had been
one of his first choices for a vocation; and that, when he
at length settled on it for good, it was to throw himself
into the task with a delicate zeal: he was to prove, it appears, the one teacher in a hundred thousand. But he was
the kind of teacher who can say: "I take a great and growing interest in being the cause of writing in others. . . .
I like to help at the incubation of poets especially." Is
there no hint here of something more than the passion of
the born schoolmaster?

It is a question, at the end, that cannot be reduced to
dialectic: you feel, or you don't, that Sill was essentially a
poet, but a poet who, in a stingy soil and under the wintry
light of a low sun, never quite came to his full growth. If
this was true, it is easy to see why. As always, we may
"blame" both the poet and the place—or the time. I shall
speak of the poet himself later, but of the place and time
here. Sprung from a line of Connecticut ministers and
physicians, and finding himself as a grown man in the
tough-minded world of the days that followed the war,
Sill could never persuade himself that being a poet was
full-time work for a Christian and a citizen. Born in New
England, and transplanted early to California, with later
sojourns in Ohio, he escaped from the hereditary pressure
toward useful labor in the vineyard only to expose himself
to the parching pragmatism of the Pacific Coast and the
Middle West. Moreover, Sill's lifetime bridged the gap—
for so many men of his temper a twilight and mournful
gap—between an age of breezy if diluted faith, the age of
Emerson, and an age over which lay the shadow, as it long

seemed, cast by the figures of Charles Darwin and Herbert Spencer. "Wandering between two worlds"—hackneyed as the phrase is, it comes first to one's lips in describing such a writer; and Sill, if he was something less than the American Arnold, was decidedly something more than the American Clough. Unable to cling to even the attenuated supernaturalism of the Unitarians, and strongly affected by Spencer's thought, even to the point of discipleship, Sill never boldly cut the cord that bound him to the long generations of godly Rowlands and Sills, or indeed to the majority of his contemporaries; and he could not cheerfully accept a universe deprived of a sanction he could not calmly dispense with. "What'll you bet we are not immortal?" he once broke out in a letter; and the jaunty phrase, trifle though it is, throws a sudden strong light on the long ordeal of a spirit *naturaliter credula*.

Such was the double conflict that had infallibly to go on in the mind of a man like Sill: on the one hand, his instincts as a man of letters at war with a conscience that harried him without pity into some form of "service" (his own word); on the other, his deep and desperate need for spiritual certainty at war with his intellectual convictions. It was, in neither case, by any means a conflict peculiar to Edward Rowland Sill; but there is no formula for these discords: in every subtle spirit they take on fresh dimensions; and you may say of Sill that he was, for American letters, the poet *par excellence* of that divided hour. Before him came Whitman; side by side with him sang Sidney Lanier, who could "heartily lay [him] a-hold on the greatness of God"; after him came a long drouth, and then the Pounds and the Eliots and the Frosts. No wonder his whole life was overcast by the shadow of a well-nigh immitigable loneliness. No wonder you come to think of him as having mainly gone it alone. "Half the weariness of my life here," he wrote from California in 1863, "consists of its terrible isolation." From Sacramento, the same year: "I am a hermit here, caring for none, cared for by none." Seven years later: "For my part, I long to 'fall in' with somebody. This picket duty is monotonous. I hanker after a shoulder on this side and the other. I can't agree in belief . . . with the 'Christian' people, nor in spirit with the Radicals, etc." During his last year at Berkeley, where he had such devoted friends, he could yet write to Holt: "I —for my part—feel a sort of vaguely lonesome desire to make a new friend or two out of the old ones—if it were possible. I *would* like to find one or two fellows who believe in something that I do—and in doing something that I believe in trying to get done. Or must we fight it out alone—solitary skirmishers—when we are come to forty year?" After the move to Cuyahoga Falls this isolation, though no more real, must have been still more acutely present to him. "The real difficulty with me," Sill wrote to Simeon Baldwin from the Ohio town, "is to get *books*. No, there is a worse one—to get *people*. But that, I suppose, we all have everywhere." "Isolation," said Carlyle, "is the sum total of wretchedness to man"; Sill must have known more than most men what those words imply. Did he, at the end, in his undergraduate phrase thank God that "life isn't long"?

He was not much known as a poet in his own day; the one volume published during his lifetime (*The Hermitage, and Other Poems*) made no great stir, though it was abused in a *Nation* review; and if, for many years, there were a few people who knew "A Fool's Prayer" and "Opportunity" through grammar-school readers, they must have constituted Sill's largest public. Mr. Robert Frost, they say, has always good words to speak of him; and Mr.

Alfred Kreymborg, last year, in his history of our poetry, gave him more attention and a juster appreciation than any of the official historians have ever done. It is well that we should be reminded of his existence, for, far as he fell short of major utterance, Sill belongs with Emily Dickinson and Sidney Lanier in the tiny group of poets—there is no fourth!—whom, in the generation that came to maturity during the Civil War, we can still read with respect. Nothing could be more absurd than to lump him indiscriminately with the Aldriches and Stedmans and Gilders of the age. Whatever his limitations, he was not merely a gentleman who wrote with ease. Unlike the poetasters of the Century Club, Sill was not content to be a genteel echo of Wordsworth or Tennyson. His insight was partial, as I shall try to say; but he *had* insight: those others had "finish." They would not be worth this little allusion if it were not that Sill has largely been remembered by being forgotten in their company.

His work at its best has a philosophic interest and even a philosophic weight. Unlike any American poet before him, or among his contemporaries, Sill had the hardihood to express in his verse a metaphysical anxiety. It is an old story to us now, this poetry of negation; but it was not an old story sixty years ago. It took an uncommon moral refinement then to have even the glimpses which Sill had into the Waste Land. In some of his poems, you come, for the first time, upon that low painful rumble of distress and apprehension and fatigue which sounds so steadily through our modern poetry. It is possible, he saw, that the universe has no concern for man; it is possible that life has no harmonic design; it is possible that there is irreparable waste and destruction and loss. Conceivably there is more to deny than to assert. All questions may be rhetorical—

and ironic. The passionate need to understand the world, to see experience as a whole, may be a special curse. One's personal fate, whatever may be true of the universe, may be—without mitigation—inglorious: "making the best of it" may be an unavoidable formula. Failure is perhaps not to be rationalized or condoned. Perhaps a man would best aim at forgetfulness, rest, or "tranquillity." "Annihilation" may be, in a modern poet's phrase, "the most beautiful word."

To characterize Sill's verse in such sentences, let me say quickly, is to give a false impression of its actual chiaroscuro. I am speaking of the areas in shadow, not of the whole picture. Sill was no Robinson, no Eliot, no Jeffers. But what is striking is that he gave so much play to negation as he did. Even in some of his boyish exercises you come upon sentiments that smack of our own twenties rather than of the American mid-century. There is an undergraduate poem called "Midnight," for example, which, after evoking a nocturnal mood of spiritual darkness, ends with these lines:

> Is it not time to tell us why we live?
> So many years we sleep, and wake, and sleep,
> While—like some Magian through the mysteries
> Leading in fear the blindfold neophyte—
> Time leads us dimly on, till angrily
> Tired life would turn and throttle its stern guide,
> Till he should tell us *whither* and *how long*.
> But Time gives back no answer, and the stars
> Burn on, cold, hushed, and changeless as before,
> And we go back baffled and stolidly
> To the old, weary, hollow-hearted world;
> To the old, endless search for life in death—
> The restless, hopeless roaming after rest.

In a much later poem, "Infirmity," a similar bewilderment gets expression, together with a more generalized bleakness of outlook: "What is the truth," it begins—

> What is the truth to believe,
>   What is the right to be done?
> Caught in the webs I weave
>   I halt from sun to sun.

After four stanzas in which the unweariable vitality of nature is set over against the declining energies of man, the poem ends:

> The youth of the world is fled,
>   There are omens in the sky,
> Spheres that are chilled and dead,
>   And the close of an age is nigh.

> The time is too short to grieve,
>   Or to choose, for the end is one:
> And what is the truth to believe,
>   And what is the right to be done?

Still later, in a poem "To the Unknown Soul," the poet, speculating on the existence of some mysteriously kindred but hidden spirit, describes *himself* in these lines:

> But well I know—since thou'rt my counterpart—
>   Thou bear'st a clouded spirit; full of doubt
> And old misgiving, heaviness of heart
>   And loneliness of mind; long wearied out
> With climbing stairs that lead to nothing sure,
> With chasing lights that lure,
>   In the thick murk that wraps us all about.

Certainly Sill was tormented more than most men by his incapacity to see into the heart of things; more painfully haunted by doubtfulness and perplexity. There is a sonnet called "The Book of Hours," in which he figures himself as a man vainly attempting to read a tale in a language he imperfectly understands, and failing to be touched by its grace:

> The Spirit of the World hath told the tale,
>   And tells it: and 'tis very wise and old.
> But o'er the page there is a mist and veil:
>   I do not know the tongue in which 't is told.

Another poem, with the title "Blindfold," expresses the same failure to grow in understanding as one advances in time—the same sense of groping for what cannot be seen:

Let me loosen the fillet of clay from the shut and darkened lid,
For life is a blindfold game, and the Voice from view is hid.

Sill was even capable of turning upon himself with a bitter smile and jeering mildly at his own hesitations and alarms. The poem called "Roland," as Mr. Kreymborg has said, foreshadows both Miniver Cheevey and J. Alfred Prufrock, with a suggestion of Senlin. The Roland of the title is a spiritual hypochondriac:

> A foolish creature full of fears,
>   He trembled for his fate,
> And stood aghast to feel the earth
>   Swing round her dizzy freight.
>
> With timid foot he touched each plan,
>   Sure that each plan would fail;
> Behemoth's tread was his, it seemed,
>   And every bridge too frail.

The world, to Roland, is a cell in which man is mercilessly caged and left to die; the dark for him is full of fanciful dangers.—

> The buds that broke their hearts to give
>   New odors to the air
> He saw not; but he caught the scent
>   Of dead leaves everywhere.

Roland is not allowed by the poet to let negation have the last word, but it is easy to imagine for what purposes of personal reproof the poem was written.

Such ironies as this are rare in Sill's work; and our whole picture would be less than faithful without at least an allusion to a few poems in which his most serious reservations are recorded. "The Blotted Page," for example, represents the poet as being allowed by the Recording Angel to delete three things from the page on which his account is kept; but the poet, trying to make a choice, sees nothing that is worth saving, and protests that the whole might better be blotted out. In "Two Views of It," a man falling from a cliff to apparently certain death is represented as passing, in a few moments, from horror at being snatched from the "glorious world" to "dull regret"—on unexpectedly recovering consciousness—that the "dark world" has come back again. In "Truth at Last," the poet speculates whether a man ever gives up hope, at the moment of some mortal disaster, and "face[s] the grim fact, seeing it clear as day." If so, he concludes, it would be a kind of victory:

> 'Tis something, if at last,
> Though only for a flash, a man may see
> Clear-eyed the future as he sees the past,
> From doubt, or fear, or hope's illusion free.

In "The Organ," finally, Sill gave expression to his nostalgic aspiration toward fruitful harmony and his hopelessness of achieving it:

> O soul, that sittest chanting dreary dirges,
>   Couldst thou but rise on some divine desire,
> As those deep chords upon their swelling surges
>   Bear up the wavering voices of the choir!
>
> But ever lurking in the heart, there lingers
>   The trouble of a false and jarring tone,
> As some great Organ which unskilful fingers
>   Vex into discords when the Master's gone.

I have mentioned the poems, of course, in which Sill's untimely pessimism comes most boldly to the surface; but you might well make quite as much, to the same end, of those still more frequent poems in which is embodied, in some form or other, the longing for rest, and forgetfulness. It is present conspicuously in the undergraduate lines I have quoted; and the very titles of six or eight poems betray the prevalence of the mood: "Serenity," "Sleeping," "A Prayer for Peace," "Tranquillity," "Peace," "A Resting-Place," "Desire of Sleep," "My Peace Thou Art," and "Night and Peace." Two or three of these poems have a spontaneity and at the same time a formal perfection that Sill did not elsewhere go beyond: you feel somehow that no theme was quite so intimate or so continuously present to him as this. But it is not only in these poems that the desire for repose finds utterance. A poem entitled "The Things that Will Not Die," which as a whole is almost as unsatisfactory as the banal title would suggest, helps us to round out our view of the man, in this connection, very memorably. He represents himself, at the verge of death, turning without reluctance from the earth; and adds, at the end:

> But they who love me best
>   Will be most glad
> That such a long unquiet now has had,
> At last, a gift of perfect peace and rest.

Sill was not the first poet, nor the last, who could strongly desire, at least at times, only the cessation of desire.

It was not in his temperament, however, to be either so much or so little as a poet of thorough-going negation. On one level his stature is enhanced, if on another it is diminished, by the repeated attempts he made to get beyond doubt, to see chagrin and failure in a larger frame, to arrive at some positiveness of view and of expression. At the very least, it can be said of Sill that he was too clear-eyed and too austere to be content with the sentimentalism of Futility. Something tough, arduous, and manly in his New England ancestry kept him from conceding the last foot to spiritual relaxation. Again and again, you find him, in particular poems, straightening himself with what seems almost a bodily motion from a posture of despair, and forcing into his voice the tones of affirmation. Sometimes this yea-saying takes the form of a Transcendental strenuousness; everyone who has even heard of Sill remembers the king's son, in "Opportunity," who finds the broken sword on the battlefield, flung there in despair by a coward, and brandishing it with a battle-shout,

> Hewed his enemy down,
> And saved a great cause that heroic day.

Similar calls to action are sounded in other poems. They always, however, ring with a less personal truth than the

affirmations which take the form of a quietistic suspension
of scrutiny, an "as if" recommendation to provisional faith.
Perhaps there is a meaning behind the veil; behave, at
least, as if there were one, and all will be well. It is this
decision that Roland comes to:

> Till on a day he came to know
> He had not made the world;
> That if he slept, as when he ran,
> Each onward planet whirled . . .

> The weary doubt if all is good,
> The doubt if all is ill,
> He left to Him who leaves to us
> To know that all is well.

So, in "The Secret," after recording a vain search for a
meaning formerly apprehended, and suddenly rediscov-
ered not directly but obliquely in self-forgetful labor, Sill
concludes:

> The blessing came because it was not sought;
> There was no care if thou wert blest or not:
> The beauty and the wonder all thy thought,—
> Thyself forgot.

And the same solution is in "A Reply":

> Child! it is not thine to see
> Why at all thy life should be,
> Wherefore thou must thus abide,
> Foiled, repulsed, unsatisfied . . .
> Careless what shall come to thee,
> Look but what thy work shall be.

Elsewhere the positive line leads rather to a mild Wordsworthian nature-worship or a fugitive pantheism. This is hardly to say more, perhaps, than that Sill was a nineteenth-century poet; that he too was prepared to protest: "I love not man the less, but nature more." Yet this much at least *can* be said; and, indeed, the undertones of weariness in his verse give his allusions to natural life a warmth and intimacy that are not merely of the convention. He seems to have brought himself into a real relation especially with the massive beauty of the north-California landscape; and he has some delicate poems about the upland meadows and the mountains and the redwoods. Occasionally he even managed to adopt the stale mythology of the "Earth-Mother" and the like; but you feel that it was without much freshness of conviction.

And, in short, you have only to follow him sympathetically in his attempt to see things as a whole, to rise above the partiality of the pessimist, in order to see why Sill's stature as a poet is no greater than it is. I said just now that his figure grows in dignity as you watch him resisting the temptation to complete surrender; but it is a moral dignity, in the limited sense, that it gains: it is not the dignity of the victorious imagination. If he had been a lesser man, he would have looked at pain and mortification and perplexity less honestly than he did; if he had been a greater man, he would have looked at them, and into them, and beyond them. A poet of high endowment, it goes without saying, is always a man in whom positive powers of some sort prevail; and whether these take the form of religious insight, or metaphysical penetration, or dramatic knowledge of men, or even sensuous refinement and physical buoyancy, they invigorate his work with affirmativeness and unify it from a commanding center. It is in this sense that Sill's imagination was natively a limited and partial one, and that he remains a minor writer. With a certain capacity for religious feeling, he was incapable of religious ecstasy; with a real concern for ideas, he had but little philosophic acuteness; with a temper naturally humane, he knew nothing special about men and saw nothing in them from a new angle; and his sensitive love of beauty he was unable to erect into a ruling principle. He was a true enough New Englander to have a natural bent toward morals, and certainly there is no reason why an interest in conduct cannot stand at the center of a poet's view of things: but Sill had not the ethical, which is to say the heroic, imagination. For *that* a man must establish some true affinity with the whole life of his time, must speak for others by speaking for himself; but Sill was out of sympathy, as we have seen—and it was inevitably so—with the real life of his period; and he could not even envisage any relevant goal toward which it might move. He was reduced, in consequence, to vacillating between acceptance and rejection; and the earmarks of that fruitless alternation are strewn over all his work.

To say that a major poet must be, in the literal sense, a poet of affirmation, is to turn your back on the great pessimists; there is of course no reason why the sense of destruction and despair cannot be translated by a poet into a consistent metaphysic. What makes the true poetry of pessimism so positive in its effect is that it comes from men who go the whole way with their tragic vision, who are willing to put pain and defeat at the center of their world and relate the rest of experience to it. Conceivably Sill might have been the Leopardi or the Heine or the Hardy of American letters in his time. But he had, as we have seen, too much virility of one kind, too little of another, to trust his own perceptions as fully as, for this, he would have had to do. As a result, to borrow the Frenchman's remark about Browning, his center was not in the middle. He moved back and forth between darkness and light, but he established no balance between them. You are reminded of what Swinburne said, I think à propos of Matthew Arnold: "Nothing is to be made by a poet out of half-hearted or double-hearted doubts or creeds: nothing out of mere dejection and misty mental weather. Tempest or calm you may put to use, but hardly a flat fog." There is a too prevailing mistiness in the weather of Sill's poetic world; and his brave attempts at affirmation fail to dispel it. His strenuousness is morally admirable, but it is vague and conscientious and impersonal. His recommendations to patient faith and unquestioning dutifulness have a suspicious quaver in them: you feel him whistling to reassure his own heart. Even his invocation of natural presences falls short of having the emphasis of ingenuous pantheism; the "one impulse from the vernal wood" never spoke to him, after all, with clear and single authority. He went too far not to have gone much farther; he saw more, alas, than he was ever willing to report. It is on this ground that he may be said to have failed, comparatively, as a poet, just as he failed, in a less real sense, as a man.

Yet "failure" is a poor word at best to use of such a man and such a writer; and to end with a mere reservation would be to do violence to your natural esteem for the finest part of Sill's poetry. Indeed, it is exactly because he was so much more than just another cultivated and facile verse-writer that his work proposes such questions at all. His poems may have been written, as Miss Shinn says, "without serious artistic purpose"; but the best of them do not have the air of improvisation. It is true that no one should go to Sill's poetry for imagery of a passionate hardness or for the utmost density of phrase and line; true too that no one should go to him for sweep and sonority. His endowment was neither that of Sidney Lanier nor that of Emily Dickinson. Certainly his note is the note of unhurried gravity: he challenges comparison, if with anyone, with the Wordsworths and Lamartines and Arnolds of his century; and his occasional union of warmth and sobriety is not unworthy of the parallel. Gravity is not to be mistaken for tameness; and, at his most characteristic, Sill is a disciplined poet, not a tame one. A score of his pieces are the fruit of genuine insights, genuine gleams of perception, genuine purities of feeling; they were certainly written in states of mental clarity and collectedness; they have the inner soundness of organization that Emerson was pointing to when he said: "Ask the fact for the form." He had need of subjecting his imagination to a private discipline, for he chose to say things that were not being generally said around him; it was not until another generation had elapsed that American poets could go the whole distance along the road he indicated. You feel that he alone, of the serious writers of his day in America, would have been at home in our milieu as he could never be in his own. This is naturally not the ultimate tribute to what he achieved, but it largely accounts for the special pleasure with which he can be read. He should not be left to the catalogue and the textbook.

HENRY ADAMS

A WARNING; NOT AN EXAMPLE

"THE BLACK DISTRICT [of Birmingham] was a practical education," says Henry Adams somewhere in his autobiography, "but it was infinitely far in the distance. The boy ran away from it, as he ran away from everything he disliked." It was the truest among many true things the man said of himself; and now we have, in this thick volume of his letters,* what is so far the completest revelation of our most distinguished American fugitive. There is scarcely a page of the more than five hundred that one would have had Mr. Ford suppress; yet there are not many more painful books in American literature. The *Education* was painful enough, but *that* one could regard as the expression of an embittered elderly man; the letters, on the other hand, force one to follow step by dreary step the long process of spiritual dessication from the doubtful prognostics of the young Harvard graduate in Germany to the bitter truculence of the restless old man in Tahiti and Paris and London. "Men are certainly the most successful invention the devil ever made, and when they arrive at a certain age, and have to be constantly amused, they are even harder to manage than when they are young, mischievous

* *Letters of Henry Adams, 1858–1891,* edited by Worthington C. Ford.

194

and tormenting." Such are virtually the last words on humanity in these letters: such, at the end of our great century, was our American style in sageness, ripeness, mellowness, and mansuetude: such was the final verdict of our best critical mind after the Civil War—of the mind that should have been that of our Goethe, our Voltaire, our Tolstoi, or at least our Arnold. No wonder the volume induces gloomy thoughts!

To tell the truth, it is hard to distinguish, in reading these letters, as in reading the *Education,* between one's distaste for the age he lived in, and one's distaste for the personality of Henry Adams. There are moments when this book, like the other, tempts one to cry out against the author as the coldest snob, the purest egotist, the most tedious grumbler, in American literature. This of the man of whom, as I say, one knows that he had no intellectual superiors in his generation, save perhaps Charles Pierce. Granted that his coldness, his superciliousness, his querulousness, were the vices of a man born out of his due time: granted that his Adams heritage would have been an incubus on the shoulders of even a larger man, Henry Adams remains a figure who preserved the ancient New England harshness without the ancient New England manliness and passion. Vanity is by no means always repellent, for it is often expansive and vital; but there was no expansiveness in Henry Adams's self-regard: occasionally amusing, because drolly expressed, it is for the most part merely tiresome. When he writes to his brother Charles, "You know by this time my canons of art pretty well, and you know that what pleases the crowd would have a poor chance of pleasing me," there is no mirth in his voice, and no irony; he is speaking literally, with the simple arrogance of an Adams. It is this, of course, that in the *Education* makes the protracted parade of modesty, of ignorance, of ingenuousness, so unendurable: it is the falsest of all modesties—the modesty of a man who believes himself never to have been properly appreciated. And part of what makes the letters painful reading is the undignified alternation between the expression of self-esteem and the expression of self-belittling.

II

If he was a snob, too, as well as an egotist, one has to remind oneself that he was not the first man of great parts, nor the last, who has succumbed to the littleness of prizing place and family and power. But it is not easy to feel warmly about a man whose relations with human beings were so entirely confined as Henry Adams's to men and women who were socially or intellectually "distinguished"; who seems never to have approached and cultivated some plain, unpromising man or woman without premeditation and for the simple sake of friendliness. When, early in life, he urges his brother Charles to cultivate the distinguished men of Boston, one feels that, wise as the advice is, it betrays something more than wisdom; when he complains of the dulness of London society, one detects the soreness of the inconspicuous outsider; when he repeatedly reminds his English correspondent Gaskell of his closeness to influential men in the Washington government, one wishes the note were not so insistently forced; when he satirizes the stiff self-consciousness of General and Mrs. Grant at the White House; when he recommends to Cabot Lodge the "social dignity" of being a "literary lion" in Boston; when he reports that the natives of Samoa "evidently know a swell when they see one" because they are impressed by the Adams name—at all such points, one makes many allowances for playfulness and for something deeper and finer than that; but, after all is said, one regrets that in the makeup of so brilliant a man there should have been so large an element of the inexpansive. He might well have been a happier man if he had been less concerned about the forms of success.

That he was *not* a happy man it did not take these letters to inform us; but perhaps one apprehends the whole dreariness of his misery only after reading them. There is nothing, for example, in the *Education,* quite so piercing as the remark in a letter to Mrs. Cameron: "Life is not worth much when the senses are cut down to a kind of dull consciousness, but it is at least painless. As for me, waste no sympathy. My capacity for suffering is gone." One vacillates here, it is true, between sympathy for a man stricken by irremediable disappointment, vexation, and grief; and impatience with Adams's peevishness, his indulgence in habitual self-pity, his failure to achieve even a provisional austerity. From an unsympathetic point of view, it would be easy to argue that there were many men in the nineteenth century more justly entitled to self-pity than the prosperous heir of Peter Chardon Brooks, the editor of the *North American Review,* the Professor of History at Harvard, the Washington householder, the companion of Hay and King and LaFarge, the traveller and the curio-collector. To say nothing of the victims of that plutocracy which Henry Adams reviled—but not too openly—one thinks of the valor of such men as Sidney Lanier and Edward Sill and Paul Hayne: men who had talents, they too, and who struggled under handicaps of which Henry Adams never knew the meaning, but who, in that miasmatic post bellum atmosphere, donned such fragmentary pieces of the armor of faith as they could lay their hands on. With him, it was as much a defect of the will as of the "way": some inner incompetence kept him, as he himself knew, from embracing any positive philosophy even when it thrust itself upon him. "By rights," he said in the *Education*, "he should have been also a Marxist, but some narrow trait of the New England nature seemed to blight socialism, and he tried in vain to make himself a convert." Even to Cabot Lodge he could write, in 1879, "I am, as you know, a little of a *communard* myself"; and one reflects that a little communism is a safe thing. It is perhaps grotesque to suggest that Henry Adams might have been an American Morris or Shaw, but at least the hint is in his own confessions. At any rate, this rather spineless refusal to go beyond negation cannot but modify one's sympathy with his pessimism. "The sad truth is," he wrote to Gaskell at the age of thirty-one, "that I want nothing and life seems to have no purpose." The blackness of that mood we need not question or belittle, but we should have liked to see more evidence of a brave attempt to throw it off.

Yet if all this were less true, the letters of Henry Adams would not have the peculiar value they do have for this generation. Shaw has observed somewhere that if parents must hold themselves up to their children as object lessons, they should hold themselves up as warnings and not as examples. The career of Henry Adams is the most salutary possible warning to the American intellectual classes, to American men of letters, against the vices to which they are peculiarly liable. The habit of dosing oneself on "the purposelessness of life," the indulgence in self-pity, did not go out of fashion on that spring day in 1918 when Henry Adams died; and he was not the last American *littérateur* to rationalize his failure to count socially by sneering at "the mass of fools who make mankind." The boy who "ran away" from the Black District in 1858 has had his successors unto the third and fourth generations. An old-fashioned moralist—perhaps, indeed, a wise moralist of any fashion—could point to the almost Æschylean retribution which he thus prepared for himself. Probably every futilitarian and every indifferentist still in his twenties or thirties could learn something by reading the letters Henry Adams wrote in his fifties and sixties. An elderly intellectual to whom "the dread of a bore [has grown] to horror," who has reached a point where literature and "so-called usefulness" also bore him, who passes an hour every afternoon at his greenhouse watching his roses, who "longs for the Cannibal Islands," and who in fact sets out on a long, restless, and unprofitable search, not for experience, but for diversion, in the South Seas; who is pleased to find that his old friends in London are "more pessimistic than I myself," and "see nothing before mankind except infinite ennui diversified by vice"—the spectacle of such an elderly man is not edifying, but it has a moral. Yes, on the whole, Henry Adams was a man America did well to produce—that once.

LETTERS OF HENRY ADAMS

SHORTLY after Lincoln's election in the fall of 1860 Henry Adams accompanied his father to Washington, where the elder man was a member of Congress; and there they remained until the following March and the inauguration of the new President. Young Adams had gone to Washington partly to write a series of political letters for a Boston newspaper, but the work of composing them evidently failed to exhaust his literary energies, which were abounding. There were subjects, moreover, that would find no natural place in a newspaper correspondence. "I propose," Adams wrote to his brother Charles in December, "to write you this winter a series of private letters to show how things look. I fairly confess that I want to have a record of this winter on file, and though I have no ambition nor hope to become a Horace Walpole, I still would like to think that a century or two hence when everything else about it is forgotten, my letters might still be read and quoted as a memorial of manners and habits at the time of the great secession of 1860."

A series of such letters did follow, and now, nearly a century later, though "everything else" about that winter has hardly been forgotten, Adams's wish seems in a fair way to be modestly realized. More of that in a moment. Meanwhile, perhaps it is true that, as he said, he had no serious hope of becoming the Horace Walpole of his time, but certainly the example of the earlier letter-writer was much in his mind, not only then but later. Nine years afterward, again in Washington, he remarked to another correspondent that he had taken up the "ever youthful" Horace Walpole once more. "What surprises me most," he went on, "is that he is so extremely like ourselves; not so clever of course, but otherwise he might be a letter-writer of today. I perpetually catch myself thinking of it all as of something I have myself known, until I trip over a sword, or discover there were no railways then, or reflect that Lord Salisbury and not Lord Carteret lives over the way."

Without a clue like this, the parallel between the two men would probably not occur to most readers. It requires a rather forcible effort to make a connection in one's mind between the author of *The Castle of Otranto* and the author of *Mont-Saint-Michel and Chartres,* between the son of the not very austere Sir Robert Walpole and the offspring of such earnest characters as John Quincy and Charles Francis Adams, between the amiable, gossipy, pleasure-loving, assiduous dilettante of Strawberry Hill and the partly fictionalized Henry Adams with whom the *Education* has familiarized us—depressive, anxious, estranged from the life of his age, and corroded by the longing for an impossible unity. One scarcely needs to suggest the manner in which Horace Walpole would have dealt with either the Virgin of Chartres or the Second Law of Thermodynamics: it would not have been the Adams manner, one can leave it at that.

Yet it was a sagacious instinct that led Henry Adams to detect a kind of kinship with his eighteenth-century predecessor. Both men were the sons, and felt it keenly, of men who had played commanding roles in the historic drama: the status of the epigone was vital to both Walpole and Adams. They had in common the personal, the family involvement in the high politics of their respective eras, they themselves were both active, too, from time to time, and mostly behind the scenes, in political manipulation and maneuver, and the gap is no great one between Walpole's Whiggish libertarianism and the republican liberalism of Adams's early years. What is more important here, the two men took, after all, a very comparable interest in what Adams calls the "manners and habits" of their contemporaries, and aspired to very much the same sort of recognition by posterity of their achievement as observers and chroniclers. Adams may have abandoned this aspiration in the end, as he abandoned so many things; but he had begun with it.

He had begun, moreover, with a sense, inherited from the eighteenth century, of the letter as a serious literary form, a form with its own exacting demands on the feeling for structure, for movement, for tone, for narrative and picture; and this he did not abandon. He had come by it as naturally as possible, not only through his reading of letter-writers like Walpole, but through family inheritance. The writing of letters was an Adams property, almost an Adams privilege, like the mission to England or the keeping of the republican conscience. Except for Franklin, the best letter-writers of the Revolutionary period were John Adams and his wife, and John Adams himself had even theorized informally on what might pompously be called the aesthetic of the letter. The epistolary style, he remarks in a letter to Abigail, is essentially different from the oratorical and the historical. "Letters, like conversation," he observes, "should be free, easy, and familiar. . . . Affectation is as disagreeable in a letter as in conversation, and therefore studied language, premeditated method, and sublime sentiments are not expected in a letter." To our own taste there are passages of rather studied diction and "sublime" sentiment in both his own letters and his wife's, but the wonder is that there is so little of either, and so much that, in the midst of great and grave events, is easy, spontaneous, unaffected, and intimate.

Henry Adams himself had a high opinion of them, or at least of Abigail's: he once observed in a letter to his friend Gaskell on the subject of American writers generally that "in the way of letters there is nothing but my old great-grandmother Abigail Adams's that are worth reading." This suggests that he rather undervalued his great-grandfather's, and that he had no special esteem, either, for the letters of his grandfather, John Quincy Adams. And in fact the epistolary style of the sixth President is far from winning; if his father ever urged "familiarity" upon him, it was in vain; his letters mostly have the air of state papers that happen to be addressed to private friends. Even in the next generation the old easiness had not quite been recaptured, and the letters that Charles Francis Adams wrote from London, during his years as Minister, are more solid than spirited. They are at any rate carefully composed, and the point is that the epistolary habit was handed on from father to son like a family heirloom. It is clear that the practice was enjoined upon Henry Adams and his brothers from an early age. In a memoir which he prefaced to his edition of John and Abigail Adams's letters, Charles Francis Adams alludes to this subject in his rather stately manner: "Perhaps there is no species of exercise, in early life, more productive of results useful to the mind, than that of writing letters. Over and above the mechanical facility of constructing sentences, which no teaching will afford so well, the interest with which the object is commonly pursued gives an extraordinary impulse to the intellect."

Doubtless there is something a little dampening here in the insistence on intellectual utility ("results useful to the mind"); and "the mechanical facility of constructing sentences" falls coldly on the heart. Another sort of man than Henry Adams might have been discouraged forever, by his father's rather arid high-mindedness, from expressing himself with any spontaneity whatever in this or any other form. Fortunately the expressive instinct was too strong in him for that, and "the interest with which the object is commonly pursued" carried the day over all mere conscientiousness. In no Adams before him had the expressive instinct been so strong: he was the first of them all who was born to be a writer and not a public servant or a wielder of political power, and it was partly because the mirage of political power thrust itself between him and his true aim so deceptively, though so inevitably, that his course as a writer was as impeded, as full of detours, as frustrated as it was. There were whole periods in his life, at any rate, when his powerful literary gift found its real outlet in correspondence; and the editor of this volume would maintain that, if one sets aside the *History*, it is in his letters that Henry Adams realized himself most completely, with the least uncertainty and unnaturalness, as a writer.

By the time, late in life, when he came to write the books on which his reputation usually rests—*Mont-Saint-Michel* and the *Education*—he had been driven, or had driven himself, into a painfully false and unwholesome relation with the audience he should normally have counted on. His publishing those books privately, with all the mystifications, the jittery precautions, the elaborate disparagements in which he enveloped the process, was a symptom of something basically unhealthy in his position as a man of letters. The consequence is that, for all their brilliance, all their weight, the two books, taken as wholes, are somehow dissatisfying to the critical sense. We dislike writing that, as Keats once said, has a palpable design upon us, and the mask of Failure in the one work, the mask of rather mawkish Mariolatry in the other, are too palpably, too insistently, too heavy-handedly thrust before our vision not to end by impressing us less as personae, in the great poetic sense, than as literary false faces. The two novels Adams wrote in his forties, *Democracy* and *Esther*, are remarkable books, more remarkable than they have usually been recognized as being; but even they were published anonymously or pseudonymously, almost clandestinely, and their publication was accompanied by a thousand facetious disclaimers of authorship. The nervous self-consciousness of all this does something to explain what is unsatisfactory about these novels; for Adams's unwillingness to *commit himself* as a writer was obscurely associated with his failure, in both *Democracy* and *Esther*, to invent an action, a set of narrative symbols, that would bear up the pressure of his moral meanings.

For a man to whom the basic facts of the literary profession itself were as problematic as all this, the letter was an ideal medium. Here there was no reason to be tormented by the elementary problems of authorship, no reason to agonize over the question of an audience and one's right relation to it. An audience was at hand, and usually it was an understanding and responsive audience. First-rate letters depend almost as much on their recipients as on the man who writes them, and just as Byron was lucky in having Tom Moore and Hobhouse and Lady Melbourne to write to, so Adams was lucky, and must have known that he was, in having correspondents so congenial and so appreciative as Charles Gaskell and John Hay and, perhaps most of all, Elizabeth Cameron. One gets the strongest impression in reading these letters that, when Adams sat down to write them, the discomfort that so often afflicted him elsewhere quite fell away and he became simply a man with a pen—a man for whom, moreover, the pen was a predestined implement. Now he was wholly at one with himself and with his perfect audience of a single person, and all his powers as a writer—powers of sharp attention to people and things, of responsiveness to impressions, of insight and judgment, and above all of expression in language—found themselves in free and unembarrassed play.

The series of Adams's published letters covers a period of just sixty years: it begins with his letters from Germany as a young student in 1858 and ends with a letter to Gaskell a few weeks before his death in 1918. As the expression of a life so many-sided as his was, these letters are bound to exert their interest on a variety of levels. Their interest as a social chronicle—as "a memorial of manners and habits," to put it in his way—is exerted on only one of these, but on that level it is undeniable. The letters that have this value were mainly written in Adams's early years—in those months in Washington that followed Lincoln's election, in the years he spent as private secretary to his father in London, and then, again in Washington, in the disenchanting year or two that followed his return. As soon as Adams joined the Harvard faculty his attention was drawn off elsewhere; even after his resignation and the return to Washington, the writing of his *History* was his great preoccupation, and after the death of his wife he withdrew too completely from social life to think of himself as in any way a recorder of it. He emerged rather warily and briefly from this seclusion when his friend John Jay was Secretary of State, and when his friend Theodore Roosevelt was President he even ventured so far out of his retreat as to attend one or two dinners at the White House. The result was a handful of letters that have something of the old animation as chronicle. In general, however, after 1870 Adams appeals to one as a letter-writer on other grounds.

It is the letters he wrote in the sixties that chiefly show how capable he was of competing with Horace Walpole on his own terrain. He is at one disadvantage here: he was never present at any event that offered itself to the chronicler quite so gratefully or so enviably as the trial of the rebel Scotch lords or the coronation of George III. And in any case Adams's writing rarely has just the qualities of briskness, amenity, and careless precision—as of eighteenth-century music—that one comes to expect of Walpole. It is usually a little lower in pitch and more astringent in savor than his predecessor's. If it has less sprightliness and charm, however, it of course has greater density:

Adams's mind, only too obviously, was a far more complex one than Walpole's, and yet his eye was no less quick and keen. It need hardly be said now that his interest in the events that passed before him was a philosophical, not a gossipy, one—but along with this he had some of the gifts of the novelist too. And what gives his letters of the sixties their special character is the union one finds in them of the general and the particular, of the broadly historical and the sharply personal, of the sense of large affairs sweeping on their way and the eye for the human actors, not always heroic actors, who are carried along with them.

How marked this is in the letters of the "great secession of 1860"! Never for more than a moment or two does one lose sight, in reading them, of the large issues that are on the verge of settlement or the failure of settlement, and of how much depends, for the future of the republic, on the outcome. The hardly bearable tensions of that winter are all here; the ebb and flow of anxiety and hopefulness; the rumors, the reassurances, the hours of optimism, the recurring shocks and setbacks. One hears much of the Congressional Committee of Thirty-Three, of the Peace Convention, of the problem of the Border States. But the potential novelist makes his voice heard also along with that of the sober young politico, and one relaxes, in the midst of these solemnities, to watch a leading figure like Seward, "with his big nose and his wire hair and grizzly eyebrows and miserable dress," smoking his eternal cigar, sprawling, snorting, belching, and doing "all sorts of outrageous things"—even patting Mrs. Charles Francis Adams on the head, like a little girl, in a manner that, instead of offending, rather flatters her. At a crush ball one sees Mrs. Stephen A. Douglas smiling and shaking hands with her guests quite as if her husband were not a drunken brute and a ruined politician; in another part of the room one observes the "ancient buffer," John Tyler, the ex-President, in the "cerements of his forgotten grave," surrounded nonetheless by a crowd of admiring devotees. How pleasurably one feels the *frisson historique* as one's eye falls on them!

There are scantier touches of this particular cinematic sort in the letters from London during the war. The unease that young Adams felt in English society may have had a bearing on this, and doubtless, too, there was a distraction in the long series of oscillations between dejection at bad news from the war front and elation over Union victories. What the London letters mostly yield up is not so much the sharply pictorial as the historically atmospheric—the intense and troubled emotional quality of a moment in British and American history, a moment of deep and potentially dangerous crisis, as a particularly proud and touchy young American would experience it. No doubt it is a partial picture that one gets, this picture of almost universal hostility toward the Union on the part of the governing groups and of hardly concealed eagerness at the prospect of its destruction; but however partial it may be, it is extraordinarily animated, personal, and infectious. The illusion of participation, of contemporaneity, is at certain moments complete. Sometimes, too, it does depend on incident and scene, as when, in the gallery of the House of Commons, the Confederate commissioner, Mason, offends against the rules of the House by crying, "Hear! hear!" to an anti-Union speech; or when, one Sunday afternoon in May, Henry Adams comes home from a walk and encounters his father, "the Chief," dancing across the entry and crying out, "We've got New Orleans!"—while the newsboys in the street outside begin shouting the news, and the whole of London is seized with excitement "as though it were an English defeat." But the letters from London are by no means exclusively obsessed with the

American war, and one is reminded again of Adams's reserve powers as a reporter of the social and political scene by a letter like that in which one sees Garibaldi at a reception at the Duke of Sutherland's—the republican and revolutionary Garibaldi, in a red shirt and a blue cape lined with red, stalking through the apartments of Stafford House with the young Duchess of Sutherland, glittering with diamonds, hanging on his arm.

No reader of the *Education* needs to be told what a genius Adams had for the personal sketch, for the quick penciled drawing of the individual subject that, isolating a detail or two and giving them their full salience, has an effect of serious and truth-telling caricature. Everyone remembers the portrait of Swinburne at Monckton Milnes's country house, looking like a tropical bird, "high-crested, long-beaked, quick-moving," or the sketch of Lord Palmerston receiving his guests at a reception, with his slow, deliberate, mechanical laugh, "a laugh of 1810 and the Congress of Vienna." This gift of portraiture exhibits itself in the letters too—intermittently, to be sure; with more intermissions than one could wish; one misses any serious attempt to evoke Disraeli in the House of Commons or Grant at the White House—but at times it is in full play. The group of drawings of Seward in Washington is a case in point, and even in the London letters one comes upon glimpses like that of John Stuart Mill, dining at the Duke of Argyll's, "a curious looking man with a sharp nose, a wen on his forehead and a black cravat . . . very retiring and embarrassed in his manner." The great display-piece of Adams's achievements in this vein, however, is certainly the wonderful series of sketches of Stevenson, whom Adams encountered several times when he was in Samoa in the early nineties.

What was it—unless it was Stevenson's effortless and

untroubled adoption of a vagabondage that Henry Adams could only gaze at from an envious distance—that called forth the particular vivacity, half satirical and half respectful, of this portrait? One hardly knows, and yet Adams was certainly never more inspired than when he summoned up for his correspondents the apparition of that strange, emaciated figure with the morbidly intelligent and agitated eyes, garbed in dirty striped-cotton pajamas and unmatched woolen socks, moving restlessly about "like an insane stork," and brandishing his long thin arms above his head "as though he wanted to throw them away." Every stroke of the pencil is expressive, and the cumulative effect of uncanniness is so complete that one accepts without difficulty Adams's own conclusion: Stevenson is no mere mortal but, as the Samoans would say, an *a-itu* or spirit. A not very respectable *a-itu*, either; the final word is a disparaging, and probably an unfair, one. The contrast between Stevenson's raffishness and the fineness of Adams's companion La Farge is the last note: "the oriental delicacy of La Farge seems to be doubled by the Scotch eccentricities and barbarisms of Stevenson who is as one-sided as a crab."

The picture itself may be a one-sided picture, a brilliant caricature rather than a sober portrait, but of its brilliance, at all events, there can be no question. Quite by itself it would make the fortune of the letters in which it appears, yet as it happens these letters from Samoa are so rich, so spirited, even so genial, that, if the remarks about Stevenson were entirely deleted from them, they would still remain among the purest triumphs of Adams's career as a writer. In general, he was never more consistently good— never more uninterruptedly animated and vivid, or less liable to his special vices of mind and style—than in the great body of letters he wrote on his very considerable travels about the globe. If ever a man was a good traveler Henry Adams was, as he quite properly boasted in a letter to Mrs. Cameron. It is true that he went on to minimize this claim by pretending it only meant that, in any given situation, he was more comfortable than his fellow travelers. But that, as he surely knew, was a ludicrous understatement. He was a good traveler, to put it on the surface level for the moment, partly because he was extraordinarily philosophical about the discomforts and hardships of travel. There is a world of difference between Adams sitting in his study on H Street and Adams journeying on foot up a narrow river valley in Fiji or bumping along in an ox-cart through the forests of Ceylon; the same man who could be plunged into gloom by a headline seems never to have much minded a gale at sea, a snowstorm in the mountains, or the necessity of dining on squid.

That, however, was the least part of his genius as a traveler, without much more significance than his baggage. What was far more important was his real love of the various world—of the world as one sees it not in newspapers or even in historical records but literally, as it unrolls itself, in travel, before the physical senses: the landscape, the city streets, the native villages, the monuments of the past, the men and women, the very animals. Can one read these letters without discerning how strong and how genuine this loving interest was, contradictory as it may seem to the bleak repudiations that form the more familiar side of Henry Adams's mind? Clearly there was a strain of magic for him in the mere fact of movement from scene to scene, and whatever his state of mind may have been, in a Berlin boardinghouse or a Washington study, however he may have despaired and denied, he seems only to have had to board a train or embark on a steamer (despite his sufferings from seasickness) to be set free for the time from his intensest anxieties and to become the other Adams, the born poet with a poet's gust for experience. One feels it at the beginning and almost as truly at the end; one feels it in the days when, with two or three other young Americans, he sets off on a walking tour through the Thuringian Forest; it is there in the period of his grief-stricken middle life when he roams with his friend La Farge through Japan and the islands of the South Seas, and even at the time when, a solitary and embittered man in his sixties, he finds himself alone, well within the Arctic Circle, gazing upon the "terribly fascinating and fantastic" landscape of glacier-laden mountains and "silent, oily, gleaming sea" that surrounds Hammerfest in Norway.

If few letters of travel anywhere are superior to these it is because Henry Adams had so fortunate a mingling of talents for the purpose. As he moved about the world, his senses were awake and aware of everything, his feeling for the tone of places was continually at work, and at the same time his mind, with its special penetrations and its rich equipment of knowledge, was restlessly taking note of all the intangibles, the "supersensibles," the impalpable analogies and contrasts and meanings. He can give one the impression of being primarily and essentially a landscape-painter in prose, a La Farge of language. He can catch what seems to be the whole quality of a moonlight night over a Hawaiian island—as he sits on a verandah and absorbs it—with his image of two palm trees on the terrace before him, glistening in the moonlight, "their long leaves waving . . . with the human suggestion of distress which the palm alone among trees conveys to me." He likes to mythologize the features of the physical world, as he does with the volcanoes on Hawaii itself, and Mauna Loa becomes a credible deity when Adams points to its huge flat bulk stretching down an interminable slope ahead of him, "with the strange voluptuous charm peculiar to volcanic slopes, which always seem to invite you to lie down on them and caress them." Very unlike Mauna Loa, but no less mythological in their way, are the sad and silent mountains about Hammerfest, which "never knew what it was to be a volcano": "They lie, one after another, like corpses, with their toes up, and you pass by them, and look five or ten miles up the fiords between them, and see their noses, tipped by cloud or snow, high in behind, with one corpse occasionally lying on another, and a skull or a thigh-bone chucked about, and hundreds of glaciers and snow-patches hanging to them, as though it was a winter battlefield; and a weird after-glow light. . . . They never can have really enjoyed themselves." It is the whole Scandinavian pantheon against the Polynesian.

Meanwhile, there is the human scene, the cities and the farms and the archaic villages, the ruined temples and the medieval churches, the human beings and the animals. The animals ought not to be forgotten; animals like the oxen that drew Adams and La Farge through the Ceylon jungle by moonlight: "our little white oxen, with their mystical straight horns, and their religious sacred humps," tripping along, "sometimes trotting and sometimes running, their bells tinkling in the quaintest way." One is unlikely to forget these charming oxen, but of course the human figures take precedence over the beasts. One recalls, for example, how in Japan "everything laughs," not only the dragonheads on the temples, but the jinrickshaw men as they run at full speed in a sizzling sun, the doll-like women, the shopkeepers when you tell them their goods are forgeries, and even the Mikado himself in cabinet council. Once recalls the Mexican peasants who "have the peculiar look, though all really Indians, that the Roman empire left forever on its slave-provinces." And of course one is least likely of all to forget the "old gold" people of Polynesia; the men and women of Hawaii, Samoa, and Tahiti; the tall, strong, broad-backed, glistening young women, wreathing in near-nudity through the intricate movements of the Siva; the "splendid young men, dressed only in their waist-cloths . . . with garlands of green leaves round their heads"; the grave and ceremonious old men on whose handsome countenances one discerns "the usual rather pathetic expression of these islanders." They are all tremendous aristocrats, these Polynesians, especially the Samoans, and make one feel like "the son of a camel-driver degraded to the position of stable-boy in Spokane West Centre." Though, to be sure, they recognize other aristocrats when they see them, and it is clear that the chief Seumano and his people are aware that Henry Adams is not quite a plebeian.

He himself, Henry Adams, at any rate, sees at once what gentlemen they are, and in general these letters of travel owe half their power to his ingrained habit of going beyond the mere surface of things, the mere look of foreignness and picturesqueness, and making the difficult effort of social and psychological understanding. It is what all good travel-writers do, of course; but how many travel-writers have Henry Adams's acuteness, his malleability, his freedom from the formulated and the preconceived? Freedom even from his own formulas—for he has no sooner yielded himself, for example, to the romantic and archaic charm of Samoan life than his critical sense too comes into play, and he begins to see that the reality of that life is many-sided, and that some of its sides are not very poetic. One cannot resist the sweet temper, the gaiety, the gentleness of the Samoans, to be sure, or their nobility of appearance and manner, but the fact is, the more one sees of them, the

more oppressively one becomes aware that there are virtually no individuals among them, that they are all more
like one another than the inhabitants of a Yankee small
town, and that they are singularly practical, unimagina-
tive, unromantic, without intellectual curiosity or reflec-
tiveness. "I begin to understand," writes Adams, "why
Melville wanted to escape from Typee." At any rate, he
had begun to understand something about primitive life
that no sentimental stereotype would have prepared him
for.

He may or may not have been "right" in his own re-
formulation of it—"right" in the literal and wholly objective sense—but he had got at something, as he almost
always did, that by no means leapt to the eye, and it is
these repeated flights of penetration into the intangibles
that largely make his letters from abroad so absorbing. That,
and the imaginative use he was constantly making of his
erudition as a historian. The mingling of these elements is
very striking in such a letter as the one from Moscow in
which, describing a high mass at a Greek Orthodox cathe-
dral, Adams remarks that it is a marvelous composite of
the Jewish tabernacle and the First Crusade, with robes
like those of Saint Louis or Godfrey of Bouillon and ceremonies like those of Solomon's Temple. What makes the
illusion more powerful, he adds, is "the wonderful tenth-
century people" taking part, with a formal devoutness such
as western Europe perhaps never knew. "In some ways," he
says, "I feel sure, the Russian of today is more primitive
than the Frenchman or German ever was, if you call this
passive attitude of subjection primitive. I never met with
it in any primitive race I have struck before, and even a
monkey shows occasional scepticism." A frigid breath from
the future sweeps over these sentences, as indeed it does
over much that Adams wrote from central and eastern

Europe in 1901. And in any event one knows oneself in the company of a traveler who is not only a landscape-painter but an ideologue touched with the poetic sense.

If he had not been an ideologue, Henry Adams's letters would have lacked one of the strands of interest which of course they have. And this remains true even if one feels that some of the general ideas propounded in his later books—the ideal unity of medieval culture, the merely chaotic multiplicity of modern culture, the application to history of the Second Law of Thermodynamics, and the like—deserve a good deal less solemn and literal attention than has often been accorded them. The sheen of novelty has worn off some of these "views" by this time, and it is easier now to see the admixture in them, along with their solid elements, of wishfulness, caprice, and intellectual dice-loading. The position Adams finally arrived at was once described by Paul Elmer More as "sentimental nihilism," and the phrase will do as well as some others to suggest its particular quality. Saying so by no means implies that Adams's mind was not one of the most interesting, in its foibles as well as in its power, in American intellectual history; one of the most complex, restless, wide-ranging, and supple. And the letters enable one to follow the *development* of his mind from phase to phase as, of course, none of his books or even all his books taken together quite do. The intellectual story they tell is, quite naturally, much less artfully shaped and organized than that in the *Education*, but it is a more complex, shifting, indecisive, and credible story.

What one gets in the letters, and fails to get in the *Education*, is the whole process by which Henry Adams moved from the great Unitarian synthesis of his fathers—from its pure, cold, arid, eighteenth-century rationality and optimism—to the mechanistic catastrophism with which

he ended. This latter was, of course, his final testament to
posterity, but only the reader of the letters has a full sense
of the delicacy with which Adams's mind was for many
years balanced between the poles of hopefulness and despair, affirmation and denial, belief and skepticism. The
uncertain poise was there from the beginning, as he himself, with his peculiarly Yankee type of introspective acuteness, once observed. Still in his middle twenties, writing
to his brother Charles from London, he confesses that his
mind is by nature balanced in such a way "that what is
evil never seems unmixed with good, and what is good always streaked with evil." Ultimately he was to reach the
point where "what is evil" seemed quite unalloyed with
any ingredients of goodness, and that was the state of
mind in which the *Education* was written. But in writing
it Henry Adams—quite properly, from the stylistic point
of view—simplified, distorted, and misrepresented his own
intellectual and emotional past.

No reader of the *Education* would gather that Adams
had ever entertained any serious hopes for the future,
even in his boyhood days in Quincy. Yet the truth is that
he had oscillated between gloom and the inherited optimism to a far later period than perhaps he himself could
recollect. "As I belong to the class of people who have
great faith in this country," he wrote to Gaskell in 1877,
"and who believe that in another century it will be saying
in its turn the last word of civilisation, I enjoy the expecta-
tion of the coming day." Yet this was written nearly a decade after the period when, according to his later fable,
the evil spectacle of Grantism had disabused him once for
all of any dreams for the republic. Four years later still,
when Garfield lay dying of an assassin's bullet, Adams was
undismayed by the prospect: "Luckily," he wrote to
Wayne MacVeagh, "we are a democracy and a sound one.
Nothing can shake society with us, now that slavery is

gone." Nor did he limit himself, in these sanguine views of his mid-forties, to the American future; at least at moments he was still capable of extending them to the human outlook generally. "There are some difficulties," he said to Gaskell, "in the path of all pessimistic reasoning which make its conclusions doubtful, and for some centuries yet may seem to confute its truth. Man is still going fast upward."

These years of the early eighties in Washington with his wife and their small circle of intimates, engrossed as he was with his great *History*, were happy years in Adams's life, and his happiness sometimes expresses itself quite directly in his correspondence. Clearly one has to see the unrelieved nihilism of his old age as the product of more than purely intellectual or historical influences: of course the social disasters of the nineties played their role in inducing it, and so, too, did the intensifying pressure upon Adams's mind of developments in the physical sciences and technology. But the strictly personal dimension cannot be left out, and the letters would tell one, if nothing else did, that the final tipping of the balance of his mind to the side of darkness was as much the consequence of personal tragedy as it was of historical decay. What his wife's suicide did to Adams was to destroy for good all the capacity he had ever had for reading the auguries cheerfully.

It did that, and at the same time it confirmed in him all the somber views he had ever taken of man's status in a soulless multiverse and especially in the multiverse of the approaching twentieth century. For it is quite true that such views had presented themselves to his mind at an early hour: in that sense the *Education* is faithful to the biographical reality. There was obviously some inner bias, very youthfully acquired, toward the darker hues of the philosophic spectrum, and one can only guess at its emotional origins—at the possibility of some obscure early injury inflicted by the necessarily exaggerated role of the father in the whole Adams order of things. A man is not with impunity the son, the grandson, and the great-grandson of a series of masterful "chiefs," and what Henry Adams may have suffered under all this is at least dimly suggested by the belatedness of his marriage, the tragedy in which it ended, and the slightly hysterical quality of his cult, in old age, of the Virgin and the Feminine Principle generally. Something of this nature was surely the emotional seedbed in which the disenchantments of Darwinism and the frustrations of Grantism could put down their roots so deep and sprout so rankly as they did.

The young Henry Adams did not need either Darwin or Grant to inspire black thoughts in his heart: Abraham Lincoln was still President, and Adams had probably not yet drunk deep of Darwinism, when, writing to Henry Lee Higginson from London, he broke out: "Meanwhile I only hope that your life won't be such an eternal swindle as most life is." And it was probably not on either scientific or political grounds that, five years later, back in Washington, he confessed in a letter to Gaskell that, even if in a few years he should have made a great reputation for himself, he would not be prepared to say what it was really worth: "The sad truth is that I want nothing and life seems to have no purpose."

The vibrations one detects in such utterances are those of an essentially personal dejection. Yet a merely private woefulness is no more characteristic of Adams's mind in his twenties than in his sixties, and already in the early letters one finds him speculating in the most impersonal terms on the nature of the world system—so evidently not a Unitarian one—that contemporary knowledge seemed more and more to be evoking. If the letters of his early and middle life reveal that he then had far higher hopes than he would later have confessed to, they also reveal how early he had arrived, tentatively anyway, at some of the grimmer conceptions that were to be characteristic of his latest thought. Something like a mechanistic theory of nature and of history had long been in his mind. "The truth is," he writes in 1863, "everything in this universe has its regular waves and tides. Electricity, sound, the wind, and I believe every part of organic nature will be brought some day within this law. But my philosophy teaches me, and I firmly believe it, that the laws which govern animated beings will be ultimately found to be at bottom the same with those which rule inanimate nature, and . . . I am quite ready to receive with pleasure any basis for a systematic conception of it all."

It was more than thirty years after he wrote these sentences that Adams got round to Willard Gibbs and Lord Kelvin, to the Law of Phase and the Second Law of Thermodynamics; but it is evident how long his mind had been wholly prepared for them. And not even at the end was he to take an essentially bitterer view of the doom to which science was hurrying mankind than he had taken in 1862: "Man has mounted science," he then wrote, "and is now run away with. I firmly believe that before many centuries more, science will be the master of man. The engines he will have invented will be beyond his strength to control. Some day science may have the existence of mankind in its power, and the human race commit suicide by blowing up the world." In 1910 he was saying not "may" but "will," and he was saying it with a gloomy eloquence of manner he had not commanded in his twenties. He was speaking, too, as one has to recognize, in the ghastly light of more evidence than there had been at hand in 1862. But he was giving voice to fears that, in one guise or another, had long tormented him.

This is not to say that there was no development what-ever in Adams's intellectual life but only that the development was more continuous (as well as more contradictory) than the reader who limits himself to the late and best-known books is likely to guess. And it is certainly not to say that his intellectual interests were limited to these large historical and philosophical matters: no reader of the *Education* would suppose that they were, but only a reader of the letters will quite realize how great was the variety of ideas to which at one time or another Adams turned his mind, or with what agility and boldness his mind played over most of them. Now it is the shallow careerism of Alexander Hamilton, now the particular place of sex in Japanese life, now the vulgar mercantile quality of the architecture of the Valois and Touraine. He glances at Anglo-Saxon poetry, and his quick, offhand remarks might have come from a literary critic of genius; he animadverts on the evolution of finance capital, and seems to have given most of his life to the problem; he finds himself reflecting on the unself-consciousness of his father and that whole generation of New Englanders, and suggests in half a dozen sentences a sustained and searching essay in psychological history. Meanwhile he has been willful, petulant, illiberal, and superficial at a hundred points; he has ridden a few hobbies—and even a few phrases (his "gold bugs," for example)—to the brink of prostration and over; he has obstinately shut his eyes to every manifestation of new life that he does not wish to consider, and allowed his prophetic catastrophism to waste and weaken itself in senile hysteria. It has all mattered relatively little to the responsive reader: the foibles of a first-rate mind are always a small price to pay for its real fruits, and among the fruits of Adams's mind his letters come very close, at the least, to holding first place.

JAMES WHITCOMB RILEY

THE PLACID INTERVAL

TO ANY ONE who was born and schooled in Indiana at any time between the administration of General Harrison (of Indianapolis) and the Vice-Presidency of Tom Marshall (of Columbia City), the name of James Whitcomb Riley will evoke a whole cluster of private recollections. Various "Riley Days" in successive Octobers, when the usual educational routine was suspended for special exercises and early dismissal, will be lively in his memory; and household allusions that never gained wide currency will pop into his mind when he comes upon that familiar name. Almost all Americans will "react," and many of them with a groan, to the name of little Orphant Annie; but probably it is only the native son who will recall the Little Cousin Jasper who so fortunately lived in Rensselaer—

> Wisht 'at his folks they'd move *here*,
> An' *we'd* move to Rensselaer!—

or Herbert Graham, the spoiled child, with his reccurent and often inopportune query, "Wuz *I* there, Ma?" Uncle Sidney and the Doodle-Bugs, the Little Man in the Tin

Shop, the Boy Lives on Our Farm—personages from whose whimsicality an adult taste would doubtless revolt —are indistinguishable in memory from the authentic heroes of legend and romance. Yet were they not invented by the writer who also maintained that

> The world is full of roses,
> And the roses full of dew,
> And the dew is full of heavenly love
> That drips for me and you?

And is not the Riley who wrote that stanza the Riley whose name is a hissing and a reproach on the lips of a later, more judicious generation?

Well, he is certainly not a writer who is ever again likely to command the esteem of critical minds as he once commanded the esteem of men like Longfellow and Lowell, Kipling and Irving, J. C. Harris and R. W. Gilder. The limitations of his period lay heavily upon him, and they were reinforced by the special limitations of his own intelligence and insight. Now that Professor Phelps has edited and published Riley's letters, one is reminded afresh of the man's suspended intellectual development, his chronic boyishness, his incuriosity, his largely empty optimism, his lazy sentimentality, and the promiscuity of his approvals. The poet who revered the name of Longfellow, but who boggled at Poe because "his influence [was] always cheerless," and "was unable," according to Professor Phelps, "to see anything in Walt Whitman," betrayed an intellectual shallowness that posterity can hardly forgive him for. "Of the general trend of society and social movements," Mr. Meredith Nicholson has said, "he was as unconscious as if he were on another planet"; and, after reading these letters, if not before, one finds it easy to credit the statement. Did ever a talented writer leave a body of correspondence more nearly devoid of acute comment or tonic judgments or the fruits of meditation? Were letters ever more consistently and tediously genial, cheery, and complacent? "Sometime everything will be right," he said in an early letter to his brother. "I feel surer of this each day that dawns and dies away." And, to the end of his life, neither personal griefs nor public calamities could jolt him out of this easy faith. The letters to Eugene Debs are in exactly the vein of the letters to Bill Nye; and, beyond that observation, the indictment of Riley need hardly go.

Yet nothing could be less necessary than to explain to the world what Riley's limitations were as a man and a poet: they are gross and palpable; they have been pointed out a thousand times; the jejune lyrist of "That Old Sweetheart of Mine" is now the orthodox Riley of the textbook and the class room. The dignity of American letters will never be threatened by an uncritical revival of his reputation. Is it possible that he deserves to be remembered a little, nevertheless? Are the ten volumes of his collected works a monument to anything but our deplorable past? Though it has become a heterodoxy to say so, I believe the answer must be Yes. In spite of Orphant Annie and the Old Sweetheart, I believe there is something modestly memorable in Riley's verse.

II

There was a period in American history, especially in the Middle West, which I have ventured to call the Placid Interval; it was a period that cried out for a true folk-poet, and, though the prayer was not too liberally answered, it was answered after a fashion by the offer of J. W. Riley.

For a decade or so before the Civil War, and for twenty-five or thirty years after it, there was a kind of lull in the swift rush of Middle Western life—a lull which we can now see to have been illusory enough, but which in retrospect has a charm, I think, legitimately sentimental. It was the sunny interlude—the *apparently* sunny interlude—between the rigors of pioneering and the ravages of industrialism, between the malarial swamp and the filling-stations of the continental motor highways; there was a moment or two when American social life really had, especially among the middle classes of the villages and small cities, a flavor and a homely grace like the social life of European provinces. It had a darker side, of course, this ingenuous culture, and I should be the last to argue that it was ever very rich or very deeply humane; but it was richer and more humane than the high-pressure civilization that obliterated it so efficiently, and we should be far enough away from it now not to feel the need of resentment and apology.

Of that culture, at any rate, Riley was exclusively the product; and, from the vantage-point of our harsher and less innocent age, we should be able to forgive him for idyllicizing it. From one point of view that life was indeed, in a quaint prosaic way, idyllic; and Riley, who had played more than one instrument in the town band, who had painted signs for druggists on straggling country fences, who had travelled in the spirit of a wandering mountebank with a vagabond medicine-show, who had mingled with the crowds of county fairs, and circuses and Fourth of July celebrations and Old Home Week, who had recited poems in many an Armory and Memorial Hall, who was only a few years too young to be a "veteran" and a member of the G. A. R., but who certainly had heard countless tales of "durin' the army,"—Riley, I say, was sent by Providence to be the voice of this age in the simple poetry of folk sentiment and folk humor. He might have been even its Hans Sachs, its Burns, its Nekrassov; and this, of course, he never became. His best is far from being so good as that. But he came closer to it than he has latterly been credited with doing. The letters show that he had a surprisingly clear sense of his role as a poet of the people, and a conscious purpose in avoiding bookishness and erudition and the exotic. "Poetry," he wrote to Madison Cawein, "should be as direct in statement as prose"; and he advised more than one versifying correspondent to eschew the stale archaism of conventional poetic language. Surviving from an age of which the literary staples were Aldrich's fake Orientalism and Stedman's fake "grand manner," there is something one would like to be able to call Virgilian in the countrified freshness of such verses as these:

> What We want, as I sense it, in the line
> O' poetry, is somepin' Yours and Mine—
> Somepin' with live-stock in it, and out-doors,
> And old crick-bottoms, snags, and sycamores;
> Putt weeds in—pizen-vines, and underbresh,
> As well as johnny-jump-ups, all so fresh
> And sassy-like!—and groun'-squir'ls,—yes, and "We,"
> As sayin' is,—"We, Us, and Company!" . . .
> No "Ladies' Amaranth" ner "Treasury" book
> Ner "Night Thoughts," nuther—ner no "Lally Rook"!

In one of his earliest poems, "The Ginoine Ar-ticle," he had said:

> What people want is facts, I apperhend;
>   And naked Natur is the thing to give
> Your writin' bottom, eh?

By "facts," alas, he unconsciously meant a limited order of phenomena; and "naked Natur" was never to thrust her bawdy presence into his verse; but it is something that he should have seen as clearly as this where his real strength lay.

For he has had the ill luck to be remembered for his feeblest and trashiest sentimentalities, not for the twenty or thirty poems in true and pungent dialect in which he showed himself—but ever so modestly!—the homespun Chaucer of the Placid Interval. One would like to see a deep pit dug for the burial of Annie the Orphant and the Old Sweetheart, and a little unpretentious corner in American literature reserved for two or three of John Hay's "Pike County Ballads," a score of Riley's rhymed sketches of Hoosier characters, and a few of his sentimental verses redeemed by their dash of bucolic humor. I am thinking of such characters—American equivalents of the Franklin and the Plowman—as Erasmus Wilson and Mylo Jones's Wife, Doc Sifers and Tradin' Joe, Jap Miller and Old John Henry. The last named, certainly:

> He's stove up some with the rheumatiz,
> And they hain't no shine on them shoes o' his,
> And his hair hain't cut—but his eye-teeth is:
>   Old John Henry!
> He feeds hisse'f when the stock's all fed—
>   Old John Henry—
> And sleeps like a babe when he goes to bed—
> And dreams o' Heaven and home-made bread,
>   Says Old John Henry.

I should like to see a place saved for such racy sentimentalities as "Griggsby's Station" ("Back where we ust to be so happy an' so pore") and "The Old Band" ("What's come of Eastman, and Nat Snow? And where's War Barnett at?") and "Down to the Capital" (where Old Flukens, Congressman from "our deestrick," lived in a building "bigger'n Masonic Hall"). There is a handful of narrative poems—"Armazindy" and "Man by the Name of Bolus" and "Tugg Martin"—so highly flavored with the manners and speech of post bellum Indiana, and even so exceptionally and dangerously close (for Riley) to "naked Natur," that they retain a curious mild charm; and, if poetry about children has ever any literary value, surely some of Riley's less well-known poems in this order have it. It was his reward for never growing up, of course, that he could so easily identify himself with the experience of small boys; and the loss, needless to say, was greater than the reward; but at least it may be worth observing that he kept the humorous tang of boyhood as well as its mental simplicity. "The Old Tramp" and "The Fishing Party" and "Our Hired Girl" and a few other poems do something to compensate for the *niaiseries* of "The Happy Little Cripple" and so many others.

III

To say all this is by no means to say that important critical issues are at stake: I am far from intending to represent Riley as one of those fine unappreciated or misappreciated writers of whom certainly we have had our share. The complete loss to the world of what he wrote could hardly be made out a major calamity. Scientists are given to speaking of an order of speculation and investigation which they call pre-science; and the sort of thing Riley went in for, even the best of it, might be defined as pre-literature. He was not even, as I say, a folk poet of the truest distinction: nothing that he wrote is capable, as the best of Burns is, of existing for its own sake in the general memory, independent of the accidents of time and place. His mind had neither the range nor the concentration, neither the rich expansiveness nor the intense precision, that are as essential to the writer of great popular poetry as to any other. And, even on his own terms, though he spoke much in his letters of the labor of the file, he was a careless, slipshod writer, too easily satisfied with the "good enough" in expression. Riley's verse is exactly the kind that does depend on the accidents of time and place. Its interest, like that of the Currier and Ives prints, is the interest of sentimental reminiscence; its "tender quality," which Lowell praised, is the tender quality of old tintypes or the melody of "O Susanna" or the illiterate domestic architecture—the cast-iron stags, even! —of the Hayes and Garfield era. One would go back and reread "Griggsby's Station" or "Armazindy" largely because one's forbears were fellow citizens of General Harrison or Tom Marshall, which is to say that one's motives would be typically extra-literary. It is the American desire, of course, in the thick of so crazy a present to have a "past" as firm as may be beneath one's feet; to affiliate oneself locally and personally with whatever forces may once have worked toward something besides business success and technical efficiency. In Riley's time men still knew how to loaf; he was himself a loafer of genius, and his "poetry" is the poetry of boyish indolence, of lazy truancy. In his restricted way, he was in favor of living, and not much in favor of getting ahead; and that is what I believe gives him, and the Placid Interval he wrote for, a certain claim even now on our regard.

HAMLIN GARLAND

RE-TRAVELLED ROADS

EVERYONE AGREES, I suppose, that *A Son of the Middle Border* is one of the most revealing autobiographies written by an American in our time: to writers, especially, this record of the beginnings of a literary career under the least auspicious of circumstances must long be certain to have the most vivid interest. Of that book Mr. Garland himself was very properly the central figure, and of course he left himself at the end on the threshold of maturity. Now, at the age of nearly seventy, he has written reminiscently rather of the famous men and women, chiefly writers, with whom he was thrown in the period of his twenties and thirties.* Needless to say, *Roadside Meetings* is very far from being another *Son of the Middle Border:* Mr. Garland is not lifted and hurried and made eloquent by his subject as he was there, and he is not the ideal writer of literary recollections. Temperamentally he has neither the humor nor the melancholy that would give a sharply personal tone to his recollections of an eclipsed epoch: his manner is too pedestrian, too imperturbably matter-of-fact, to render with their full value these memories of encounters with the great. And, from one point of

* *Roadside Meetings,* by Hamlin Garland.

view, his deep-seated ingenuousness is a real deficiency: the people he writes about are viewed at the very shortest of critical distances, and the literary stirrings of the eighties and nineties are seen in extraordinarily little perspective.

Yet, from another point of view, this is of course something of an advantage; we should be grateful to have Mr. Garland's "second thoughts," but if we had them we should miss what we could less easily replace for ourselves. As it is, *Roadside Meetings* gives us the period pretty much as it saw itself. Very nearly the whole of it is represented in this book: did anyone else of Mr. Garland's generation know more or less well so many of the American writers who filled the interval between the Civil War and the end of the century? Could any one else tell us at once so much about Howells, so much about Crane, and so much about Riley? Joaquin Miller and Henry James, Burroughs and Bret Harte, Sarah Orne Jewett and Mark Twain—they are all here in glimpses or long views, and always with at least a stroke or two of sober characterization. The author of *Main Travelled Roads* may be unbrokenly prosaic as a recorder, but there is a compensating literalness of truth in his portraits; there are glimpses here that, if I am not mistaken, no other writer about the period has ever given us.

And, whether it is in the subject itself, or an outcome of Mr. Garland's long training in the use of dingy materials, a prevailing grayness lies over all but a few patches of this territory. Were the personal lives of American writers in those days so generally arid as Mr. Garland, in his wholly unsentimental way, succeeds in making them out to have been? One speculates whether the effect can be deliberate, and is inclined to think it is not; there is nothing to suggest that any contrast with these lives has ever taken hold of Mr. Garland's imagination; he describes them, as I say, on their own terms. But could a series of literary pictures be more cheerless, even more elegiac, than this series which begins with the aged Whitman at Camden in the midst of poverty, disorder, and grime, and ends with Henry James at Rye revising his earlier books for posterity—"if people ever take the trouble to look into my books"?

> The mixture of Europe and America which you see in me [he said to Garland], has proved disastrous. It has made of me a man who is neither American nor European. I have lost touch with my own people, and I live here alone. My neighbors are friendly, but they are not of my blood, except remotely. As a man grows old he feels these conditions more than when he is young. I shall never return to the United States, but I wish I could.

"No, I shall never go back," the white-haired and decayed Bret Harte had said to him in London a few days earlier. "Sometimes I wish I had never come away." No record could be more distressing, in a peculiarly sharp way, than the whole latter half of *The Letters of Bret Harte,* published a few years ago; and the glimpse of that wrecked and stranded celebrity in Mr. Garland's few paragraphs, confirms the impression most memorably.

So it is with many of the others: the aged Lowell lecturing on English dramatists to bored and dwindling audiences at the Lowell Institute ("bending low over his paper and peering closely at it as though the light were poor or his glasses dim," going "monotonously on in a mumbling rumble"); Stephen Crane drifting about with his sallow complexion, his cough, his cigarette-stained hands, and his shabbiness; Henry B. Fuller living in obscurity and indigence in Chicago, "wandering through the ugly West

Side parks or surveying raw suburban developments, a small, lonely figure walking swiftly but eccentrically along weed-grown avenues"; Stedman complaining continually of overwork and grumbling about his duties at the Stock Exchange as "mere gambling"; Joel Chandler Harris at his desk in the office of the Atlanta *Constitution*, inveighing against the South as "a region without mental stir, unkempt and unenterprising"; they do not make a group of very gaily-colored portraits, these men of letters of the gilded age. Even the Millers and the Rileys—with all their bravado, all their careful drollery—do not really turn luminous at Mr. Garland's touch; they burn, at the best, somewhat smokily. But, whoever is to be "blamed" for that, Mr. Garland is certainly not the man: he has told what he saw and heard with praiseworthy plainness and fidelity; and, even if it is an effect he did not calculate, he has written a book that incites to considerable reflection on the quality of the society of which he has recorded one aspect.

MISCELLANEOUS

COUNTERFEIT PRESENTMENTS

EVERYONE KNOWS—we owe the knowledge to a hundred travelers and anthropologists—how intensely the "primitive man" feels on the subject of having his portrait painted or his picture taken—and how alarmingly he sometimes acts. Is it possible that such feelings survive in our civilized psyche in some unconfessed and deeply buried guise? The history of Western portrait-painting since the early Renaissance would hardly suggest such a thought, and just as little would the prosperous history of the portrait photographer since the days of Daguerre and Draper. Sir James Frazer tells us that the Tepehuanes of Mexico were once panic-stricken by the prospect of having a camera turned on them, and that, when at last they agreed to pose, it was with the conviction that death or some other great evil would follow. And indeed he alleges that even in western Scotland, in the nineteenth century, there were persons who refused to have their likenesses taken in the fear that such pictures might ruin their luck or their health. Is the distance between ourselves—contemporaries of Steichen and Weston—and the Tepehuanes or the western Scots so great as we commonly imagine?

Perhaps it is, but if so it is not because we are not, in our own manner, obsessed with the idea of the portrait. The almost mysterious formulas which prescribe, in any given age, the recurrence of favorite words or images in titles, betray this fact. Everyone, surely, has observed how often the very word "portrait" or some word like it has echoed and reechoed through the titles of our recent literature. To go, for the moment, no further backward, it has been a favorite ever since, in the early eighties, Henry James published *The Portrait of a Lady*. Walter Pater was close on James's heels, in 1887, with *Imaginary Portraits*, and then very quickly came Oscar Wilde with *The Portrait of Mr. W. H.* and of course *The Picture of Dorian Gray*. Since Wilde's time we have had a novel by Ford Madox Ford entitled simply *The Portrait*, the *Portrait of the Artist as a Young Man*, Mr. Eliot's poem ("Portrait of a Lady"), a poem of Ezra Pound's ("Portrait d'une femme"), Mr. Dylan Thomas's *Portrait of the Artist as a Young Dog*— and who can say how many other "portraits" and "pictures" in the titles of lesser writers than these? Does not all this suggest a singular preoccupation on our part with the "counterfeit presentment"?

For of course the titles tell by no means all the story or indeed the more interesting part of it. What is far more striking than these verbal echoes is the active, the essential, the "symbolic" role that pictures of all kinds, and portraits especially, have played in the fiction of the last century or so. The portrait that is not merely dimly evoked by a title but that, on the contrary, hangs on the wall in a frame, or is being painted by an artist on an easel, and makes its existence felt, sometimes decisively, in the tale— this is the portrait that solicits our attention here. How frequently it has figured in fiction or drama we rarely pause to reflect. A fairly recent instance for the stage, within the memory of all but the youngest theatergoers, is of course John Balderston's play of the twenties, *Berkeley Square;* and the notion for this piece, as most readers remember, was derived from a late and unfinished novel of Henry James's, *The Sense of the Past.*

No writer ever made use of this emblem more richly, more delicately, or with a finer witchery of interfused "reality" and uncanniness. Readers of James's fragmentary novel will remember the young American, a twentieth-century Man of Feeling, with a deeply imaginative "sense of the past," who falls heir to an ancestral townhouse in London and who finds there the singular portrait of a youth of George the Fourth's period—singular because the face of the young man is *turned away* from the puzzled onlooker. The thought forces itself on Ralph Pendrel that, when unobserved, the portrayed figure is quite capable of turning about and facing outward, in the familiar fashion; and indeed, as it eventuates, the youth in the picture proves to be capable of stepping bodily out of the frame itself, helping himself to a lighted candle, and coming to meet Ralph Pendrel as he returns, with his own taper, to the room in which the portrait hangs. The young man of 1820 turns out to have a passion of curiosity about the future which matches Ralph's own passion for the past, and the two inevitably make an exchange of epochs. In doing so, as James's notes indicate, they were only to confirm the disquieting premonitions which had visited the painter of the portrait himself.

Did ever a portrait behave so, so oddly and also so impressively, in literature before? The answer is, yes, again and again. Portraits had been behaving in this manner in European and American fiction for the better part of two centuries before James set to work on his never-to-be-completed novel. Like so many motives in literature,

James's mysteriously animated portrait comes at the end of a long series, not at its beginning. A glance at a few of this ancestral portrait's own ancestors will only fortify our respect for James's art, and perhaps have a curious interest of its own.

The subject is only one aspect of a much more inclusive one, the appearance of works of art generally in literature. That is a subject which has almost literally no beginning and is not likely to have a very early end. If one cast one's net only wide enough to take in written and not oral literature, one would doubtless have to begin with the shield of Achilles in the *Iliad*, once so familiar to at least a few schoolboys; one would not be able to pass over the pictured scenes from the Trojan War, painted on the temple walls of Carthage, which move Aeneas so deeply in the first book of the *Aeneid* (*et mentem mortalia tangunt*); and so one would work one's way gradually down to our own time and to the Botticellis and the Vermeers of which Proust made such beautiful use in *Remembrance of Things Past*. It would be a question of taking in not only pictures but statues as well, statues which also come to life, like the statue in Mérimée's famous *conte, La Vénus d'Ille*—the "source" of which can be tracked down through all the winding corridors of literary history to the dusky regions of folklore.

The same thing is true even when we limit ourselves to the narrower subject of portraits; in any collection of fairy-stories or folk-tales, one is bound to stumble sooner or later on this motif—on the notion that an individual's image can, under certain circumstances, come to life, and behave in any one of various uncanny ways which suggest a magical identification with the individual himself. The portraits of the Virgin or of various saints which, in medieval folklore, are represented as weeping or bleeding or leaving their shrines, belong unmistakably to the primordial line of which I am speaking; they are an obvious example of what folklorists call Magic Objects, and it is only because they represent individual human beings that they interest us here so much more than the bleeding branches or the speaking reeds which belong to the same broad category.

In any case, we can hardly set out on a treasure hunt through oral and written literature for painted likenesses. I am broaching only the smaller question of portraits and their use in the fiction of the last century or two. Just when these particular works of art first made their appearance, I do not know and will not undertake to say; let us assume for convenience that at least a very early example of the Romantic portrait is that grim likeness of Prince Manfred's grandfather which, in Horace Walpole's stagey little novel, *The Castle of Otranto,* steps down out of its frame and, to Manfred's consternation, stalks with a melancholy air out of the apartment in which it has been hanging. Whether it is really the very first of our modern line or not, Walpole's picture did surely indicate that the ancient emblem was about to take on a new life; the "Gothic" portrait had arrived on the scene, and a peculiarly modern quality of feeling, a peculiarly modern nuance of the poetic, the complex, the equivocal, was about to attach itself to the old motif.

It very soon became evident that Gothic or Romantic writers were going to find the portrait a device quite as irresistible to them as music or musical instruments. Mrs. Radcliffe's novels abound in mysterious miniatures which end by revealing unsuspected identities; there is a beautiful and sinister portrait in the famous shocker, *The Monk,* by M. G. Lewis, which becomes an emblem of sensual and demoniac beauty; and perhaps the most memorable of them all is the terrible picture with the frightening eyes which young John Melmoth, in Maturin's *Melmoth the Wanderer*, finds hanging in his uncle's closet and burns to ashes after his uncle's death.

No one of these portraits behaves in quite what could be called a frankly magical manner; there were plenty that did—though sometimes to the effect merely of charm or comedy, as in Gautier's witty story, *Omphale*, in which the picture of a lovely eighteenth-century marchioness comes to life for the amorous benefit of a young Parisian of a later epoch. Nor does the preternatural power reside always in the painted image itself; it is sometimes a question rather of supernormal insight or divination on the part of the artist. What must be a rather early embodiment of this long-lived theme is one of E. T. A. Hoffmann's tales, *Doge und Dogaressa:* what happens here is that a nineteenth-century painter represents in a painting two genuinely historical personages, Marino Faliero and his young bride, and quite without consciously intending to do so, imparts to the young Dogaressa's countenance an expression which is subtly premonitory of the fate that, unbeknown to the artist, did in fact befall her. The painting has revealed much more of the truth than the painter himself, in any literal sense, could have "known."

Portraits which take on a magical animation, portraits which speak of an otherwise unsuspected reality—these are two of the kinds of portraits which adorn the walls of Romantic fiction; a third is the portrait which mysteriously exercises a baleful and even a fatal influence either on the painter himself or on the sitter or on some third personage who falls under its spell. There can be few more intense expressions of this theme than a story of Gogol's called simply "The Portrait," a story in which a young painter's career is ravaged and wrecked by the mere possession of a portrait—for its subject, an evil old money-lender, is a symbol of low ambition and worldly avarice.

How often the emblem may appear in the minor Russian writers I cannot say; it was certainly a favorite with our own Gothic and Romantic writers in America. Everyone will recall the young painter in Poe's tale, "The Oval Portrait," who, in a "dark high turret-chamber where the light dripped upon the pale canvas only from overhead," paints a portrait of his young and lovely bride, which, stroke by stroke as he paints it, steals from the girl a portion of her vitality, so that at the moment when it is finished, she herself expires, having imparted to the picture the substance of her life. Like the picture of Dorian Gray—the most celebrated of all these works of art—this portrait of Poe's is a kind of inverse example of what folklorists call the Life-Token, the magic object which is vitally identified with an individual, so that it flourishes with his health and withers with his illness and dies with his death; which may even *bring on* his death if it is blighted or cut down.

The American writer for whom, even more than for James, the portrait was to be highly characteristic, was Hawthorne; but Melville, too, rather unexpectedly, turns up with a very curious example in *Pierre*. There is a likeness in Hawthorne's tale, "The Prophetic Pictures," which, in the style of Hoffmann's, anticipates more of the tragic future than even the painter himself could rationally have foreseen; and in "Edward Randolph's Portrait" the picture of the wicked governor is "rumored" to have "started from the wall, and spoken face to face" with one of his successors at a crisis in the colony's history. Most familiarly of all, in *The House of the Seven Gables*, the grim old seventeenth-century portrait of Colonel Pyncheon, hanging on the wall of the room in which he died, "seemed to sym-

bolize an evil influence, and so darkly to mingle the
shadow of [its] presence with the sunshine of the passing
hour, that no good thoughts or purposes could ever spring
up and blossome there." In *Pierre* the so-called chair portrait, a likeness of Pierre's father as a youth, "seems to
say" a whole series of things to Pierre as he sits gazing at it
in the little room where, at his mother's insistence, he has
hung it out of the way; there "seems" to lurk "some mystical
intelligence and vitality" in it; and when Pierre sets fire
to it—disenchanted as he is about his father—it stares
tormentedly at him in beseeching horror. It is an all but
literally animated portrait, and it plays a conspicuous role
in this somewhat Radcliffean novel.

Such are a few of the most striking and memorable likenesses among the many in which modern fiction, from
Horace Walpole to Henry James, has abounded. The
chances are, I suspect, that with the revival of something
like the Gothic manner in our fiction, the old symbol will
reappear, from time to time, in a fresh and unhackneyed
embodiment. Meanwhile, one cannot help wondering why
it has recurred so frequently as it has already done, and
just what the secret is not only of its curious beauty but
of its troublous, equivocal effect upon the fancy. For certainly, in the hands of a genuinely imaginative writer, a
portrait that behaves as if it were a living man or woman
ceases to be a mere pleasing work of the pictorial art; it
troubles us with a sense that the ordinary limits of conscious and rational experience have been well overpassed;
that some deeper and darker levels of existence have been
penetrated, and, their mysterious waters stirred.

Naturally, as I need not say, every appearance of an
emblem like this, in serious writing, is in a certain sense
unique, and no ingenious interpretation will fit every case
like a glove. The chances are, nevertheless, that a common

strand, however slight it may be, will run through and unite a hundred appearances of such an obsessive symbol as this has proved to be; and here, I believe, we have a clue to that common strand in Freud's remarkable essay on "The Uncanny." The point of this essay is that the word "uncanny" does not apply to all frightening things whatever, but only to the kind of things that not only frighten us but carry us back to something long known to us, something once familiar but "forgotten" with the lapse of time, buried below the drifting accumulations of later experience, or actually repressed by an inner censor which cannot allow them to obtrude into consciousness directly. Infantile wishes and fears are among these forgotten things, but so, too, according to Freud, are all those primitive beliefs, superstitions, and terrors which civilized men imagine themselves long since to have surmounted, but which lurk nevertheless in the obscure recesses of the psyche; beliefs which, though they may never emerge into the conscious daylight, are always with us, and can always be evoked, however disguised, by the imagery of a poem or a tale.

If Freud is right, then the uncanniness of the animated portrait is an admirable case in point. For certainly no primitive conviction could be deeper-rooted or more widespread than the "superstition" that lies in ambush just below the rich and dusky literary surface we have been examining. It is the superstition I began by alluding to. Primitive people, almost universally, are said to believe that every individual has a soul, but that this soul is by no means an impalpable and, as we should say, spiritual entity; it is a very palpable and substantial thing, a tiny man within a man, which resembles the individual himself in everything but its size, and in sleep or trance or illness, and of course in death, can take its leave of the body. This is the Separable Soul of anthropological lore, and belief in it accounts for a thousand fears of which primitive man is a victim; for of course if the soul can detach itself from the body, or be malignantly detached from it, the direst results may follow. It may fail to get back into the body when the man awakes; it may fall into the hands of enemies; it may sicken and die. And all these dangers are multiplied and intensified by the equally well-established "fact" that a man's shadow, his reflection, his effigy, or portrait may all be identified with his soul—separable from him in the same way and exposed to all the same risks and terrors.

No wonder primitive men attempt to defend their shadows against being trodden on or struck; no wonder they avoid gazing at their own reflections in pools and mirrors; no wonder they threaten and sometimes assault the civilized visitors who try to paint their portraits or take their pictures with cameras. And perhaps it is not surprising that vestiges of these beliefs have survived among the peasantry of Europe and in remote corners of America even into our own time. Nor is it odd that the Gothic, the Romantic imagination, which reevoked and (so to say) transliterated so much of the imagery of folklore, should have found itself peculiarly captivated by the symbol of the portrait—the symbol that fused in one whole the beauty and the grace of the civilized aesthetic and the darkness, the fearfulness, the primordial anxieties of an immemorial conviction. We literate moderns have no conscious belief whatever in a Separable Soul; most of us do not even know that our forebears once had such a belief; but the notion is by no means so far behind us as we should like to suppose. It joins hands, moreover, with an awareness which each of us does have in some degree or other, the awareness that our individuality is very far from being the simple unity it superficially appears to be, that just below the surface we are divided, confused, multifarious, and discordant, and that we do indeed have other selves, if not separable selves, besides the self in whose name we legally function. The uncanny ambiguousness of being an individual—the sense of this is a sense which, on the irrational level, primitive man and modern man share between them, and for both of them it is a perplexity and a source of pain. Of this perilous dualism or multiplicity the romantic portrait is an admirable symbol.

CONSTANCE ROURKE

THALIA AMERICANA

IT IS A MIGHTY subject, this of American humor: a subject one conceives of as approachable from ever so many unsuspected angles; and it could hardly have fallen, for the moment, into better hands than Miss Rourke's.* For one thing, it is not easy to think of many writers capable at once of her industry and of her skill, of her patience in research and her lucidity in exposition: in a word, of her balanced competence. *American Humor* is an erudite book: it is chock full of what are called "materials"; but among a thousand such it is the one book that stands on its own legs, and allows you, in spite of everything, to see the wood as well as the trees. But this is not all, or indeed the best, that one can say of it. Literary competence is one thing, and gifted insight is another; and what chiefly gratifies a reader of Miss Rourke's is her sense of the many dimensions in her subject, the free play of her mind over more than a few of its aspects: particularly, her recognition that the problem must be constantly referred to psychology and constantly posed against a background of social history. Humor not simply as a formal entity, a literary

* *American Humor: A Study of the National Character,* by Constance Rourke.

245

mode, but humor envisaged dynamically as the product
of personal needs and social conflicts, the expression of a
whole people's ambitions and disappointments and joy in
in achievement: such is the subject of her book as Miss
Rourke apprehends it. The subtitle is modestly definitive.

The whole question, as I say, is an infinitely engaging
one. Notoriously, we have been and are—other men than
Americans have said we are—a humorous people. A baby,
it appears, begins laughing only after many weeks of crying or of impassiveness; and our seventeenth, even our
eighteenth, century was in this respect infantile; but once
our career of guffawing began it was uninterrupted and,
in our own eyes, brilliant. If ever the comic spirit has had
free rein, one would say, it has been in America. Yet has
it—after all? At any rate, how many reservations, on reflection, one has to make! Granted that Americans have
laughed continuously and loud, what kind of laughter has
it been? How much of it, for example, has been that
"thoughtful laughter" which, according to Meredith's
familiar formula, is the basis of true comedy? How much
of it has been the rich and heady *Gelächter* of those who,
according to Nietzsche, "can at once laugh and be elevated"? Extraordinarily little, perhaps. With all our jolli-
ness, we have had no fine comedy in the theatre, though
we have excelled in burlesque; and, unless in the last few
years, we have found little place in our letters for genuine
satire. The fact of these defaults is of course a commonplace. It has been less observed, perhaps, that with all our
popular humorists or polite wits we have had no great
humorous literature of the sort in which the sense of the
ridiculous, deepened and purified and enriched, becomes
the mainspring of what is virtually poetry: no Aristoph-
anes, I mean, no Apuleius, no Chaucer, no Rabelais, no
Cervantes, no Gogol. Set beside such writing our best

literary humor is either tenuous or brutal, either lacking in body or lacking in tenderness; and, in this light, we seem to have vacillated between the prim and the bitter, between Oliver Wendell Holmes and Ambrose Bierce. Even Mark Twain, unlike those others, distrusted or misunderstood the poet that was in him; and this keeps him from being a true exception to the rule.

To say all this is not to belittle Miss Rourke's subject: on the contrary, it is to make some attempt at suggesting why the subject is so peculiarly fascinating. Without great comedy or great satire, without a Chaucer or a Gogol, we have nevertheless had a constant preoccupation with the ridiculous; and Miss Rourke, of course, has had to pick and choose among the crowding facts with exacting selectiveness. She has also had the wisdom not to burden herself, in a book so descriptive and appreciative, with a thesis; but she hints at one here and there, and she stimulates her reader to grope toward a generalization of his own. For one cannot fail to be struck by the fact that, as Van Wyck Brooks once said, our humor has been a humor not of extraction but of distraction; that, in other words, our laughter has mostly not been a joyful expression of our whole life, but a way of escaping from it or a way of compensating for its disappointments. The humor of evasion (the "tall tale," the burlesque) and the humor of disillusion (sarcasm, cynicism) have been our favorite forms: it is singular how much of American humor has been intensely and sometimes morosely destructive. And this is probably because we have been generally so unsure of ourselves and so unsure of one another, and have had to invent an illusory security. As a people, we have hung together very imperfectly; and only out of rich and integrated sociality does thoughtful laughter, or tender laughter, or elevated laughter, arise. If the irresponsible fantasies of our early comedy "failed to exhibit subtlety, fineness, balance," says Miss Rourke, "they had created laughter and had served the ends of communication among a people unacquainted with themselves, strange to the land, unshaped as a nation; they had produced a shadowy social coherence." A series of abortive attempts at unity, or of compensations for disunity: such appears to be the truest aspect of American humor.

This is certainly not the "thesis" of her book, as I have said; but it is because Miss Rourke seems to have some such point of reference in mind that one follows her story with an interest so cumulative. That story falls into two pretty sharply distinguished divisions: in the earlier chapters, Miss Rourke concentrates on the anonymous or quasi-anonymous humor of the American people in the early nineteenth century, on the fate of those broad typical comic inventions—the Yankee, the backwoodsman, the Negro: Jack Downing, Davy Crockett, Jim Crow—which were our earliest experiments at a folk mythology of our own; in the later chapters, she deals rather with American letters in the Golden Day and since, so far as they take humorous form or have even a philosophically comic aspect. I am not sure that the cleavage is a perfectly happy one: certainly one could wish that Miss Rourke had given detailed attention to the less strictly literary, the more democratic and journalistic humor of the decades since the Civil War, as she has done to that of the earlier period —could wish so if only because one is so sure of the acuteness with which she would treat it. Not that the later chapters, too, are not full of beautiful interpretations: one would not care to dispense with the passages on Poe and Whitman, on Henry James and Emily Dickinson; and there is a true sense in which Miss Rourke relates these to the theme of comedy. But I think they are less peculiarly her own than the early chapters: *there* she has evoked almost a complete picture, to the fancy, of our early society, with its laconic peddlers, its heroic hunters and gamecocks and flatboatmen, its darkies and strolling comedians and shanty Irish, its expansiveness and its violence and its color. And she has made it far more than a pleasant picture: she has made it a psychological study of a whole society from the point of view of its laughter.

No one who reads the book will fail to be struck by its omissions, and, if they are pointed out, it should not be by way of reproach to Miss Rourke, so much as by way of indicating the unmanageable richness of the subject. I for one could wish that this particular book had been twice as large as it is, so pointed and so pregnant are the interpretations Miss Rourke has in fact found room for. It would be worth a good deal to see what she would make of some of the cracker-box philosophers and lecturers and fashionable funny-men whom, alas, she ignores: I mean Josh Billings, and Eli Perkins, and Bill Nye, and James Whitcomb Riley, and Eugene Field, and Abe Martin. On a larger scale, she could doubtless have found a place for "polite" or genteel humor, the essayists and writers of *vers de société*, who fail to appear: Halleck and Drake and Holmes and Aldrich would certainly have suggested a few significant observations. The omission of both Ambrose Bierce and George Ade seems to me fairly serious. With so much about the early theatre, one would enjoy a parallel chapter on the comic stage, the vaudeville and the "entertainment" since the Civil War. The newspaper humorists of our own generation—B. L. T., F. P. A., Don Marquis, Heywood Broun and Irvin Cobb—are perhaps closer to the heart of the subject than Robinson and Frost and Anderson, whom Miss Rourke deals with instead. There is a true subtlety in her avoiding them, no doubt;

and the loss is perhaps less great than the gain: I should protest heatedly only against one final omission, and that is the figure of Mr. Mencken, certainly one of the two or three most accomplished humorists of his decade. But Miss Rourke has made no claim and implied no claim to being encyclopedic, and one feels that there is a reason behind all these silences: as it stands, her book is every way a notable contribution to the history of American culture.

NEWTON ARVIN

Frederick Newton Arvin (he dropped his first name early in life) was born in Valparaiso, Indiana, on August 25, 1900, and educated in the local schools. From high school he went east to Harvard University, from which he was graduated in 1921, *summa cum laude* and Phi Beta Kappa.

He taught briefly at Detroit Country Day School before accepting an appointment at Smith College in the fall of 1922. With the exception of a leave of absence (1925–1926) when he served as associate editor of *Living Age*, and occasional visiting professorships, Arvin seldom left Smith College for very long, and there he did most of his writing. For a number of years he was a member and director of the Yaddo Corporation and from 1952 a member of the National Institute of Arts and Letters. Smith College appointed him the Mary Augusta Jordon professor of English in 1960. After his retirement in 1961, he remained in Northampton until his death on March 21, 1963.

While still an undergraduate, Arvin had been invited by Van Wyck Brooks to write for *The Freeman*. Thereafter, his articles and reviews appeared in a variety of magazines, and he soon became known for his incisive thinking and supple style. *Hawthorne*, his first major work, was published in 1929. In 1935 he won a Guggenheim fellowship, from which emerged his biography of Whitman. In 1951 his full-length study *Herman Melville* won the National Book Award for Nonfiction. *Longfellow: His Life and Work* was published shortly before he died.